GEORGE ORWELL: A REASSESSMENT

Also by Peter Buitenhuis

The Grasping Imagination: the American Writings of Henry James
The Great War of Words: British, American and Canadian Fiction
and Propaganda, 1914–1933
Selected Poems of E. J. Pratt (*editor*)

Also by Ira B. Nadel

Biography: Fiction, Fact and Form
Joyce and the Jews: Culture and Texts
Gertrude Stein and the Making of Literature (*co-editor*)

George Orwell: A Reassessment

Edited by

Peter Buitenhuis
Professor of English
Simon Fraser University

and

Ira B. Nadel
Professor of English
University of British Columbia

MACMILLAN
PRESS

First published 1988

Published by
THE MACMILLAN PRESS LTD
Houndmills, Basingstoke, Hampshire RG21 2XS
and London
Companies and representatives
throughout the world

Typeset by Wessex Typesetters
(Division of The Eastern Press Ltd)
Frome, Somerset

British Library Cataloguing in Publication Data
George Orwell: a reassessment:
1. Orwell, George—Criticism and
interpretation
I. Buitenhuis, Peter   II. Nadel, Ira Bruce
823′.912   PR6029.R87
ISBN 978-1-349-19589-3   ISBN 978-1-349-19587-9 (eBook)
DOI 10.1007/978-1-349-19587-9

Contents

Acknowledgements

The editors and publishers wish to thank Harcourt Brace Jovanovich, Inc., and A. M. Heath Ltd, on behalf of the Estate of the late Sonia Brownell Orwell and Secker and Warburg Ltd, who have kindly given permission to quote extracts from the following: *Nineteen Eighty-Four, Wigan Pier, The Lion and the Unicorn* and *Homage to Catalonia* by George Orwell; and *The Collected Essays, Journalism and Letters* edited by Sonia Brownell Orwell and Ian Angus.

Notes on the Contributors

Peter Buitenhuis is Professor of English at Simon Fraser University, British Columbia. He is the author of *The Grasping Imagination: the American Writings of Henry James* (1970), and of *The Great War of Words: British, American, and Canadian Fiction and Propaganda; 1914–1933*. He has published numerous articles on American and Canadian fiction.

Bernard Crick is Professor Emeritus of Politics of Birkbeck College, London University. He retired early to live in Scotland and to work on a trilogy on the nations of the British Isles. His *George Orwell: A Life* won the *Yorkshire Post* Book of the Year Award in 1980, and his *In Defence of Politics* has been in print since 1964. He produced a critical text with commentary of *Nineteen Eighty-Four* in 1984.

Paul Delany is Professor of English at Simon Fraser University. He is author of *British Autobiography in the Sixteenth Century* (1969), *D. H. Lawrence's Nightmare: the Writer and his Circle in the Great War* (1978), and of *The Neo-Pagans* (1986).

John Ferns, Professor of English at McMaster University, Ontario, is author of *A. J. M. Smith* (1979) and of four volumes of poetry: *The Antlered Boy* (1970), *Henry Hudson* (1975), *The Snow Horses* (1977), and *From the River . . .* (1985). He is the editor, with Brian Crick, of George Whalley's *Studies in Literature and the Humanities: Innocence of Intent* (1985).

Graham Good teaches English at the University of British Columbia. *The Observing Self: Studies in the Essay* is forthcoming and he has published numerous essays on George Orwell.

Erika Gottlieb teaches at Seneca College in Toronto and has published several essays on modern literature. She is now at work on a book on Orwell.

Mason Harris is Associate Professor of English at Simon Fraser University, where he has been teaching since 1966. He has published articles on Victorian fiction and science fiction, and is working on a book on psychology and class in anti-utopian fiction in the tradition of H. G. Wells.

Samuel L. Macey is Professor of English at the University of Victoria. His books include an edition of *Henry Carey's Dramatic Works*, a volume (with R. G. Lawrence) *Studies in Robertson Davies Deptford Trilogy*, and he is the author of *Clocks and the Cosmos: Time in Western Life and Thought*. His *Patriarchs of Time: Dualism in Saturn-Cronos, Father Time, the Watchmaker God, and Father Christmas* is to be published by the University of Georgia Press.

Gerald A. Morgan is Professor Emeritus of Royal Roads Military College, Victoria, B.C. He has published papers on topics as diverse as Aristotle, Calderon, Conrad, Hopkins, Marlowe, Tiutchev, and Zamyatin.

Mary Jo Morris is completing her doctoral dissertation at the University of Toronto. This is her first publication.

Ira B. Nadel, Professor of English at the University of British Columbia, is the author of *Biography: Fiction, Fact and Form* (1984), *Joyce and the Jews: Culture and Texts* (1988), and editor, with Shirley Neuman, of *Gertrude Stein and the Making of Literature* (1988). He has published articles on George Eliot, Dickens, Beerbohm, Strachey and Joyce. He is also co-editor of *The Journal of Pre-Raphaelite and Aesthetic Studies*.

F. Quei Quo is Professor of Political Science at Simon Fraser University. He is the author of *Political Systems: An Introductory Analysis* (1972) and co-editor of *Parliament, Policy and Representation* (1980). He has published many articles on the politics of Pacific Rim countries.

Michael L. Ross is Associate Professor of English at McMaster University, Ontario. He has published on a variety of topics in nineteenth- and twentieth-century English literature. A recent essay deals with the relation between D. H. Lawrence's *Lady Chatterley's Lover* and Orwell's *Nineteen Eighty-Four*.

Preface

The plethora of world-wide conferences held in 1984 to celebrate the importance of George Orwell and his 1949 novel *Nineteen Eighty-Four* were distinguished by their versatility and range of subject matter. Politics, psychology and language competed with history, stylistics and socialism in seminars, workshops and forums held in Strasbourg, Ann Arbor and Vancouver. Orwell as critic, as journalist, as futurist were among the new interpretations offered of his work which embraced his newly-discovered broadcasts, letters and manuscripts. Volumes like *Remembering Orwell* (1984), edited by Stephen Wadham, suddenly appeared alongside ominously titled collections like *And He Loved Big Brother: Man, State and Society in Question* (1985), papers from an Orwell meeting sponsored by the Council of Europe.

The productivity of scholarship and criticism generated by the celebratory gatherings extended the already growing bibliography of materials. And in the almost twenty years spanning George Woodcock's *The Crystal Spirit, A Study of George Orwell* (1966) and Patrick Reilly's *George Orwell: The Age's Adversary* (1985), criticism of Orwell has veered from studies of his political thought such as Alex Zwerdling's *Orwell and the Left* (1974) to introductory primers such as David Smith and Michael Mosher's *Orwell for Beginners* (1984). In the seventies, *The Unknown Orwell* (1972) and *Orwell: The Transformation* (1979) by Peter Stansky and William Abrahams and *The Last Man in Europe* (1974) by Alan Sandison registered a biographical interest Bernard Crick satisfied in 1980 when he published his comprehensive biography, *George Orwell: A Life* (1980).

Following that phase of criticism, scholars turned either to schematising Orwell's work or to specialist studies concentrating on single aspects of his career. *A George Orwell Companion* (1984) by J. R. Hammond illustrates the former, *The Language of 1984* (1984) by W. F. Bolton the latter. In general the language of Orwell received more attention as the *Supplement* to the *Oxford English Dictionary* (1972–1982) documented a series of phrases that record his impact. 'Orwellian', 'Big Brother', 'Doublethink', 'Newspeak', and 'Nineteen Eighty-Four' all became codified. More recently, studies such as Daphne Patai's *The Orwell Mystique, A Study in Male Ideology* (1984) suggest a feminist approach to the man and his career, balanced by Ian Slater's *Orwell, The Road to Airstrip One* (1985), a review of Orwell's developing political and social thought. Textual work, highlighted by the May 1984 discovery of Orwell's wartime radio scripts and letters, and supplemented by the appearance of Crick's critical and annotated edition of *Nineteen Eighty-Four* (1984) suggested new areas of research.

The value of such activity, however, can only be measured by the new readings and fresh analyses of Orwell, his writing and his social thought. The editors believe the present collection accomplishes this through its diverse approach to Orwell the writer and man of action. Originally presented in October 1984 in Vancouver as part of a two-day gathering entitled 'George Orwell in 1984: A Reassessment', the papers chronicle the reactions of political scientists, literary critics, social historians and novelists to the Orwell *œuvre*. Correspondingly, the essays cover subjects from social theory and political action to communications theory and the cultural revolution. They follow no single method or approach, preferring the flexibility of response Orwell himself displayed. The combination of Orwell's honesty with his self-irony, his grasp of the absurdity and yet seriousness of a situation, is reflected in the ensuing discussions which confirm what he wrote in his essay 'New Words': 'aesthetic and moral considerations are . . . inextricable' (*CE*, II, 4).

As a whole, the collection explores the role of the critic/writer in contemporary society: whether we should listen to him as well as read him; whether he has a message as well as a language to convey. Orwell's themes of social inequality and human freedom, however, unite to resolve any apparent contradictions in his mission. Did Orwell make 'political writing into an art' as he wished to in 'Why I Write'? Did he achieve an imaginative history that was truthful as well as factual, a goal he expresses in a 1946 review, in his critique of political orthodoxy, imperialism, and lack of personal freedoms? The following essays confront these and other questions which are central to an assessment of the critic and writer, social commentator and political analyst. But it would be negligent to overlook, as his Canadian friend Paul Potts realised, that Orwell also wrote 'beautiful English prose. The kind of English that people usually embarrassed by beauty could appreciate'. Coupled with what George Woodcock has called Orwell's 'intense interest in the concrete aspects of living', his work remains a distinguished model of political and artistic literacy.

Bernard Crick's essay, 'Orwell and English Socialism', serves as an excellent introduction to the essential threads in the tapestry of Orwell's life: his evolving political thought, his devotion to good writing, and the final distillation of his ideas into the savage satire of his last novel. The three sections into which the remaining essays have been divided: *Nineteen Eighty-Four*, *Language and Politics*, and *Literary Criticism* reflect these major threads.

Samuel Macey's essay locates *Nineteen Eighty-Four* in time – past, present and future – and puts a high price on Orwell's setting the novel in a period so soon after his own. The essays of Mason Harris and Erika Gottlieb take opposing positions on the central debate over *Nineteen Eighty-Four* – whether its focus is mainly psychological or political – and each adds new insights to the debate. This section is concluded by Gerald Morgan's fresh and original essay 'False Freedom and Orwell's Faust-Book *Nineteen Eighty-Four*'. He places the novel in the larger context of the Faust legend, perhaps the dominant myth of modern western civilisation.

In the second section, Paul Delany explores the too-often ignored contradictions in Orwell's writings about language, while Mary Jo Morris's essay suggests that some of these contradictions can be resolved by seeing Newspeak as Orwell's satiric attack on the utilitarian nature of Basic English. John Ferns eloquently shows how central was Orwell's experience in Spain to his devotion to truth-telling. Finally, in this section, Quei Quo shows how this truth-telling, and Orwell's prescience about the totalitarian techniques of manipulation of ideology, accurately and devastatingly prefigured the Chinese Cultural Revolution.

In the last section, Graham Good explores a little known path – the relationship between George Orwell and T. S. Eliot. He reveals more links between them than most of us could have dreamed of, and concludes by illuminating their crucial differences. Lastly Michael Ross makes a spirited and convincing defence of Orwell as a literary critic. He examines analytically the criteria by which Orwell has been too easily criticised in the past. The essay raises the question, which was later pursued in the panel discussion, about the sad withering away of good popular literary criticism, at which Orwell was such a master.

The other points made in the panel discussion have to do with Orwell's political affiliation, and the shape of his career. Bernard

Crick deals with these points with his customary trenchancy. Ian Slater draws on his recent experience in Yugoslavia to illuminate the continuing relevance of *Nineteen Eighty-Four*. It may be that this evidence is the best counter to Samuel Macey's pessimism about the future value of the novel. The panel discussion concluded a stimulating and revealing two days of discussion. It is perhaps worth noting that, such is the richness and complexity of Orwell's work, there is little overlap between this volume and the three previous collections of essays emerging from the coming of age of *Nineteen Eighty-Four – 1984 Revisited: Totalitarianism in Our Century*, edited by Irving Howe (1983), *On Nineteen Eighty-Four*, edited by Peter Stansky (1983), and *On the Future of Nineteen Eighty-Four*, edited by Ejner J. Jensen (1984).

The conference would not have been possible without the financial assistance of the Canadian Social Science and Humanities Research Council, the Vice-Presidents Academic of the University of Victoria and Simon Fraser, the Departments of English of the University of British Columbia, Simon Fraser and Victoria, and the Department of Political Science at the University of British Columbia. For aid with the manuscript, the editors would like to thank the Publications Committee of Simon Fraser; for expert editorial advice on standardising, checking, and copy-editing, Tirthankar Bose, and for word-processing, the Dean's Office of Simon Fraser, and Anita Mahoney who did the job.

George Orwell's catholicity of interests stimulated academics from several different disciplines to participate in this conference. Given this catholicity it was therefore entirely appropriate that the three largest universities in British Columbia should collaborate for the first time in history on an academic conference. The organising committee was made up of Ira B. Nadel and George Feaver from the University of British Columbia, Peter Buitenhuis and Stephen Duguid from Simon Fraser, and Charles Doyle from the University of Victoria.

P.B.
I.B.N.

Introduction

Orwell and English Socialism

Bernard Crick

In 1946 in an essay 'Why I write' Orwell wrote, 'What I have most wanted to do throughout the past ten years is to make political writing into an art.' And he might well have added, into a popular art, for I believe that he developed his famous clear, plain, simple, colloquial and forceful style precisely in order to reach what he was more apt to call 'the common man' than the working class. His debt to Swift has often been noted, especially for the strategies of his two major satires, but his deliberate choice of rhetoric, his adopted style and conscious persona as a writer may owe more to Daniel Defoe; and he wrote for much the same kind of audience.

Orwell's pre-war novels had all been written to catch the attention of the public for whom Charles Dickens and H. G. Wells had written, a public composed of both working class and lower middle class who used and depended upon the free public library and had, like Orwell himself, missed the overrated advantages of full-time higher education. From his own experience he deeply believed in the potential moral superiority of the self-taught over the institutionally educated (there is at least this parallelism between Orwell and Rousseau!). But as his sales showed, he singularly failed to reach this audience until he became literary editor of and a columnist in the left-wing *Tribune*, which enjoyed a large readership in war-time conditions, and until he wrote *Animal Farm* and *Nineteen Eighty-Four*. Yet their very success played a trick with his reputation. Many on the Left held that it is never timely to tell salutary home truths about the home team. Many on the Right accepted his fierce libertarianism but either ignored his egalitarianism or dismissed it as silly and superficial. And perhaps ordinary readers who did not know where Orwell stood already might be forgiven for thinking that the two satires are solely against the Soviet Union and not also against all forms of power hunger and rational hierarchy. Indeed, I have met whole school classes who have skipped 'Goldstein's testimony' and so are not aware that at the heart of

Nineteen Eighty-Four is a satire on the useless manufacture of atomic warheads: they are manufactured, remember, simply to 'burn off surplus value' which otherwise would be spent on welfare which would undermine the basic conditions of an hierarchical society.

In that same essay, 'Why I Write', he remarked that 'every line of serious work that I have written since 1936 has been written, directly or indirectly, against totalitarianism and for democratic socialism, as I understand it'. The last phrase, whether honest or evasive, is not accidental. I want to try to clarify what he understood it to be. If we ignore some famous detractors on the Left and some infamous bodysnatchers on the Right, while charitably allowing that Orwell did say some intemperate and ill-defined things in the heat of polemic and that he was not a systematic political thinker (he was a writer), so he is open to honest misunderstanding (it has not always been honest) for those who go into him only on a particular occasion or at a particular stage of his rapid but by no means unilinear development, yet I conclude that he is a pretty typical English left-wing socialist in the tradition of Morris, Blatchford, Carpenter, Cole, Tawney, Laski, Bevan and Foot, and quite as influential as the last three. I say 'English socialism', for once, not 'British' for there is in 'Scottish democracy' a harsher republican and populist tradition, and in Welsh socialism, however secular it tries to be, as in the rhetoric of Aneurin Bevan and his disciple, Neil Kinnock, the language of evangelism and 'New Jerusalem' keeps breaking through. 'Tribune socialism' might convey more: egalitarian, libertarian, environmental, individualist in practice if not in theory, highly principled but somehow untheoretical, or if tinged with Marxism, then only in its broadest and most libertarian forms, and very much divided in itself about distrust of using the central state – a municipal social and quasi-communitarian strand – and a desire to nationalise and control 'the commanding heights' of industry.

Orwell's path towards socialism was slow and unsure – as Peter Sedgwick pointed out in an essay of 1969 in *International Socialism* which did much to restore Orwell's image among the new Left. His first published novel, *Burmese Days*, is certainly anti-imperialist:

You see louts straight from school kicking grey-haired servants. The time comes when you burn with hatred of your own countrymen, when you long for a native rising to drown their Empire in blood. And in this there is nothing honourable, hardly

even any sincerity . . . . You are a creature of the despotism, a
pukka sahib, tied tighter than a monk or a savage to an
unbreakable system of tabus.[1]

But beware of hindsight and myopia. Others beside socialists
have hated imperialism, British and North American radicals for
instance. Orwell was aware of socialist doctrines but did not then
claim to be a socialist. When, shortly after leaving Burma, another
young writer asked him sententiously 'Where he stood', Orwell
replied that he was a 'Tory anarchist'. There is more in this than a
joke. Some old high Tories or 'Little Englanders' took their
individualism so seriously that they held strong views against
imposing moral and cultural values on others. Almost as much as
Mr Doolittle, they disliked middle-class morality, especially its
imposition. They could accept the military necessity of Empire, but
everywhere favoured 'indirect rule', respecting, often studying
and preserving native cultures. Some of them even 'went native',
at least lived between two worlds. They opposed the missionaries,
European secondary education and the moral prejudices of white
wives. They had no hope or desire for progress, believed the
subject peoples were incapable of self-government, but were
tolerant and indulgent.

Even *Down and Out in Paris and London* is not specifically socialist.
Its tone is melancholy and descriptive. He simply went among
tramps to see if we treated our natives as we treated those in the
Empire, and on the whole he concluded that we did. It is not the
book of a stirrer, as yet, rather of – in Victor Pritchett's famous
phrase – 'a man who went native in his own country'. But it meant
that when the time came when he did speak as a socialist, he knew
more about poverty than most middle-class socialists.

When Orwell first declares clearly that he is a socialist, in *The
Road to Wigan Pier*, he straightaway adopts his persona of the teller
of home truths to the home team. He delivers a two-handed blow
at socialists for worshipping the Soviet Union simply on account
of its power and for allowing the movement to become infested
with 'cranks'. It would be a thin-skinned comrade who could not
laugh at the comic exaggeration of the famous passage: 'One
sometimes gets the impression that the mere words "Socialism"
and "Communism" draw towards them with magnetic force every
fruit-juice drinker, nudist, sandal-wearer, sex-maniac, Quaker,
"Nature Cure" quack, pacifist and feminist in England'. But one

would have to be abnormally thick-skinned not to take offence at the picture of those who come 'flocking towards the smell of "progress" like bluebottles to a dead cat'.[2] The voice of the supporter on the terraces cries, 'What a load of rubbish! Sell 'em!' Orwell's tone is uncertain at times. See how a rather laboured sarcasm precedes a noble peroration:

> It is usual to speak of the Fascist objective as the 'beehive state', which does a grave injustice to bees. A world of rabbits ruled by stoats is nearer the mark. It is against this beastly possibility that we have to combine. The only thing for which we can combine is the underlying ideal of Socialism; justice and liberty. It is almost completely forgotten. It has been buried beneath layer after layer of doctrinaire priggishness, party squabbles and half-baked 'progressivism' until it is like a diamond hidden under a mountain of dung. The job of the Socialist is to get it out again. Justice and liberty! *Those* are the words that have got to ring like a bugle across the world.[3]

Indeed, but one does not have to be a very hard dialectician to ask quite what these two words mean. And if one must rant and bang the table, what is wrong with good old 'Liberty, Equality, Fraternity'?[4] But he does make a very serious point about the image of Socialism in relation to those who need to be won over.

The Road to Wigan Pier is his remorselessly honest account of class relationships – not an abstract account, but one disturbingly specific. He was by birth, he said, a member of the 'lower-upper middle class' which was, he helpfully explained, 'the upper middle class without money'. They were a special section of the middle class, and in his opinion a specially dangerous one. He tells us that he was brought up to believe that 'the lower classes smell' and he gives that as an example of a belief, however false one knows it to be, that it is hard to be sure, if one is honest, that one can ever fully shake off. He takes for granted that socialism aims at a classless society, but he warns us, in a tone of comic pessimism, that it is not easy to achieve – there is much self-deception and what we would now call 'tokenism'.

> Many people . . . imagine that they can abolish class distinctions without making any uncomfortable change in their own habits and 'ideology'. Hence the eager class-breaking activities which

one can see in progress on all sides. Everywhere there are people of good will who quite honestly believe that they are working for the overthrow of class-distinctions. The middle class socialist enthuses over the proletariat and runs 'summer schools' where the proletarian and the repentant bourgeois are supposed to fall upon one another's necks and be brothers for ever; and the bourgeois visitors come away saying how wonderful and inspiring it all has been (the proletarian ones come away saying something different). And there is the outer-suburban creeping Jesus, a hangover from the William Morris period, but still surprisingly common, who goes about saying 'Why must we level *down*? Why not level *up*?' and proposes to level the working class 'up' (up to his standard) by means of hygiene, fruit-juice, birth-control, poetry, etc. Even the Duke of York (now King George VI) runs a yearly camp where public school boys and boys from the slums are supposed to mix on exactly equal terms, and do mix for the time being, rather like the animals in one of those 'Happy Family' cages where a dog, a cat, two ferrets, a rabbit and three canaries preserve an armed truce while the showman's eye is on them.[5]

Note that the humour only consists in its being true and specific in contexts usually inhabited by abstract generalisations – instead of the customary 'alliance of workers by hand and workers by brain' we have the middle-class socialists meeting the workers most intensely at – where else? – summer schools.

What he actually argues for is a most interesting sociological theory, that a working-class movement depends for its leadership upon members of the lower middle class, or what he sometimes calls 'the sinking middle class' or the 'rising working class' (my hypothetical class of the public-library educated). This class must be wooed, not alienated. This class, he says, could turn to fascism, or to socialism: it is essential 'for the moment . . . to go easy and not frighten more people than can be helped'. Perhaps it is just an urban version of the old myth of the yeomanry beloved of the Victorian radicals and the early socialists; but it also anticipates a key concept in post-war historical and sociological accounts of the rise of European Fascism and Nazism. In specific terms he looks to the kind of people who make the corporals and the sergeants, the ward secretaries and the shop stewards, neither the rankers by themselves, nor the traditional officers, nor renegade gentlemen adventurers like himself. Several times he talks about the growth of a new 'intermediate class'. A fierce egalitarianism only emerges in *Homage to Catalonia*, his account of what happened when he went to Spain to fight Fascism and save the Republic. 'I have seen wonderful things and at last really believe in Socialism, which I never did before'. The stress in this sentence must be on 'really' and on 'believe', as if, before he saw the anarchist and the independent Marxist militias (the quasi-Trotskyist POUM) in Catalonia, his socialism had been cerebral or intellectual, perhaps even just anti-capitalist and little else: the Catalans had made him feel a socialist and convinced him that an egalitarian society was possible. 'The essential point of the system', he recalled, 'was social equality between officers and men. Everyone . . . mingled on terms of complete equality . . . . Of course there was not perfect equality, but there was a nearer approach to it than I had ever seen or than I would have thought conceivable in time of war . . . . I was breathing the air of equality, and', he admitted, 'I was simple enough to imagine that it existed all over Spain. I did not realise that more or less by chance I was isolated among the most revolutionary section of the Spanish working class'.[6] There was a deep feeling for justice in *The Road to Wigan Pier*, only the egalitarianism was lacking. But egalitarianism by itself is not English socialism, nor necessarily democratic. The values of *moral individualism* and *honesty* transfuse both books. It was he who told us in *The Road to Wigan Pier*, not his critics, 'that you do not solve the class problem by making friends with tramps', and that at that time 'I had carried my hatred of oppression to extraordinary lengths. At that time failure seemed to me the only virtue'; and that it took him a long time to get away from 'the simple theory that the oppressed are always right and the oppressor always wrong'. Some of us never have. How much the public might respond to such shattering honesty from party leaders rather than so many easy lies, half-truths and evasions!

Another characteristic of English socialism that is so Orwell-like is the attempt to strike a balance between the interests of humanity in nature and in manufacture, or between town and country. His novel of 1939, *Coming Up For Air*, shows a warm love of a traditional England of the 1900s that is being gradually destroyed by urban development, and will shortly be utterly destroyed by the bombing planes in a meaningless war – he links two themes that come together today in the strange alliance in Britain between the environmentalists and the CND. But Orwell is careful not to resurrect the pastoral utopianism of William Morris. Indeed he mocks it. His character 'George Bowling' has an excess of nostalgia which pulls him backwards from what he dimly senses needs to be done. Orwell sees that industry alone can create the higher standard of living which is needed for the health and well-being of the people, not simply for the meaningless accumulation of goods or 'the worship of the money god'. He seeks some balance, which is sensible if somewhat banal: the kind of thinking that lay behind the Town and Country Planning Act of 1947, to control the growth of housing and industry. But beneath this there is something deeper. In his own life-style Orwell clearly shows that he believes that a person who loses touch with the activities and rhythms of the countryside becomes less human. In the novel *Nineteen Eighty-Four* there is the vision of the 'golden country', but also the symbol of the final torture chamber as the place where it is never dark, though the rat is the king of darkness. Mankind, he is saying, cannot live at extremes of light or dark, goodness or evil, nor all in the natural country nor all in the built town. This belief that there is something deeply moral in attachment, however part-time, to the land, even minimally to gardening or allotments, is a characteristic both of Orwell and English socialism. Every working man wanted a small house of his own with a patch of land. Orwell sensed a deep cultural dislike for purely urban, terrace or apartment living. And he had an almost pietistic love of ordinary solid things and actions, natural substances and do-it-yourself.

His experience in Spain led him to join the Independent Labour Party. He later wrote that a writer 'cannot be a loyal member of a political party' – the stress must have been on 'loyal'. The ILP regarded itself as to the Left of the Labour Party, an arguable proposition domestically, depending on which section of the Labour Party one considered; but in foreign policy the difference was clear. The ILP in foreign affairs had a position hard to distinguish from that of Trotsky: that a war was coming, but it would be an imperialistic war of British, French and German rivalry for the control of markets. As late as July 1939 Orwell published an article with the sardonic title, 'Not Counting Niggers', which mocked the preparations for war, a war that was purely in the interests of the governing class, and reminded his readers 'that the overwhelming bulk of the British proletariat does not live in Britain, but in Asia and Africa'. They are never counted. 'Nothing is likely to save us except the emergence in the next two years of a real mass party', he asserted, 'whose first pledges are to refuse war and right imperial injustice'. He adopted the stance of a revolutionary socialist opposed to all capitalist wars.

When the war broke out, he changed his mind almost overnight. Chamberlain's England, even, was preferable to Nazi Germany and Nazi conquest. And, furthermore, the war could only be won if there was a social and political revolution. He argued in *The Lion and the Unicorn* that not merely had the old order got us into this Dunkirk mess, but that it had to be swept away if the country was to survive. He convinced himself, for a while, that 'the English revolution started several years ago, and it began to gather momentum when the troops came back from Dunkirk'.[7] He briskly synthesised his Catalan revolutionary fervour with a left-wing version of civic patriotism:

> Patriotism has nothing to do with conservatism. It is devotion to something that is changing but is felt to be mystically the same . . . . To be loyal both to Chamberlain's England and to the England of tomorrow might seem an impossibility, if one did not know it to be an everyday phenomenon. Only revolution can save England, that has been obvious for years, but now the revolution has started and it may proceed quite quickly if only we can keep Hitler out. Within two years, maybe a year, if only we can hang on, we shall see changes that will surprise the idiots who have no foresight. I dare say the London gutters will have to run with blood. All right, let them, if it is necessary. But when the red militias are billeted in the Ritz I shall still feel that the England I was taught to love so long ago and for such different reasons is somehow persisting.[8]

Patriotism and traditionalism are characteristics of English socialists. Their world did not begin in 1789 and 1917 but in 'the long revolution' of the peasant revolts, the English Civil War, agrarian riots and Chartism. The proles in Oceania, it will be remembered, 'had stayed human. They had not become hardened inside. They had held onto the primitive emotions which he himself had to relearn by conscious effort'. Indeed Orwell implies, both in *The Lion and the Unicorn* and in *Nineteen Eighty-Four*, that the common people had retained a sociability, a mutual helpfulness or 'decency' which the middle classes, power-hungry and economically competitive, rivalling each other, had lost. True individualism is mutual recognition or sociability, not competitive.

The image of the family, as the primary social group, is thus important to Orwell. He cannot begin to imagine why some way-out socialist theorists 'reject' the family as inherently inegalitarian: Orwell sees it as a natural institution and as the source of morality and sociability – hence 'the Party' in *Nineteen Eighty-Four* has to destroy the family and get children to denounce parents in order to remove the very source of individuality. But families are not all of a kind. '[England] is a family in which the young are generally thwartèd and most of the power is in the hands of irresponsible uncles and bedridden aunts. Still, it is a family. It has its private language and its common memories', he says, 'and at the approach of an enemy, it closes its ranks. A family with the wrong members in control – that is, perhaps, as near as one can come to describing England in a phrase'.[9]

How a writer rather than a theorist works can be seen when, almost as an aside in a typical peroration in *The Lion and the Unicorn*, he advances a most challenging social theory which found academic support only long after the end of the war.

The inefficiency of private capitalism has been proved all over Europe. Its injustice has been proved in the East End of London. Patriotism, against which the Socialists fought so long, has become a tremendous lever in their hands. People who at any other time would cling like glue to their miserable scraps of privilege, will surrender them fast enough when their country is in danger. War is the greatest of all agents of change. It speeds up all processes, wipes out major distinctions, brings realities to the surface. Above all war brings it home to the individual that he is not altogether an individual.[10]

'War is the greatest of all agents of social change', a dark thought for a socialist; but most post-war histories of the British welfare state, while they trace the ideas back much earlier, see its actual emergence in the conditions of the war, not simply in the post-war legislation. Orwell was original and thoughtful, but not a systematic theorist; yet he throws out, almost as asides, more important, speculative generalisations, of this kind, than many famous social theorists ever possessed.

He is fully aware that his advocacy of revolution on the one hand, and of traditional values on the other, appear to some as contradictory. He is fully aware of the Marxist position on values, but regards it as so foolish as to be unworthy of explicit refutation: that all values are a product of bourgeois property relations, until the classless society. He adopts the position, with an almost perverse commonsense, that we know instinctively what values to pursue, liberty, equality and fraternity (or 'decency' or sociability). They have been known in the past, but suppressed in extent by greed and property relations: they do not need to be 'subsumed' or 'transformed', but simply made general and liberated from constraints:

> An English Socialist government will transform the nation from top to bottom, but it will still bear all over it the unmistakable marks of our own civilization . . . .
> It will not be doctrinaire, nor even logical. It will abolish the House of Lords, but quite probably will not abolish the Monarchy. It will leave anachronisms and loose ends everywhere . . . . It will not set up any explicit class dictatorship. It will group itself around the old Labour Party and its mass following will be in the Trade Unions, but it will draw into it most of the middle class and many of the younger sons of the bourgeoise. Most of its directing brains will come from the new indeterminate class of skilled workers, technical experts, airmen, scientists, architects and journalists, the people who feel at home in the radio and ferro-concrete age. But it will never lose touch with the tradition of compromise and the belief in a law that is above the State. It will shoot traitors, but it will give them a solemn trial beforehand and occasionally it will acquit them. It will crush any open revolt promptly and cruelly, but it will interfere very little with the spoken and written word . . . . It will show a power of assimila-ting the past which will shock foreign observers and sometimes make them doubt whether any revolution has happened.
> But all the same it will have done the essential thing. It will have nationalised industry, scaled down incomes, set up a classless educational system.[11]

Orwell never changed his values after 1936. There is no biographical evidence that his socialism waned; on the contrary there is much that it matured. *Animal Farm* is a democratic socialist polemic against Soviet Communism; and *Nineteen Eighty-Four*, when read as a Swiftian satire, is compatible with this same position. Orwell had consistently said, since his first commitment in *The Road to Wigan Pier*, that totalitarianism could come from the Left as well as the Right. This does not make him anti-socialist; it makes him anti-Communist. But what did change, between the writing of *The Lion and the Unicorn* and the publication of *Animal Farm*, was the wild hope that he had from 1936 onwards that 'the revolution' was around the corner, albeit a relatively benign 'English revolution'. He was not alone in hoping that 1945 would see the beginning of 'the Republic', but he was quicker than many to see that Mr Attlee's government was not embarked on a revolutionary process, yet could be defended, much as he had defended 'Chamberlain's England' in 1940, as a relative good, something better than before but by no means as good as it might have been.[12] He did not cease to believe in 'the Republic' but, like many, he grew more realistic in considering time-scales. The creation of an egalitarian Britain would be a task for generations: 'revolution' became a process, not an event. He no longer seriously hoped to see a socialist Britain in his lifetime. This seems to me a sensible and realistic perspective, neither a sign of changing ideology nor of abnormal pessimism.

Everything else found in *The Lion and the Unicorn* remained: his traditionalism, belief in the moral superiority of the common people, his pietism towards nature, and above all his belief that liberty and equality were not merely not antithetical, but that more liberties could actually be exercised in an egalitarian society: they were conditions of each other. He had a very positive sense of freedom: liberties were to be exercised, not simply enjoyed, and the results could be turbulent. In some ways Orwell's ideas of civic freedom owe as much to the Roman and the French Jacobin traditions as they do to nineteenth-century English liberalism. hence his desire to be 'in on the action', his belief in direct participation and also his tough-guy talk about shooting traitors after 'a solemn trial' and crushing 'open revolt promptly and cruelly' – not the Orwell most often quoted by his liberal admirers.

He is clear about the best possible outcome. But he is realistic about the post-war world and says quite explicitly that he would prefer to live under the relative tolerance of American capitalism than under Soviet power. Yet these alternatives exclude a middle position which he continued to believe (which took some optimism) was both preferable and realistic: a United Socialist States of Europe.[13] What is remarkable about Orwell as a practical political thinker is that he is both idealistic about best-possible outcomes and realistic about second-bests, a curious mixture of optimism and pessimism, of rhetoric and plain honesty. He believes in the basic decency of human nature and that we *could* attain 'the Republic', but he does not believe in inevitable progress and recognises that things could go terribly wrong again, as they did under Stalinism and Hitlerism and imperialism. The outcome depends not on 'impersonal forces', 'economic formations' or 'determining social structures' but on a collective aggregation of individual will power and morality.

Thus Orwell is an ethical socialist. Consider this well-known review of Hayek's *The Road to Serfdom*:

> In the negative part of Professor Hayek's thesis there is a great deal of truth. It cannot be said too often . . . that collectivism is not inherently democratic, but, on the contrary, gives to a tyrannical minority such powers as the Spanish Inquisitors never dreamed of.
>
> Professor Hayek is also probably right in saying that in this country the intellectuals are more totalitarian-minded than the common people. But he does not see, or will not admit, that a return to 'free' competition means for the great mass of people a tyranny probably worse, because more irresponsible, than that of the State. The trouble with competitions is that somebody wins them. Professor Hayek denies that free competition necess- arily leads to monopoly, but in practice that is where it has led, and since the vast majority of the people would rather have State regimentation than slumps and unemployment, the drift towards collectivism is bound to continue if popular opinion has any say in the matter . . . .
>
> Between them these two books sum up our present predica- ment. Capitalism leads to dole queues, the scramble for markets, and war. Collectivism leads to concentration camps, leader worship, and war. There is no way out of this unless a planned economy can somehow be combined with the freedom of the intellect, which can only happen if the concept of right and wrong is restored to politics.[14]

The implication is that freedom of the intellect must be qualified by morality. Presumably we should exercise our freedom with responsibility towards others. And Orwell also seems to believe that there are some things that the State can do which it should not do. Interests may attach to groups but they should not override certain rights attaching to individuals. There are, indeed, difficulties in this position; but such is his position.

Orwell's socialism is libertarian. As *Animal Farm* shows, he has a speculative sympathy for anarchism – indeed, personal sympathies too. But he is too tough-minded to adopt that position philosophically. He sees the State as a necessary evil, acknowledges its function in general but distrusts it in all its particular actions. This was characteristic of the old *Tribune* Left: in theory a demand to nationalise nearly everything and to seize control of the 'commanding heights', but in practice an intense suspicion of leadership and a rooted belief that all power tends to corrupt. In *The Lion and the Unicorn*, even, Orwell had warned:

Centralized leadership has very little meaning unless the mass of people are living roughly upon an equal level, and have some kind of control over the government. 'The State' may come to mean no more than a self-elected political party, and privilege can return, based on power rather than on money.[15]

Thus in commonsense terms, but perfectly clearly, he is one of the first socialist thinkers to say that class structure can be a product of power-hunger and office-holding, not simply of economic exploitation. He rejects Marxism as too simplistic rather than as wholly false. I read the sociology of the 'Outer Party' in the novel *Nineteen Eighty-Four* as a savage satire on bureaucracy: intellectuals deserting their, to him, historic task of 'education and agitation' among the masses, for the comfort and security (or so it seemed at first) of desks and departments. The concept of 'bureaucratisation' has caused almost as much trouble to orthodox Marxism (I mean has proved as 'problematic') as nationalism. Orwell, in essays and asides, was on to this before my colleagues, the high-brow polysyllabic neo-Marxists. Dislike of bureaucracy links to his concern with immediate experience, rather than abstract benefits, to place him firmly in the small-group, decentralist tradition of socialism rather than either the Fabian or the Marxist versions of *étatism*.

His libertarianism is also typical of English socialism in his

undisciplined commitment to free speech and truth. In the famous
essays on censorship, propaganda and the control of literature, he
not merely restates the classic liberal argument that the dangers of
censorship are always greater than its benefits, but more arguably
tries to establish that plain language speaks the truth whereas
polysyllabic neologisms are either obfuscations or lies. Well, it
isn't as simple as that. Syntactically there is no way of telling
whether plain words lie or not, whether there was such a person
as 'Robinson Crusoe' and whether such things happened to him
(or whether Orwell shot an elephant or saw a hanging). But it is a
good rule of thumb. And one is for ever grateful to him for pointing
out that a phrase like 'ideologically correct' simply means 'a lie for
the party'. He has the robust commonsense to believe that a good
cause can afford to admit errors and mistakes. And if the guardians
of the cause will not make these admissions themselves, then he
will: 'liberty is telling people what they do not want to hear'. Such
men are always happier in opposition.

A characteristic of English socialism, in contrast to Marxian
socialism, has been to recognise that there are some areas of life
which have to be preserved from politics: a good politics even sets
up barriers of laws, institutions and customs against itself; and
similarly while economic factors condition and limit everything to
some extent, yet they determine nothing. Only an English socialist
could talk, as Morris, Tawney and Orwell did, about the importance
of privacy in the good life. But to Orwell the most important of
these 'reservations' was literature itself. He had said that above all
else he wanted to make 'political writing into an art'. He saw that
his best writing was political, but it was his best because it was
good writing or art, not for the truth or relevance of the message.

He recognised a tension: 'My book about the Spanish civil war
. . . is, of course, a frankly political book, but in the main it is
written with a certain detachment and regard for form. I did try
very hard in it to tell the whole truth without violating my literary
instincts'.[16] And he recognised the peculiar problems of his times:
'Any writer or journalist who wants to retain his integrity finds
himself thwarted by the general drift of society rather than by
active persecution . . . . Everything in our age conspires to turn
the writer . . . into a minor official, working on themes handed to
him from above and never telling what seems to him the whole of
the truth.'[17] He may be forced by the state, or even by his
conscience, into writing propaganda, but then:

he should do so as a citizen, as a human being, but *not as a writer*
. . . . To suggest that a creative writer, in a time of conflict, must
split his life into two compartments, may seem defeatist or
frivolous: yet in practice I do not see what else he can do . . . .
To yield subjectively, not merely to a party machine, but even
to a group ideology is to destroy oneself as a writer.[18]

Indeed to destroy not merely oneself, but any distance between
politics and culture. He is quite happy to say that a culture can be
thoroughly political, both good politics and bad politics; but not
wholly and exclusively political. If it does, it becomes both bad
writing and actually anti-political – while politics is the medium of
freedom. Thus Orwell's position is essentially dualistic. Moral and
aesthetic judgements are not the same. He is not saying 'l'art pour
l'art', he is saying 'culture for humanity'; but part of that humanity
is this very dualism, not merely that a good man can be a bad
writer, but that an evil man, say Ezra Pound, can be a great poet.
What contempt he has for those socialist theorists who cannot
allow a class enemy to be a good writer nor a class hero to be a
bad one!

Any kind of socialism contains a systematic critique of society as it
is and a prophecy of society as it could and – most advocates try
to argue – will be. Marxian socialism has tried to brush aside
moral dilemmas and awkward thoughts (such as that economic
oppression is not the only kind of oppression) by claiming to be
scientific, deterministic, historical, certain – at least in broad terms –
about the stages and direction of social change. But Orwell's
critique of society as it is would be true, in his perspective, even if
there was no future. What should be done should be done; we
can never be quite sure of the consequences; and to do evil for the
sake of the future is always either a bad excuse or a self-deception.
We do not act freely for the sake of future happiness, but because
it is good to act freely. We cannot be sure of the future. He did
have a vision of the future, but it was both perennial and long
term. While socialist writing, precisely because it is committed
both to critique and prophecy, is commonly so rhetorical, Orwell's
mixture of a short-term pessimism with a long-term optimism is
peculiar, and salutary.

In 1946 he reviewed a group of books under the heading, 'What
Is Socialism?' It was a particularly revealing piece and a particularly

unfortunate omission from the familiar four volume *Collected Essays*:

> a Socialist or a Communist . . . is a person who believes the 'earthly paradise' to be possible. Socialism is in the last analysis an optimistic creed and not easy to square with the doctrine of original sin . . . . At this moment it is difficult for utopianism to take shape in a definite political movement. The masses everywhere want security much more than they want equality, and do not generally realise that freedom of speech and of the Press are of urgent importance in themselves. But the desire for an earthly paradise has a very long history behind it.
>
> If one studied the genealogy of ideas for which writers like Koestler and Silone stand, one would find it leading back through Utopian dreamers like William Morris and the mystical democrats like Walt Whitman, through Rousseau, through the English diggers and levellers, through the peasant revolts of the Middle Ages, and back to the early Christians and the slave revolts of antiquity. The pamphlets of Gerrard Winstanley, the digger from Wigan, whose experiments in primitive communism were crushed by Cromwell, are in some ways strangely close to modern Left Wing literature.
>
> The 'earthly paradise' has never been realised, but as an idea it never seems to perish, despite the ease with which it can be debunked . . . . Underneath it lies the belief that human nature is fairly decent to start with, and is capable of indefinite development. This belief has been the main driving force of the Socialist movement, including the underground sects who prepared the way for the Russian revolution, and it could be claimed that the Utopians, at present a scattered minority, are the true upholders of Socialist tradition.[19]

But does he really mean that utopians are a 'scattered minority', and not rather that there must be a touch of utopianism in every socialist thinker and writer, even in a realist like himself? The categories are not exclusive: they exist on different levels of experience and on different time-scales. Even intense optimism and intense pessimism go side by side in the socialist mind, certainly in Orwell's. That 'optimistic' passage was written when he was beginning to compose *Nineteen Eighty-Four*, his allegedly totally pessimistic novel.

Now consider a very black and pessimistic passage (until the very end) written in 1943 when he was still in his revolutionary phase. He devotes most of a *Tribune* column to 'reactionary writers' (few socialists have written so fairly and sensibly about their enemies):

> The danger of ignoring the neo-pessimists lies in the fact that up to a point they are right. So long as one thinks in short periods it is wise not to be too hopeful about the future . . . .
>
> The real answer is to disassociate Socialism from Utopianism. Nearly all neo-pessimist apologetics consist in putting up a man of straw and knocking him down again . . . . Socialists are accused of believing that society can be – and, indeed, after the establishment of Socialism, will be – completely perfect; also that progress is inevitable . . . .
>
> The answer is . . . that socialism is not perfectionist, perhaps not even hedonistic. Socialists don't claim to be able to make the world perfect: they claim to be able to make it better. And any thinking Socialist will concede to the Catholic that when economic injustice has been righted, the fundamental problem of man's place in the universe will remain. But what the Socialist does claim is that the problem cannot be dealt with while the average human being's preoccupations are necessarily economic. It is all summed up in Marx's saying that after Socialism has arrived, human history can begin.[20]

That is, indeed, a curious way of disassociating oneself from utopianism; to which, in any case, in a modified or speculative way, he returned. The logical contradiction is fairly obvious, except again it may be a question of time scales, whether he is thinking in 'short periods' or the longest possible term of human history. But what is as interesting is the psychological ambivalence, again typical of 'English socialism': on the one hand a sensibility and perception that is close to observable experience and intensely practical, but on the other hand Pilgrim with his eyes raised towards Zion, head-in-the-air while feet necessarily tramp through the Slough of Despond and Vanity Fair. But perhaps only the plodding Pilgrim could sustain the idealistic Pilgrim through the hard work and daily disappointment that gradualism is heir to.

Part One
Nineteen Eighty-Four

1

George Orwell's *Nineteen Eighty-Four:* The Future that Becomes the Past

Samuel L. Macey

Since the eighteenth century, utopias and dystopias have been very much concerned with both clock time and chronology. The revolutionary improvement in the accuracy of clocks during the third quarter of the seventeenth century can be directly related not only to the heightened concern with time and chronology but also to the new meaning of the word 'progress'. Since the seventeenth century, progress has come to mean a progressive material improvement through time rather than the progress of a person through space. Modern utopias favour the new progress through time while dystopias question its values. A hundred years after Huygens' invention of the pendulum clock, which epitomised the modern mania for accurate time measurement, the use of chronometers by such seamen as Cook, Bligh, and Vancouver resulted in a world that became increasingly too well surveyed to permit imaginary settings for either utopias or dystopias. As a result, a whole series of such works, beginning with Mercier's *L'An 2440* (1768–71), are now projected into the future but comment directly on the present.

In our century, the three major dystopias – Zamyatin's *We* (written in 1920), Huxley's *Brave New World* (1932), and Orwell's *Nineteen Eighty-Four* (1949) – are projected into the future like the Wellsian works by which they are influenced. Though all these works share a compulsive concern with clocks and time, one related aspect of Orwell's novel makes it unique. The comparatively short time projection that Orwell gave to *Nineteen Eighty-Four* in 1949 – when contrasted with the more normal projections like Zamyatin's one thousand years or Huxley's 632 After Ford –

involved him in certain time-related problems that provide the subject for this paper. Orwell's *Nineteen Eighty-Four* is concerned with a protagonist during what is probably the last year of his life. But, unlike the protagonists in all the other major dystopias, Winston Smith can remember what the world has been like since the year when the dystopia was published. Winston, who is in his fortieth year, lives in a society in which time is very precisely measured, whereas chronology is blurred by the efforts of the Party to change the past. We shall consider this apparent paradox by concentrating first on time and then on chronology.

In terms of time, we find that the novel opens when the clocks are striking thirteen (*Nineteen Eighty-Four*, p. 157). This combines a symbol that connotes disaster[1] with an indication that society, in using the twenty-four-hour day, has rationalised the measurement of time. O'Brien – who, as a leader of the Party's Thought Police, represents his society – is constantly concerned with precise time. When we first meet him, he 'glanced at his wrist watch' (p. 165). Much later, in a space of six pages, he looks at his wrist watch on no fewer than three separate occasions (pp. 304, 306, 309). Just as with its leaders, the use of time by all members of the Party is carefully regulated. Winston's working week was sixty hours and Julia's even longer. During Hate Week he had worked more than ninety hours in five days, and the Records Department worked 'eighteen hours in the twenty-four, with two three-hour snatches of sleep' (p. 314).

Long working periods necessitate the careful regulation of time, but so do shorter periods of organised ritual like the Two Minutes Hate or the 'Physical Jerks' controlled by the telescreen (pp. 164–70, 183, 186–8). The type of temporal control exercised by the Party is illustrated by the short paragraph: 'The telescreen struck fourteen. He must leave in ten minutes. He had to be back at work for fourteen-thirty' (p. 180). As Winston informs us, 'In principle a Party member had no spare time, and was never alone except in bed' (p. 226). The activities of the day occurred between 'nought seven fifteen', when Winston, like others, was awoken by an ear-splitting whistle from the telescreen (p. 183), and twenty-three thirty, when the lights to his room were switched off at the main (p. 244).

Since the temporal control of Party members makes them operate like machines, it is not surprising that Orwell uses the pejorative connotations for machinery that correspond with our post-

Romantic prejudice regarding machines and automata. The Two Minutes Hate begins when a 'grinding screech, as of some monstrous machine running without oil, burst from the big Telescreen' (pp. 165–6). We are told that, though machines would end human drudgery, 'the dangers inherent in the machine are still there' (p. 320). The Party employs a system of continuous warfare in order to 'keep the wheels of industry turning without increasing the real wealth of the world' (p. 321). They thus pervert the intended use of machinery, because 'a hierarchical society was only possible on a basis of poverty and ignorance' (p. 321).

Juxtaposed to the strict temporal control by the Party and the related diabolism of its clocks are the old clocks and watches in Mr Charrington's junk shop, which have benevolent connotations. This dichotomy in clocks between the efficient and diabolical, and the old and benevolent gained its first prominence with the nineteenth-century novelists. In Dickens, for example, one can compare the expensive gold repeaters of Scrooge and Mr Jaggers with Master Humphrey's old clock or Sam Weller's large old watch. The same is true in Hardy's *Far From the Madding Crowd* when one compares the gold repeater of the diabolical Sergeant Troy with the large and benevolent old watch of Gabriel Oak.[2]

Consciously or otherwise, we recognise in *Nineteen Eighty-Four* the symbolically benevolent quality of old clocks. When we first meet Mr Charrington in his antique shop, we readily associate his 'long benevolent nose, and mild eyes' with the 'tarnished watches that didn't even pretend to be in going order', and the 'friendly ticking' of the 'old-fashioned glass clock with a twelve-hour face . . . on the mantelpiece' (pp. 237–9). In *Nineteen Eighty-Four* the old-fashioned clock's twelve-hour face is as much an anachronism as the old-fashioned miles, pints, and pounds that the Party has long since changed to the metric system. Julia – who is only twenty-six or twenty-seven, and therefore born after the publication of *Nineteen Eighty-Four* – examines 'the absurd twelve-hour clock with a sort of tolerant amusement' (p. 282). Winston frequently refers to it or translates its time into that of the twenty-four-hour day into which he must always return (pp. 274, 280, 316, 330, 346, 351).

Part of the benevolence related to old clocks derives from the fact that they do not control men as absolutely as modern timekeepers. The escape into the antique shop is in some measure an escape from the control of time. Although Winston had bought

the book in which he surreptitiously writes his diary from Mr
Charrington's shop, that was before the story began. His first
purchase in *Nineteen Eighty-Four* is that of the antique glass
paperweight (pp. 238–9). Later, Julia and he examine it and its
embedded piece of red coral immediately after she is amused by
the old clock. Winston feels that 'The paperweight was the room
he was in and the coral was Julia's life and his own, fixed in a sort
of eternity at the heart of the crystal' (p. 283). Eternity is, of course,
a condition to be both desired and feared, a condition in which
time no longer exists. Later, Winston feels that 'the room [above
the antique shop] was sanctuary. It was as when Winston had
gazed into the heart of the paperweight, with the feeling that it
would be possible to get inside that glassy world, and that once
inside it time could be arrested' (p. 287). Even when Winston and
Julia visit the country, he is escaping from time, and this is not
merely because he finds himself in a landscape that he recognises
out of memory. Paradoxically, despite the 'military precision'
(p. 256) of the journey that he has made, we learn that on this
occasion Winston 'had no watch' (p. 258).

The peripeteia in the plot comes when Winston discovers that
the antique shop is controlled by the Thought Police (or, on another
level, that they understand the innermost workings of his mind).
At this point, 'Someone . . . picked up the glass paperweight from
the table and smashed it to pieces on the hearth-stone. The
fragment of coral, a tiny crinkle of pink like a sugar rosebud from
a cake, rolled across the mat' (p. 350). Winston notes that the time
on the old clock is eight-thirty; but because he is in the antique
shop his temporal sense is not fully under control and he does not
know whether he had slept until eight-thirty in the evening or
eight-thirty on the following morning (p. 351). Ironically, Winston
now moves immediately from the apparently benevolent antique
shop, where he had been able to lose his sense of time, to the so-
called Ministry of Love, where his knowledge of time is intentionally withheld as part of a carefully calculated process of torture.
Here, since there are 'no clocks and no daylight[,] it was hard to
gauge the time' (pp. 354, 356, 358).

It was equally hard to gauge the longer temporal periods to
which we will be referring under the headings of chronology and
history. At the Ministry of Love, Winston estimates that he might
have been there 'Days, weeks, months – I think it is months'
(pp. 377, 394–7). As O'Brien says of the Party's control over both

chronology and history, 'Do you suppose it is beyond us to produce a dual system of astronomy? The stars can be near or distant, according as we need . . . . Have you forgotten doublethink?' (p. 388). In Room 101, it is only after Winston has shouted frantically that Julia's body should be thrust 'between himself and the rats' (p. 406) that he finally proves himself worthy of loving Big Brother. Immediately thereafter he is thrust back into time. At the beginning of the last chapter, we find him sitting in the Chestnut Tree Café at 'the lonely hour of fifteen' (pp. 407, 409, 413).

The hopelessness of the tone at the end of *Nineteen Eighty-Four* is reflected by the 'biting day in March' at the conclusion of the seasonal cycle of one year through which the novel passes. The work begins on a bright cold day in April, and the first date in the diary is 4 April 1984, when Winston is thirty-nine. Winston 'came out of the Ministry [where he worked, and] the balminess of the April air had tempted him' (p. 227); he then made his visit to Charrington's junk shop, and bought the paperweight. This leads to his meetings with Julia and her seduction in the country when 'It was the second of May', and 'The air seemed to kiss one's skin' (p. 257). Though they only succeeded in making love once more during the month of May (p. 276), they met no less than seven times during June (p. 286). This would be symbolically appropriate for the month containing the summer solstice. At the very moment of the peripeteia, Winston had wondered, 'Would not the light be fading at twenty-one hours on an August evening?' (p. 351). During the ensuing autumn and winter, their love is due to be tested and found wanting, but neither season nor month is mentioned again until the final chapter. Then, Winston meets Julia once more; this time, however, it is 'on a vile, biting day in March, when the earth was like iron and all the grass seemed dead'. Even the few crocuses that might represent hope have been 'dismembered by the wind' (p. 410). Easter is undoubtedly approaching but for Winston, in March 1985, only gin symbolises the spirit of 'his life, his death and his resurrection' (p. 412).

Though time is precisely measured in *Nineteen Eighty-Four*, the Party feels obliged to distort chronology and history. Because people as old as the protagonist might still remember how things had been in 1949 when the novel was published, the Party by changing history makes them question their own memories. But

Winston cannot find his refuge on the other side of Zamyatin's glass wall or in one of Huxley's islands.[3] When he tries to escape out of time, in the real world of 1984, there is no other refuge but the dreams and memories in his own skull. Though Winston dreams, for example, of the Golden Country that he remembers from the past, Julia is nevertheless with him there in the present (pp. 182–3, 262–3, 396). On one level, his dreams themselves might suggest a form of solipsism or the esemplastic reality created out of the mind of which Coleridge writes in *Biographia Literaria*.[4] Further, if the dream is caused by Julia's sidelong look of 'curious intensity' it is reflected later in the song: 'A look an' a word an' the dreams they stirred' (pp. 209, 275). We know of the visit to the junk shop that 'the instant [Winston] had allowed his thoughts to wander, his feet had brought him back here' (p. 237). At the beginning and end of Part Two we learn in precisely the same words that as Julia is hurt Winston feels 'the pain in his own body' (pp. 247, 350). Again the close identity between Winston's mind and the very existence of Julia is emphasised as he tells us that when she pulls at her zipper, 'it was almost as in his dream' (pp. 264, 251, 182). He tells her 'the story of his married life, but curiously enough she appeared to know the essential parts of it already' (p. 270). Indeed, the very idea of inviting Julia into Charrington's room 'had first floated into [Winston's] head in the form of a vision' (p. 274).

But the same esemplastic quality relates Winston's dreams and thoughts to O'Brien, a leader of the dreaded Thought Police who seems also to have doubled as the 'benevolent' Charrington. Winston says of O'Brien (as he might have done of Julia), 'what evidence had he in reality that O'Brien was any kind of political conspirator? Nothing but a flash of the eyes . . . beyond that, only his own secret imaginings, founded on a dream' (pp. 302, 177, also 415). Winston's parallel relationships with Julia and O'Brien strongly suggest that on one level they, too, may result from dreams that have become reality: both Julia and O'Brien can cap the rhyme that Mr Charrington taught him (pp. 282, 311, 241); they both slip a crucial message into his hand at the same place (pp. 248, 293); Julia readily approves of divulging their mutual secrets to O'Brien (p. 288); and, finally, though Julia claims to have seen a rat in Mr Charrington's room, it is O'Brien who knows about Winston's secret dream of rats, and uses that dream in Room 101 (pp. 281, 404). Indeed, Room 101 is the place where each prisoner's individual nightmare is turned into reality after having been uncovered by the Thought Police (p. 383).

But Winston's individual brand of solipsism must be eliminated by the Party. O'Brien admits that 'Reality is inside the skull'. He insists, however, that only 'collective solipsism' is acceptable, since only 'Whatever happens in all minds, truly happens', and 'We [the Party] control matter because we control mind' (pp. 387, 389, 399). For this reason, O'Brien also maintains that 'reality is not external. Reality exists . . . only in the mind of the Party' (p. 374). That is why Winston, from now onwards, 'must not only think right; he must . . . dream right' (p. 401).[5]

Since Winston's job involved the re-writing of library copies of old newspapers, he hardly needed to be reminded by O'Brien that since the Party controls all records and memories it also controls the past (pp. 190–91, 373). For the Party, 'history was a palimpsest, scraped clean and re-inscribed exactly as often as was necessary' (pp. 190, 197). Inventions were claimed, citizens were eliminated, and alliances were changed at will (pp. 187, 284, 312, *passim*). As a result, no-one can learn from the past or be sure of the future (pp. 327–8, 341–2). Hence also the paradox of a society which is as sure of the present time of the day as it is unsure of the most elementary chronology. Winston, for example, says of the past that he 'believed that he had been born in 1944 or 1945', and writes of the present, 'at this moment . . . in 1984 (if it was 1984)' (pp. 162, 185).

The relationship between past, present and future is essential to Orwell's *Nineteen Eighty-Four*. Winston, in 1984, claims to be writing his diary for the future and the unborn (p. 162), whereas the appeal is clearly to the readers of 1949. He writes *'To the future or to the past, to a time when thought is free . . . when truth exists and what is done cannot be undone'*. Though he 'recognised himself as a dead man it became important to stay alive as long as possible' (p. 180). But the Party thinks otherwise. Their slogan – repeated in the first and last part of the novel – is that 'Who controls the past . . . controls the future: who controls the present controls the past' (pp. 186, 373). The events of the four seasons during 1984–85, which structure the novel, may occur in Winston's mind, or occur externally, or occur on both levels. But wherever they take place they clearly demonstrate the inevitability of punishment, confession, repentance, and reintegration before death of anyone who has strayed even in thought from the love of Big Brother. As

Winston read in Emmanuel Goldstein's book: 'The mutability of the past is the central tenet of Ingsoc' (p. 341) or English Socialism, but the future is no longer 'softened by promises of compensation in an imaginary world beyond the grave' (pp. 332, 417).

Winston had known from the beginning that in his world there was no longer the Christian hope of eternal bliss. His forecast that 'The past was dead, the future was unimaginable . . . . And in front of him there lay not death but annihilation' (p. 179) is confirmed by O'Brien in the last part of the novel: 'You will be annihilated in the past as well as in the future. You will never have existed . . . . Nothing has happened that you did not foresee' (pp. 378, 395, 415). There seemed to have been a parallel inevitability seven years earlier when O'Brien speaking out of the darkness had appeared to predict in a dream that 'We shall meet in the place where there is no darkness' (pp. 177, 310, 369). And so they do. In a civilisation where there is only 'predestined horror . . . fixed in future time, preceding death as surely as 99 precedes 100' (p. 277), they are predestined to meet again in Room 101, the room bathed in light. There everyone must face the secret horror that has been carried around locked within the self (p. 245). 'The last step was something that would happen' in the ironically named Ministry of Love. What happened there would only confirm for Winston that 'The end was contained in the beginning' (p. 294).

In conclusion, then, the control by the Party in *Nineteen Eighty-Four* represents a control not only through clocks and time but also through the manipulation of chronology, history, memory, and even dreams. The elimination of the past and future through the control of the present means that 'Nothing exists except an endless present' (pp. 290, 287). The Party will continue, but it would seem that the annihilation of its individual citizens is as predestined as the fate of a Greek tragic hero. Though Winston is denied the ability of the tragic hero to meet his fate with a dignity worthy of emulation, the novel does offer a minimal ray of hope when one considers the chronology of its structure. Winston's diary written for the future between April 1984 and March 1985 does in fact become Orwell's *Nineteen Eighty-Four*, the potent novel of warning that has been reprinted almost annually since 1949. While the diary remained a warning aimed at Winston's past and our present, it permitted us to hope that we might still do something about the malevolent potential of Ingsoc. Even the threat – repeated four times – that the Party was to last a thousand years could be regarded as offering a faint ray of hope. In 1949, it would have been considered an echo of the Nazi party's vain boast that it would endure for the same period (pp. 308, 348, 380, 385).[6]

But hope is by no means the dominant tone in Orwell's *Nineteen Eighty-Four*. By projecting his work a mere thirty-five years into the future, he had given to his novel a more frightening immediacy than the other major dystopian writers had dared to risk. By doing so he could examine aspects of memory and dreams much more relevant than they would be in a novel projected hundreds of years into the future. Yet a price has been paid for Orwell's courageous stand. As the period between 1984 and the time of reading narrowed, the credibility gap clearly widened. We know now, for example, that there were no purges, no civil wars, and no atom bomb attacks in England after the publication of Orwell's novel (pp. 181, 297, 325, *passim*). Moreover, as 1984 recedes into the past the very title of the book must become an anachronism. The true martyr, then, is not Winston Smith but Orwell himself. In order to impress upon us the immediacy of the dangers of Ingsoc, Newspeak, doublethink, Big Brother, and so much else in our current society, Orwell deliberately chose to project his novel to 1984. When he did so, he surely foresaw that the price would be the inevitable annihilation of his own greatest monument.

2

From History to Psychological Grotesque: The Politics of Sado-Masochism in *Nineteen Eighty-Four*

Mason Harris

I

Nineteen Eighty-Four is probably the best political satire of the twentieth century, but its status as one of the most disturbing horror stories of all time is mainly due to its relentless psychological study of the disintegration of its main character. Winston Smith's ordeal and collapse in the Ministry of Love is so appalling that some critics assume that here the author must have collapsed as well. Frightening as the society of Orwell's imaginary future may be, it is the failure of the self in this society which provides the basis for the widespread assumption that *Nineteen Eighty-Four* is Orwell's testament of despair. In an influential critique Isaac Deutscher accuses Orwell of succumbing to the political madness he set out to criticise.[1] According to Deutscher, *Nineteen Eighty-Four* is the hysterical product of the failure of Orwell's inadequate, rationalistic socialism in the face of irrational aspects of modern history, which is why it so easily lent itself to the right-wing interpretation so convenient to the Cold War.

Deutscher assumes that the irrationality of the novel's world reflects the author's state of mind. Here I will argue that in *Nineteen Eighty-Four* Orwell undertakes a study of the psychological nature of totalitarianism, a study that grows naturally out of his previous work. Through the collective insanity of the future world, and the struggle and defeat of his main character, Orwell investigates both the basis of individuality and the threat presented to it by the appeal of absolute authority. In *Nineteen Eighty-Four* Orwell makes an important contribution to the psychological analysis of fascism and of the authoritarian personality, which gained momentum in European thought in the thirties and has been elaborated by Erich Fromm, Erik Erikson, and others.

Although Orwell identified himself primarily as a political moralist, a strong interest in psychological attitudes towards authority is manifested in his early fiction and acquires a political dimension in *The Road to Wigan Pier* and later essays. The problem of authority also plays a central role in the anti-utopian tradition of Wells, Zamyatin, and Huxley, which Orwell continues and revises in *Nineteen Eighty-Four*. I will first outline the tradition of fantasy in which Orwell was working, then briefly trace the development of his interest in the psychology of fascism, and finally show how some psychological ideas first defined in the essays are worked out in the novel. My goal here is not to provide a full psychological interpretation of *Nineteen Eighty-Four*, but to indicate intentions on the part of the author which any psychological approach must take into account.[2]

II

In anti-utopian fantasy Orwell found an emphasis on the psychology of class and on the submergence of the self in a social whole, both closely related to major themes in his own work. Wells's stories of the future – *The Time Machine*, 'A Story of the Days to Come', and *When the Sleeper Wakes* – depict a world where the classes are rigidly separated; the ruling class has become indolent and passive, the workers primitive and aggressive. In *Brave New World* Aldous Huxley depicts a whole society that has fallen into the state of indolence which Wells attributes to his upper class. Reacting against both Wells and Huxley, Orwell reverses the class-psychology of Wells's future world, making the workers passive and the ruling class – the Party – insanely aggressive.

Wells is much preoccupied with the problem of aggression in human nature, but retains a rationalist perspective. While there is some aggression in Huxley's *Brave New World* and Zamyatin's *We*, both depict worlds which are pleasant to most of the characters and with which these characters seek mystical union – a theme not present in Wells. To explain the appeal of fascism, Orwell makes aggression a characteristic of the dominant class while incorporating the idea of the ecstatic loss of self in a social whole from Zamyatin and Huxley. The result is a world of aggression which also offers mystical union and loss of self. Orwell thought Zamyatin's anti-utopia superior to Huxley's because in Huxley's future world the conquest of the self is effected entirely through physical pleasure – 'There is no power hunger, no sadism, no hardness of any kind' – while Zamyatin possesses an 'intuitive grasp of the irrational side of totalitarianism – human sacrifice, cruelty as an end in itself, the worship of a Leader who is credited with divine attributes . . . .'[3] Orwell sees the ritual executions in this novel as a reversion to the world-view of primitive religion. I would argue that he somewhat exaggerates the cruelty of Zamyatin's world because he is projecting into it themes which he plans to develop in his own fantasy of the future.[4]

Nineteen Eighty-Four and *We* have in common some aspects of plot, an oppressive atmosphere of constant surveillance, and a drastic annihilation of the self, but the affinity of Orwell's novel with Wells's emphasis on the psychological characteristics of the classes in the future world is equally important. Wells is mainly concerned with the dangers of a degenerate working class, while Orwell focuses on the tensions of the lower-middle class, represented by the Outer Party to which Winston belongs, and on the authoritarian world which has been generated by these tensions. This state of affairs is the culmination of two themes which run through much of Orwell's work: the misery of being lower-middle (or 'lower-upper-middle') class, and the problem of absolute authority embodied in an all-powerful institution which threatens to engulf the individual self, but which also emanates a seductive attraction fatal to the individual's attempt to escape.

Orwell's interest in the relation between class and institutions springs from the respectable near-poverty of his family combined with his experience in boarding school and the Burma police. In his first two novels the institution is represented by the British Empire and the Church of England, respectively. In *The Road to Wigan Pier*, where he announces his conversion to socialism, he broadens his perspective by linking the psychological tensions of the middle class to fascism, thus discovering the combination of class and evil institution which will dominate his imagination for the rest of his career. A brief summary of some of his political ideas will provide a background for his interest in the psychology of identification with power.

III

From the second half of *The Road to Wigan Pier*, 'Inside the Whale', and other essays we can put together an outline of Orwell's vision of political alternatives for the future. According to Orwell, the failure of capitalism has resulted in economic chaos and the collapse of middle-class values. This crisis in values is intensified by a corresponding decline in religious belief. Orwell announces 'the break-up of *laissez-faire* capitalism and of the liberal-Christian culture' (*CE*, I, 525), and proposes an egalitarian, common-sense socialism as the only alternative. He fears, however, that in Britain the middle class will turn to fascism, as it did in Germany and Italy, and he never tires of pointing out that upper-middle-class intellectuals of the left have already turned to Stalinism, which he regards as fascism in disguise. Orwell sees the turn towards authoritarianism in the thirties primarily as the result of the frustration of the need of the middle class for order and traditional values. He feels that because of the failure of capitalism western civilisation must make a choice in the near future between socialism and fascism. *Nineteen Eighty-Four*, first planned in the early forties, is intended to serve as a negative example, warning against the wrong choice and emphasising by way of contrast the need for the moderate socialism he outlines in *The Lion and the Unicorn* (1941). (Bernard Crick points out that Orwell assumed that readers of *Nineteen Eighty-Four* would be familiar with his writings in support of socialism.[5])

Orwell sees aggressive lower-middle-class fascism and the intellectuals' Stalinism as variations on the same state of mind: both arise from the confusion of values resulting from the crisis of capitalism, and both are secular substitutes for religion, providing an infallible set of doctrines embodied in a powerful organisation which invites the confused individual to gain a sense of security by surrendering his ability to think and feel for himself. The fashionable Stalinism of the British intellectual is a secular religion – 'The patriotism of the deracinated' (I, 515) – which resurrects in

disguise all the traditional values which the disillusioned intellectual claims to have repudiated.

Unfortunately, the new secular religions are far more primitive
than the values they replace. Both fascism and Stalinism are more
dynamic than nineteenth-century liberalism because they awaken
atavistic feelings from the Middle Ages and beyond. Orwell
complains that neither liberal nor Marxist historians have been able
to explain the popular success of fascism. He acknowledges that
the German ruling class sought to use Hitler for its own advantage,
but makes a sharp distinction between the relatively limited upper-
class interests which benefit from fascism, and the psychological
appeal of fascism to millions of devoted followers who may have
little to gain from it in a material sense.[6] He continues to explore
the psychology of fascism in some later essays, and makes this the
central theme of *Nineteen Eighty-Four*. It is to isolate the psychological appeal of fascism that Orwell eliminates material incentives
to power in *Nineteen Eighty-Four* – what he thinks of Stalin's Inner
Party can be seen in the pigs of *Animal Farm*.

Two essays of the mid-forties work towards defining a psychological pattern of submission and domination which underlies all
forms of identification with authority. In 'Raffles and Miss Blandish'
Orwell interprets a contemporary taste for brutality in detective
stories in terms of an alternation between 'masochism', the submergence of the self in all-powerful authority, and 'sadism', the
right to inflict such power ruthlessly on others. The atmosphere
of such fiction resembles O'Brien's depiction in *Nineteen Eighty-
Four* of a world where love, friendship, and sexuality no longer
exist.[7] In the Americanised gangster novels of James Hadley Chase,
'such things as affection, friendship, good nature or even ordinary
politeness simply do not enter. Nor, to any great extent, does
normal sexuality. Ultimately only one motive is at work throughout
the story: the pursuit of power' (CE, III, 217). Orwell concludes
that the popularity of this kind of fiction is symptomatic of a
growing trend towards the abandonment of traditional standards
in favour of identification with the ruthless assertion of power: 'The
interconnexion between sadism, masochism, success-worship,
power-worship, nationalism and totalitarianism is a huge subject
whose edges have barely been scratched' (CE, III, 222). Although
politics are never mentioned in such stories, they provide a perfect
reproduction of the 'mental atmosphere' of fascism. Here Orwell
explores the tendency towards fascism on the part of ordinary

people, who find in these stories power-worship 'in the form in which they are able to understand it' (*CE*, III, 224).

In 'Notes on Nationalism', an essay which outlines many of the major themes of *Nineteen Eighty-Four*, Orwell seeks to define the psychological essence of power-worship by analysing identification with power on the part of the intellectual. He stretches the word 'nationalism' to cover identification with a race, nation, church, or political party, 'Nationalism . . . is inseparable from the desire for power. The abiding purpose of every nationalist is to secure more power and prestige, *not* for himself but for the nation or other unit in which he has chosen to sink his own individuality' (*CE*, III, 362). The 'sinking' of the self in an infallible whole represents the masochistic side of the pattern. Such identification with authority then brings out the sadistic side, promoting a wilful fabrication of external reality and a ruthless attitude towards those not included in the group: 'Loyalty is involved, and so pity ceases to function' (*CE*, III, 379).

'Nationalism' is inherently hostile to the acknowledgement of external reality because this would interfere with 'dreams of power and conquest which have no connection with the physical world' (*CE*, III, 372). In Orwell's earlier work the tendency of totalitarian parties to fabricate reality is attributed to political self-interest, but here the external world is rejected mainly because it would interfere with enjoyment of the authoritarian state of mind: 'What remains constant in the nationalist is his own state of mind: the object of his feelings is changeable, and may be imaginary' (*CE*, III, 368). Orwell says that 'in this essay I am trying to isolate and identify tendencies which exist in all our minds and pervert our thinking, without necessarily occurring in a pure state or operating continuously' (*CE*, III, 377). This also describes the motivation for *Nineteen Eighty-Four*, an imaginary world where such 'tendencies' can find a 'pure' and 'continuous' manifestation.

One of the most striking ideas in this essay is the concept of 'negative nationalism'. Orwell observes that nationalism 'may work in a merely negative sense, *against* something or other and without the need for any positive object of loyalty' (*CE*, III, 362). Fanatical opposition to a group or leader involves the same psychology as fanatical identification. As evidence that 'nationalist feeling can be purely negative' (*CE*, III, 363) Orwell cites Trotskyism – not so much 'Trotsky himself, who was by no means a man of one idea', as mediocre followers who identify themselves entirely in terms of hostility to Stalin (*CE*, III, 376). Such negative identification is a fallacy to which the alienated intellectual is particularly liable. We will see that Winston Smith falls into it when he joins the Brotherhood' under O'Brien's auspices.

The use of psychological concepts in 'Raffles and Miss Blandish' and 'Notes on Nationalism' indicates that by the mid-forties Orwell had become interested in the interpretation of the authoritarian personality. He never explains to what extent he was influenced by contemporary psychological theory, but it is interesting to note that a similar definition of sadism and masochism is developed in Erich Fromm's *Escape from Freedom* (1941), which also parallels aspects of the philosophy O'Brien expounds to Winston in *Nineteen Eighty-Four*.[8] Like Orwell, Fromm defines sado-masochism as a means of escaping, through identification with absolute power, from the sense of helplessness which capitalism inflicts on the isolated individual. Wilhelm Reich's *Mass Psychology of Fascism* (1932) is another possible influence. In his emphasis on the sense of self Orwell seems closer to Fromm than to Reich, but the Party's use of repressed sexuality in the service of fascism may owe something to Reich. The general influence of Freudian thought is evident in *Nineteen Eighty-Four*: Winston's successful interpretation of his dream in Chapter Seven indicates an interest on Orwell's part in the basic concepts of psychoanalysis, while O'Brien's manipulation of Winston's guilt suggests familiarity with Freud's concept of the super-ego. Orwell's interest in the appeal of fascism, first made clear in *The Road to Wigan Pier*, inevitably prompted his thought in a psychological direction. By the mid-forties he was adopting ideas from the Freudian analysis of fascism in the course of constructing his own concept of the authoritarian state of mind.

IV

Nineteen Eighty-Four first plunges us into a nightmare version of contemporary problems of politics and class, and then moves towards the psychological problems raised in 'Raffles and Miss Blandish' and 'Notes on Nationalism'. The totalitarian world of the future has emerged as the result of social disruption caused by a series of world-wide political catastrophes, including nuclear war: 'It was only after a decade of national wars, civil wars, revolutions and counter-revolutions in all parts of the world that Ingsoc and its rivals emerged as fully worked-out political theories' (p. 334). (Thus we should not see Oceania primarily as the product of a socialist revolution, as was assumed in the Cold War interpretation.) This society has been constructed by the intelligentsia of the middle class: 'bureaucrats, scientists, technicians, trade-union organisers, publicity experts, sociologists, teachers, journalists and professional politicians' (p. 334).

The division of the Party into two strata designates Winston's impoverished Outer Party as the lower middle class. Winston's world maintains a state of political frenzy reminiscent of Hitler's Germany – a sort of continuous Nuremberg rally. (As a condensation of 'English Socialism', 'Ingsoc' corresponds to 'Nazi' for 'National Socialism'.) With very few exceptions the members of the Outer Party lack the capacity for abstract thought, and thus Winston feels intellectually isolated – a minority of one. The Outer Party does contain intellectuals like Syme, the expert on Newspeak, Ampleforth the poet, and Winston himself, but more characteristic of the Outer Party is Winston's neighbour Parsons, 'a mass of imbecile enthusiasms' (p. 175) who combines slavish devotion to the Party with admiration for the sadistic activities of his children in the Junior Spies – an admiration which continues unabated when his daughter denounces him to the Thought Police for supposedly talking against Big Brother in his sleep: 'It shows I brought her up in the right spirit, anyway' (p. 360).

If the Outer Party is a lower-middle-class phenomenon, the intellectual direction of this world, supplied by the Inner Party, is a parody of Stalinism. Though they are intended to destroy thought, yet doublethink, Newspeak, and the constant rewriting of history, all require intelligence to conceive and maintain. Orwell grafts onto the lower-middle-class hysteria of the Outer Party the self-deception and dishonesty of the Stalinist intellectual – the consequence of the willing submission of the mind to absolute power. There is a peculiar nihilism in the Inner Party's attack on language and reason, as though the intention were to destroy even the possibility of meaning: 'linking-together of opposites . . . is one of the chief distinguishing marks of Oceanic society. The official ideology abounds with contradictions even when there is no practical reason for them' (p. 344). This sometimes results in a macabre humour which increases the grotesque effect without becoming comic.

Winston revolts against this world with more determination and consciousness of purpose than the main characters of Orwell's early fiction, yet his implication in the evil institution is also more dynamic. Winston's diary is the symbol of his rebellion, but an element of sadism appears when he begins this diary by describing with relish a news film of refugees being bombed in a lifeboat. Again, his initial fantasies about Julia combine rape and torture: 'Vivid, beautiful hallucinations flashed through his mind. He would flog her to death with a rubber truncheon. He would tie her naked to a stake and shoot her full of arrows like Saint Sebastian. He would ravish her and cut her throat at the moment of climax' (p. 169). There is nothing like this elsewhere in Orwell's fiction; these fantasies are a more imaginative version of the torments inflicted on the heroine in the detective novel Orwell summarises in 'Raffles and Miss Blandish'. Also, the rubber truncheon is the favourite torture weapon of the Party.

Despite these fantasies Winston is in fact rather mild and hesitating, quite prepared to give Julia the lead in their relationship. His fatal characteristic is not his latent sadism but the stronger reverse side of his personality, his masochistic admiration for O'Brien. At the height of the Two Minutes Hate Winston's 'secret loathing of Big Brother changed into adoration, and Big Brother seemed to tower up, an invincible, fearless protector . . .' (pp. 168–9). Winston repudiates this feeling by writing 'Down with Big Brother' over and over in his diary, yet he also feels 'deeply drawn' to O'Brien, a substitute authority-figure who, he imagines, must share his most secret ideas (p. 165). Winston decides that he is writing his diary to O'Brien, and dreams or imagines that O'Brien has whispered to him, 'We shall meet in the place where there is no darkness' (p. 177), both a suggestion of paradise and a mysterious prevision of his torture by O'Brien in the Ministry of Love. 'Winston had never been able to feel sure . . . whether O'Brien was a friend or an enemy. Nor did it even seem to matter greatly. There was a link of understanding between them, more important than affection or partisanship' (p. 178).

This imagined relationship with O'Brien, which seems more intimate and intellectually significant than his relationship with Julia, is actually a regression to an infantile level where subject and object cannot be distinguished. With Julia, Winston encounters difficult problems in relating to another person. He must anxiously ponder whether her note is genuine, overcome the obstacles to communication and meeting, and finally appreciate the vitality of a world-view quite different from his own. On the other hand, Winston does not have to evaluate his feeling for O'Brien because his sense of relationship to him is so deep that the difference between friend and enemy seems superficial. He does not have to communicate with O'Brien because 'It was as though their two minds had opened and the thoughts were flowing from one into the other through their eyes' (p. 171) It is not necessary to plan any meeting in a real time or place because Winston has an inexplicable confidence that they will meet 'where there is no darkness . . . . Winston did not know what it meant, only that in some way or another it would come true' (p. 178). The relationship with Julia is furtive, limited, and rewarding. The sense of mystical union with O'Brien is in fact a surrender to irrationality which links Winston to the authoritarian world against which he attempts to rebel.

For much of the novel, however, the temptation to masochistic submission to O'Brien remains in the background while Winston struggles to develop a sense of self, both through personal memory and his relationship with Julia. Even in describing the news film Winston performs an act of self-consciousness alien to the world of the Party. As he begins the diary he also wrestles with dreams and memories of his mother. Here his progress is blocked by an overwhelming sense of guilt, yet he persists in trying to remember his childhood and to place it in the now-suppressed historical past. After making love to Julia in the room above the antique shop, Winston has a dream in which the glass paperweight, representing the inner world of the self, expands to contain an infinite world, while at the same time the gesture of protecting a child, made both by his mother and a woman in the news film, becomes meaningful to him. As a result of this dream he comes to terms with his guilt over a childhood death-wish towards his mother and sister. He is now able to accept his mother's love for him as a sustaining force and to affirm the world of personal values she represents (pp. 294–8). Later, standing at the window of the same room, he makes this insight the basis of an affirmation of the vitality of human life everywhere and a hope for future revolution (pp. 346–8). Whatever the ambiguities of the proles, the most important aspect of this moment is Winston's uncharacteristic optimism.[9] Through facing the anxiety and guilt of self-exploration, Winston achieves an affirmation both of the self and the world. In doing so he profoundly threatens the Oceanic state of mind.[10] Later O'Brien will instruct him on how to escape from the problems of possessing a self into the joys of infantile dependence on authority.

Unfortunately, when Winston attempts political action, the most difficult step of all, his vague sense of dependence on O'Brien leads him into the fallacy Orwell has defined as 'negative nationalism'. At the beginning of their relationship, both Winston and Julia naively define their sexual love in terms of blind opposition to the Party: 'If he could have infected the whole lot of them with leprosy or syphilis, how gladly he would have done so! Anything to rot, to weaken, to undermine' (p. 264). At this point such sentiments seem part of the vitality of their newly-discovered relationship in a world where 'No emotion was pure, because everything was mixed up with fear and hatred' (p. 265). Later, this attitude is transcended in Winston's revelatory dream and his subsequent meditations, where he finds a value in life beyond mere opposition to the Party.

When Winston joins the 'Brotherhood' with O'Brien he takes a crucial step towards his final defeat. O'Brien gives the playful negativism of the lovers the doctrinaire codification required for the 'nationalist' state of mind. He administers a parody oath which requires blind obedience and willingness to commit an absurd series of sadistic actions: 'You are prepared to cheat, to forge, to blackmail, to corrupt the minds of children, to distribute habit-forming drugs, to encourage prostitution, to disseminate venereal diseases . . . to do anything which is likely to cause demoralization and to weaken the power of the Party?' (p. 305). Here Winston submits to the sadistic authoritarianism against which he seeks to conspire; nothing O'Brien says suggests an interest in creating a better world. O'Brien also emphasises that as rebels they will not be allowed to experience a sense of solidarity with others: they will work in isolation and never know the reason for their orders – conditions under which Winston already works in the Ministry of Truth.

After taking the oath, 'A wave of admiration, almost of worship, flowed out from Winston towards O'Brien . . . it was impossible to believe that [O'Brien] could be defeated. There was no stratagem that he was not equal to, no danger that he could not foresee' (p. 308). Here Winston duplicates the official view of Big Brother which the Two Minutes Hate inspired in him against his will; certainly there is some irony in joining a 'Brotherhood' to oppose Big Brother. (During the torture, O'Brien demolishes Winston's claims to humanist values by playing a recording of Winston taking the oath.) In asserting the homoerotic bond of a male power-structure O'Brien ignores the presence of Julia. O'Brien's power over Winston is made evident when Julia immediately answers 'No' when Winston is asked whether he and Julia would be willing to 'separate and never see one another again', while Winston hesitates for some time before refusing – 'For a moment he seemed even to have been deprived of the power of speech' (p. 306).

Orwell's concept of Trotskyism as 'Negative nationalism' illuminates the role of the mysterious book by 'Goldstein', the hate-figure now become prophet. The status of this volume as *'the book'* suggests the religious worship of a text. Deutscher complains that it reads like a simple-minded version of Trotsky; this was probably Orwell's intent. Also, the vision of history as endless power-struggle provided in the book's opening paragraphs suggests James Burnham, a thinker in whom Orwell found a consistent strain of power-worship, and whose ideas contributed much to the basic concept of the insane world of *Nineteen Eighty-Four*. 'Goldstein' asserts that 'no advance on wealth, no softening of manners, no reform or revolution has ever brought human equality a millimetre nearer' (p. 332). This denial of historical process seems a better argument for the static world of the Party than for revolution.[11] The passages Winston reads from 'Goldstein's' book combine Burnham with simplified Trotsky to provide a bitterly accurate account of Oceanic society without much sense of a more human alternative. Thus it is symbolically appropriate that O'Brien should claim to have helped write the book; it remains within his universe of discourse. 'Goldstein' makes clear that Ingsoc is the opposite of true socialism, but does not say what true socialism is, thus contributing to the problems readers have had in assessing the political perspective of the novel. We never get to 'Goldstein's' vision of a better future, but O'Brien may be right when he says it isn't very convincing (pp. 384–5).

Winston's failure is not intended to invalidate his struggle for independence, but to show the vulnerability of the intellectual isolated in a world which despises humanist values. Julia has more confidence and emotional vitality than he, but she refuses to think beyond the immediate present. She has no interest in the course of history, the difference between truth and falsehood, or even in the possibility of a world different from that of the Party. We should remember that it is she who gleefully accepts as a self-definition Winston's remark that she is 'only a rebel from the waist downwards' (p. 291). Winston's recurring sense of futility stems from his need to look beyond his present situation: he shoulders the burden of historical time, confronting the dubiousness of being able to reconstruct the past or communicate with the future, if there is to be one different from his present. Like Orwell's Stalinist or Trotskyist contemporaries, he risks intellectual suicide by turning to an authority-figure to make his world secure, though in his perilous isolation he has more excuse for this weakness than they do.

V

In the Ministry of Love, O'Brien treats Winston as a case for religious conversion. If Winston turned to O'Brien to bolster a faltering attempt at independence, O'Brien states that the very coherence of the Party's world depends on Winston's voluntary submission, his enthusiastic acceptance of the faith: 'When finally you surrender to us, it must be of your own free will. We do not destroy the heretic because he resists us: so long as he resists us we never destroy him. We convert him . . . we bring him over to our side, not in appearance, but genuinely, heart and soul' (p. 379).

O'Brien tortures Winston not so much to intimidate him as to break down his sense of self and cause him to develop a love-relationship with his torturer. In Winston's vision, O'Brien 'was the tormentor, he was the protector, he was the inquisitor, he was the friend' (p. 369). As the treatment proceeds, he experiences a 'peculiar reverence for O'Brien, which nothing seemed able to destroy' (p. 395). He comes to feel that O'Brien's mind entirely contains his own, and that he is a helpless infant cared for by O'Brien. The more helpless and ashamed Winston feels, the more he experiences himself through O'Brien's consciousness, as part of O'Brien's strength.

O'Brien reveals to Winston a utopia of sado-masochism where the highest joy is the loss of self to absolute authority, accompanied by regression to infancy and escape from time into the immortality of the Party: 'The individual only has power in so far as he ceases to be an individual . . . if he can make complete, utter submission, if he can escape from his identity, if he can merge himself in the Party so that he *is* the Party, then he is all-powerful and immortal'

(p. 387). O'Brien describes this ideal world in terms which alternate between submission and domination. It will be 'a world of trampling and being trampled upon' in which 'there will be no emotions except fear, rage, triumph and self-abasement' (p. 389). Here the fear is essential to the rage, and the self-abasement to the triumph. 'Utterly penitent', Winston will crawl into a 'world of victory after victory, triumph after triumph' (p. 390). O'Brien promises, 'Always, at every moment, there will be the thrill of victory, the sensation of trampling on an enemy who is helpless. If you want a picture of the future, imagine a boot trampling on a human face – for ever' (p. 390).[12]

The key word in this famous statement is 'imagine'. The citizens of Oceania are not allowed to do much face-trampling on their own; that is reserved for specialists in the Ministry of Love. Rather, the 'sensation' of triumph is experienced vicariously through victories reported on the telescreen, news films such as the one recorded in Winston's diary, public executions of traitors and prisoners of war, and the various 'hate' periods. The new Winston produced by O'Brien's therapy is a gin-sodden, sentimental masochist, but still capable of experiencing 'triumph' when a blast of trumpets from the telescreen announces a great military victory. In this final scene, Winston's fear of a 'smashing defeat in Africa' is actually ambivalent – it might bring about 'the destruction of the Party!' (p. 409) – but he does not know this because he no longer attempts to understand his feelings. When victory with great slaughter is announced, he sits drunkenly while experiencing vicarious action: 'Under the table Winston's feet made convulsive movements. He had not stirred from his seat, but in his mind he was running, swiftly running, he was with the crowds outside, cheering himself deaf' (p. 415). Thus the sense of triumph can be enjoyed in complete passivity. Only at this moment does Winston achieve the 'healing change' by projecting his ambivalence into love for Big Brother and hatred for the enemy.

In addition to representing submission to external authority, the relation between O'Brien and Winston could represent the super-ego sadistically tormenting the ego. The Party with its all-seeing telescreens could be an extreme manifestation of a guilty conscience. Freud says that the cruellest aspect of the super-ego lies in its refusal to distinguish between thoughts and actions: 'nothing is hidden from the super-ego, not even thoughts . . . the intention is counted as equivalent to the deed'.[13] Early in his ordeal, Winston understands that 'in the eyes of the Party there was no distinction between the thought and the deed' (p. 368). O'Brien confirms that 'The Party is not interested in the overt act: the thought is all we care about' (p. 377). In 'The Prevention of Literature', an essay of the mid-forties, Orwell describes, in terms close to Freud's concept of repression, the 'self-censorship' which a writer may be led to impose on himself by dogmatic political loyalties: 'Even a single taboo can have an all-round crippling effect upon the mind, because there is always a danger that any thought which is freely followed up may lead to the forbidden thought' (*CE*, IV, 65). As he recovers from torture, Winston becomes adept in a technique of mental hygiene called 'Crimestop': 'The mind should develop a blind spot whenever a dangerous thought presented itself. The process should be automatic, instinctive' (p. 399). Winston's ego sinks in self-esteem until he becomes dependent for his moral being on O'Brien and Big Brother. Social authority can gain complete control over the individual only by crushing the ego and appropriating the super-ego, thus setting up a sado-masochistic relationship within the self as well as between the self and others.

O'Brien's lectures to Winston originate with Dostoyevsky's Grand Inquisitor, who explains that he takes away the burden of freedom in order to give humanity perfect happiness. In the anti-utopian tradition, the Inquisitor provides a model for authority-figures who justify the oppressive future world. Mustapha Mond of *Brave New World* and the Well-Doer of *We* both follow the Inquisitor's argument in their own terms, but O'Brien makes a dramatic departure from it. When Winston, asked to answer the crucial question of *why* the Party maintains itself in power, gets ready to explain that 'the choice for mankind lay between freedom and happiness' (p. 385), O'Brien angrily silences him, turning up the torture-dial to emphasise the gravity of his error, and begins his exposition of the joys of sado-masochism as the whole basis of Oceanic society. Deutscher claims that this explanation reveals a hopelessly naive interpretation of history on Orwell's part – no social hierarchy could be maintained by sadism alone. (Winston makes the same objection, but is overruled [p. 391].) It is important to note that Orwell introduces this explanation with a clearly-marked revision of the tradition of anti-utopian fantasy, indicating that he wants to make his own fantasy more extreme than those of his predecessors. *Nineteen Eighty-Four* should be seen as a deliberately Gothic world, an experiment in isolating extreme states of mind, rather than as a prophecy intended to sum up the whole meaning of modern history.

A crucial difference between *We* and *Nineteen Eighty-Four* appears in O'Brien's insistence that Winston's submission must be voluntary. In Zamyatin's novel heretics are publicly executed and sometimes tortured, but little is made of repentance. Finally an operation is discovered which can render everyone permanently loyal by removing part of the brain. Such a physical solution would be unacceptable to O'Brien: despite all his apparatus he must rely in the end on persuasion, including a large amount of bluff. He repeatedly tries to convince Winston of the non-existence of his self: 'You do not exist' (p. 383). 'You will be annihilated in the past as well as in the future. You will never have existed' (p. 378). He also claims that through torture Winston's psyche will be permanently damaged: 'We shall crush you down to the point from which there is no coming back . . . . Everything will be dead inside you . . . . We shall squeeze you empty, and then we shall fill you with ourselves' (p. 380).

If taken literally, these statements contradict O'Brien's stated intent. If his methods could produce this result against Winston's will, then the whole process would be defeated. The shock treatments which seem to remove a piece of Winston's brain may descend from the operation in *We*, but O'Brien explains that they have only a temporary effect intended to show Winston that total doublethink is really possible (pp. 380–2). Winston must learn to block voluntarily the ability of his brain to distinguish truth from falsehood. O'Brien makes such grim predictions about the effects of torture in order that eventually Winston will be convinced that they have come true: after being worn down enough he will believe that he is indeed 'empty' and choose to embrace the masochistic solution. Again, when O'Brien taunts Winston about his physical condition, he commits a *non sequitur* in equating his body with his mind: 'We have broken you up. You have seen what your body is like. Your mind is in the same state. I do not think there can be much pride left in you' (p. 395). This statement will be true to the extent to which Winston accepts it.

O'Brien stages his ultimate bluff by threatening Winston with rats in Room 101. If Winston had been able to think at this point, he would have realised that O'Brien could not allow the rats to attack him, since O'Brien has stated that he cannot destroy the heretic before the 'cure' is complete: Winston must be kept alive and more or less intact until he has stopped resisting. Also, it is hard to see in objective terms why Winston's 'betrayal' of Julia here is so different from all the other 'betrayals' made in the automatic confessions elicited by torture. It would seem that the threat of the rats sets off psychological processes in Winston which undo the therapeutic effect of his dream and his interpretation of it, where he discovered that despite a hunger-driven death-wish against his mother and sister, he was not in fact responsible for their disappearance.

Winston probably associates his childhood aggression with the hungry rats, and is overwhelmed by the thought that he has directed a similar death-wish against Julia, thus becoming unworthy of loving her, and sinking so much in his self-esteem that he must take refuge in infantile dependence on O'Brien and Big Brother. The apparently permanent damage which Winston and Julia acknowledge in their final meeting is actually a problem of self-esteem which they no longer have the courage to grapple with. It is indicative of the greater psychological complexity of Orwell's novel that Zamyatin's hero, anaesthetised by the operation, calmly watches his lover being tortured, while Winston sacrifices Julia only in his imagination, and then believes that he has committed an irreparable crime.

VI

Nineteen Eighty-Four provides a remarkable solution to some difficulties in Orwell's previous work. In the essays, Orwell's preoccupation with the psychological nature of totalitarianism is expressed in a series of harsh and rather repetitious attacks on Stalinist intellectuals, with occasional reference to the Catholic Church. His great political fantasy divides this subject into social and psychological levels where its various aspects can be developed more effectively. By providing a surface-level of topical reference to Nazi Germany, Stalinist Russia, and censorship in wartime Britain, Orwell gives himself full scope as political satirist, detailing the means by which governments coerce behaviour: surveillance, intimidation, torture, and the suppression of the historical past. His 'naturalistic' description of Winston's Outer Party also grounds the authoritarian world in the tensions of the middle class.[14]

On the psychological level, Winston's exploration of the self through memory and his growth towards emotional maturity with Julia are set in polar contrast to the flight from time and self offered by O'Brien. The horror of O'Brien's victory has caused readers to exaggerate the novel's pessimism. Winston's struggle to maintain his inner self shows the possibility of resistance; he fails because he has already conceded part of himself to O'Brien. O'Brien defeats Winston through a series of bluffs reinforced by the demoralising effect of torture. Because the totalitarian world is an illusion lacking social and intellectual content, it can succeed only by persuading the individual to abandon critical reason; to think about such a world is to see through it. Despite all his outward submission Winston maintains a secret resistance until he succumbs to bluff in Room 101. Even the converted Winston must rely on alcohol to maintain a sense of participation in the world of the Party. The 'gin-scented tears' which trickle down his nose at the end comment on the quality of his love for Big Brother.[15] Winston's defeat is intended to warn against all forms of identification with authority. Orwell's defence of the experiential self in this novel implicitly rejects any temptation, religious or political, to merge the self in a larger whole.[16]

The disturbing intensity of O'Brien's assault on Winston's psyche arises from the difference between Orwell's anti-utopian world and those of his predecessors. Both Huxley and Zamyatin construct coherent future societies, while Orwell's future is only a mass hallucination. The world of *Nineteen Eighty-Four* is much more frightening than that of *We* because it is less substantial and hence must use more extreme means to maintain its reality in the minds of its inhabitants. Zamyatin's United State functions efficiently, has a consistent rationale, and, in its own terms, provides well for all who co-operate with it.[17] At the end the Well-Doer pleads with D-503 to reaffirm a world he once enjoyed, and in which he played a valuable role. O'Brien, on the other hand, must persuade Winston to surrender everything he values in order to embrace an acknowledged illusion which can be maintained only through constant hysteria. The very excessiveness of the means O'Brien uses to defeat Winston reveals the vulnerability of his mad utopia.

Ingsoc is not an attempt to build a new society, but a regressive state of mind created to fill the void left by the failure of capitalism. The Party is so concerned with the control of inner feelings because any form of individual subjectivity threatens to expose the illusory nature of a world which has abolished the self and the relation between subject and object. O'Brien must defeat Winston because he feels that Winston resembles himself; that is, Winston is what O'Brien would be like if he had a self (p. 382). If Winston does not submit, O'Brien might fall back into the world of the self, where he would encounter doubt, inner conflict, and mortality. The gains Winston has managed to achieve on this route mean nothing to O'Brien; in a world where the self does not exist, self-knowledge and personal love can only be seen as dangerous perversions. O'Brien's world becomes the final reality of the novel, but this should not invalidate the ideal of the self as expressed in Winston's best insights. Through a drastic revision of the anti-utopian tradition Orwell created a world where he could give unified expression to his ideas about politics and psychology, thus combining an elaborate satire of the politics of the thirties and forties with a dramatisation of the deepest levels of psychological response to authority.

3

Room 101 Revisited: The Reconciliation of Political and Psychological Dimensions in Orwell's *Nineteen Eighty-Four*

Erika Gottlieb

I

As a political allegory against totalitarianism, *Nineteen Eighty-Four* is in the company of such great documents of twentieth-century humanism as Huxley's *Brave New World* and Camus's *The Plague*. Yet *Nineteen Eighty-Four* is unique in its achievement of what has rarely been attempted before, and not accomplished even by Camus or Huxley – the successful meshing of a consistent allegorical structure with a psychologically plausible, realistic texture.

Nineteen Eighty-Four also stands apart from all of Orwell's other books because it successfully combines two distinct aspects of his own work: the impassioned allegorical vision of *Animal Farm*, reminiscent of the satire and vision of Swift, even Blake; and the documentary approach of his naturalistic novels with their almost painstakingly close observation of character and environment.

We only have to recall the opening of the first chapter, indeed the first two pages, to recognise Orwell's unerring eye for detail: he makes us feel, touch, and smell the poverty and neglect as Winston ascends the ugly, run-down staircase of Victory Mansions, enters his barren, drab apartment, takes a gulp of foul-tasting Victory gin, and lights a poorly rolled Victory cigarette.

As the scene leads unobtrusively to Winston's overview of the sprawling gray city dominated by the overpowering structures of the four Ministries, we are face-to-face with the source and the eventual explanation of the ironic contrast between so many 'Victories' and the undeniable economic failure of Oceania. Guided by the convincingly realistic detail, we are scarcely aware of Orwell's mastery: by now the casually naturalistic description has imperceptibly turned into the scaffolding of the allegorical structure.

Still on the same flight of stairs, we pick up Winston's growing sense of uneasiness as he observes the Party's incessant vigilance: the ever-watching eyes of Big Brother on the posters, the helicopters snooping through windows, the omnipresence of the Thought Police, and the telescreen in the very centre of his own apartment. Without the use of explicit comment, we have been prepared to recognise the ironic contrast between Big Brother's World and the Word used to describe it. Having understood that Victory stands for failure, we can now proceed to solve the next puzzle: what is the true meaning of 'minitrue, minipax, miniluv, and miniplenty' (p. 160).

Within the space of the same two pages we get to know Winston, the middle-aged central character of the novel not only in terms of his physical characteristics, but also in terms of his intellectual and psychological attitudes. As a result, the unfolding political allegory touches us with an intimacy unknown in novels of this genre. Through Winston we sense, as if on our own skin, what it is like to be living under the ever-watching eye of the Police State. (It seems to me that it is precisely this exceptionally convincing power of Orwell's vision right from the opening that may account for the initial reluctance of many a young contemporary reader to 'enter' into the novel.)

Yet, in spite of the novel's undeniable power and stature in twentieth-century fiction, few of its critics have shown appreciation for the complexity and consistency of Orwell's achievement. On the one hand, there is the voice of the critic who concentrates exclusively on the political prophecy or warning, ignoring the psychological dimension of the book, and, perhaps as a result of this, talks about various flaws in form or structure. It is the political critic who describes the novel as 'didactic phantasy',[1] or 'a satiric dream',[2] speaking of its 'essentially didactic approach',[3] pondering whether it should be regarded as 'a flawed masterpiece'[4] or even the work of a writer who 'as a controversial critic and pamphleteer

. . . was superb, as good as any in English literature' but 'as a novelist was not particularly gifted'.[5]

On the other hand, critics who concentrate exclusively on the psychological analysis often reach conclusions I find startlingly contradictory to Orwell's professed goals in the political allegory, because they read the novel fundamentally as a projection of the writer's paranoid or sado-masochistic tendencies: Murray Sperber, for one, argues that the novel is only 'ostensibly about the future, but much of its political intensity comes of the author's past, not only about his feelings about school, but much earlier experiences as well'.[6] (In other words, the horrors in *Nineteen Eighty-Four* are due to the fact that Orwell had a horrible childhood, and that he also happened to hate school.) Another of the 'psychological' critics suggests that Orwell's emphasis on the cruelty of Big Brother's regime should be regarded as yet another projection, that of the writer's physical pain and fear of his own death, of a pessimistic state of mind caused by the advanced stage of tuberculosis.[7] (In other words, here the horrors of *Nineteen Eighty-Four* are due to the fact that Orwell didn't feel particularly well at the time of the writing of the novel.) Although I appreciate the attention these critics pay to the psychological dimension in the novel, I feel that looking at Winston's character as a projection of the author's well-being – physical or mental – leads to a shortsighted interpretation that will regrettably block the reader from understanding the novel.

The critic insisting on Orwell's sado-masochistic tendencies or on Winston's paranoia inevitably overlooks an important factor: Freud's definition of the neurotic personality has been so influential that it is often accepted as axiomatic that the source of neurosis resides in the individual's failure to adjust to a societal standard, a commonly accepted 'norm' of sanity. Orwell's *Nineteen Eighty-Four* is one of the first works which genuinely and systematically challenges this assumption.

One cannot come to grips with the novel without understanding that Orwell here introduces a paradox of numbers. By juxtaposing the single individual's sanity and humanity with the insanity and inhumanity of an entire state, he proposes that in certain societies the exclusive norm of sanity may indeed reside in the 'minority of one' (p. 225). The dictator of a totalitarian society can hold on to power only by convincing the masses that the unnatural, hate-filled and topsy-turvy world he created out of his insane obsession with power is normal. Orwell's political allegory contains the psychological warning: in a totalitarian state paranoia becomes the norm. Consequently, in a society which is based on suspicion, spying, fear and hatred, Winston is not a paranoid when he feels persecuted.

Therefore, it is really quite beside the point here whether or not *Nineteen Eighty-Four* reflects the writer's paranoia or sado-masochistic tendencies related to an unhappy childhood; what is essential is that we realise that the novel is based on the uncannily accurate analysis of the paranoid and sado-masochistic tendencies of dictatorship as exemplified by Stalin's Russia and Hitler's Germany.

Readers of *Nineteen Eighty-Four* who have lived under totalitarian rule have often been amazed at the novel's exceptional insight into the workings of the Police State,[8] an insight more likely to come from Orwell's wide reading in contemporary history, including first-hand accounts of political prisoners in Germany and Russia, than from the subconscious projections of his own psycho-pathological problems.

Also, whether or not Orwell's political insights were accurate, his definition of totalitarianism in *Nineteen Eighty-Four* matches those of his political commentaries, and no intelligent reader has yet come forward to claim that these commentaries are distorted by the essayist's paranoia.

Indeed, Orwell has explored the psycho-dynamics of the contemporary dictators' power over their subjects in many of his essays:

> The interconnection between sadism, masochism, success worship, power worship, nationalism and totalitarianism is a huge subject whose edges have barely been scratched . . . . Fascism is often loosely equated with sadism, but nearly always by people who see nothing wrong in the most slavish worship of Stalin.[9]

Confronted with ample historical evidence about mass insanity, Orwell is understandably concerned about the prospects of dictatorship on an even larger scale, should the Western world not recognise the falsehood of *both* Hitler's and Stalin's propaganda.

> The truth is, of course, that the countless English intellectuals who kiss the arse of Stalin are not different from the minority who give their allegiance to Hitler or Mussolini . . . . All of them

are worshipping power and successful cruelty. It is important to notice that the cult of power tends to be mixed up with a love of cruelty and wickedness *for their own sakes.*[10]

Whether or not Orwell was on his deathbed when he conceived of Winston's torture scenes (as a matter of fact, there is evidence that he had a detailed outline for the book under the title, *The Last Man in Europe* as early as 1943, well before his last illness),[11] *Nineteen Eighty-Four* emerges as a dramatic warning against the dehumanising power, the 'successful cruelty' of the totalitarian state. Reading *Nineteen Eighty-Four* as a case study of Winston's or Orwell's private neurosis clouds the issue that *Nineteen Eighty-Four* is a harrowing indictment of totalitarian governments because it happens to be a strikingly accurate anatomy of the way such governments have been functioning in the past and are still functioning in the present.

When in search of latent references to the author's childhood tendencies for paranoia, the 'psychological' critic may completely miss Orwell's explicit and by now widely accepted political diagnosis of the paranoia inherent in a totalitarian regime. The Two Minutes Hate which at its climax turns into the ecstatic worship of Big Brother is the daily ritual of the dictatorship turned state religion. Only by whipping up hatred against the arch-enemy, Goldstein, the satanic Betrayer, can the Inner Party prepare the atmosphere for the worshipful prayer to Big Brother the 'Saviour' (p. 170). What Orwell is pointing out in this scene is the theological underpinning of both Stalin's and Hitler's cult of leader worship. Both relied on justifying the persecution of a scapegoat accused of the treachery of Satan (whether we look at Hitler's use of the Jew linked to a Jewish world conspiracy, or Stalin's use of Trotsky linked to imperialist hirelings and counter-revolutionaries). In both cases the whipping up of hatred against this Satanic enemy allowed the dictator to justify his persecution of any individual or group he chose to associate with the scapegoat – an effective ploy leading to the subjugation of his own people to slavery.

Of course, what concerned Orwell in the novel was not merely the analysis of atrocities actually committed by Hitler's or Stalin's regimes, but what he felt was the Western intellectual's susceptibility to the psychosis of nationalistic leader worship. He was also concerned that prolonged periods of war may call forth or increase this susceptibility.

. . . we are in danger of . . . the centralised slave state, ruled
over by a small clique who are in effect a new ruling class,
though they might be adoptive rather than hereditary. [The]
dynamic [of such a state] would come from some kind of rabid
nationalism and leader worship kept going by literally continuous
war.[12]

Concerned with the impact of totalitarianism on the Western
mind, in *Nineteen Eighty-Four* Orwell presents us with a haunting
demonstration of the psychodynamics of this particular political
system; the political and psychological aspects of the novel are
inextricably intertwined. To recognise the organic unity of political
and psychological dimensions is also essential to the recognition
of *Nineteen Eighty-Four* as a well-integrated work of art – something
neither the political nor the psychological critic has been ready to
acknowledge without reservations, in spite of the novel's undeniable power and success.

To demonstrate the thematic unity of Orwell's vision and also
his mastery of form and structure, the rest of this paper will
concentrate on the scene of Room 101. This scene, I suggest, is in
effect the dramatic climax and the symbolic centre of the novel
because it brings together the psychological, political and mythical
dimensions of the major theme. That theme is betrayal.

In Oceania Big Brother has created the condition, or rather the
illusion of perpetual war. By creating the myth of the fictitious
enemy outside, he is able to foment hatred and fear against the
equally fictitious enemy inside. It is this combined threat of the
enemy without and the traitor within that gives Big Brother a free
hand to enslave his *own* people through the relentless persecution
of the 'culprits' – in fact anyone singled out practically at random
from the population. Public purges, mock confessions, or private
mock trials are simply ritual enactments of the same religious
myth – rituals designed to perpetrate awe and fear of Big Brother
as Divinity.

Betrayal also becomes the major theme on the personal-political
level – that is, in terms of Winston's actions in society – and it puts
the structure of the first two books (Part I and Part II) into an ironic
perspective. At first glance, one would see this entire movement
as Winston's ascent on the staircase (our first glimpse of him in
the novel) leading to self-understanding, liberation, and moral
regeneration. Yet, in the light of Part III in the Ministry of Love,

the whole ascending movement was mere illusion. Winston has been watched throughout: what he thought to be his liberation was part of the systematic process leading to his fall, humiliation, and degeneration.

A variety of critics have been trying to come to terms with the reasons for Winston's defeat. Some political interpretations define his goals as unrealistically Utopian, and blame Winston for being unaware of reality.[13] Others point out that as a member of the Underground, Winston was ready to become as ruthless as Big Brother himself; he would lose himself simply by entering political action. Psychological interpretations tend to blame different aspects of Winston's neurosis, even his death wish, for actually foreseeing, even provoking his own punishment.[14]

I feel, however, that Winston is made to lose his battle neither because he is lacking in political judgement, nor because he is a personally flawed, neurotic human being. Throughout the book he is fighting for self-awareness, understanding, for an ability to detect and act upon the Truth. Purchasing the diary, buying the glass paperweight, renting the room which will become his shelter with Julia – these acts should not be seen as expressions of a death wish. On the contrary, these are the only means by which he can assert his will to live. It is only in a deadly, unnatural society that expressions of basic human instincts lead to death; in Oceania the wish to live is judged to be a deathwish.

When, for instance, Paul Roazen claims that it is 'the tormenting capacity of memory [which] lends *Nineteen Eighty-Four* its nightmarish air',[15] he overlooks the fact that in a world of constant lies, in a world with all reliable records eliminated, Truth must reside in the past; memory is Winston's only means to search for historical Truth, his only means to search for personal Truth, his only road to break his bondage to his past and thereby rid himself from his nightmares.

The nightmarish air of the book actually comes from the opposite direction: from the collective nightmare imposed upon an entire civilisation by a successful dictator. It is Big Brother who deliberately creates and maintains the nightmarish condition of confusion and mass hysteria intended to cover up for the one and only real betrayal in Oceania. It is the thief who cries 'Thief' the loudest. It is his own crimes Big Brother blames on Goldstein and on all the other thought criminals; it is Big Brother who had originally betrayed the dream of human liberation through the Revolution.

The children's history book with its official description of the mythical past is indeed full of lies: Big Brother did not stage the Revolution to establish Paradise for the oppressed; he staged the Revolution in order to obtain power.

On the political level of the betrayal, Winston comes to understand that the Party is omniscient indeed. O'Brien had been watching him for seven years, aware of his every move, every entry in the diary, covertly encouraging him all the time, lying in wait for him to join the Underground.

Finally, and on the most intimate level, the psychodrama of Winston's self-betrayal is at the very heart of the dramatic structure. The greatest 'horror that had lain embedded in the future' is what awaits Winston in Room 101, posing Winston's final test of loyalty to his own sense of decency and humanity. When in the final crisis he is made to betray Julia, he will, in effect, lose his own self. This is where all the various levels of treachery finally come together to bear their combined effect on the reader. When in Room 101 Winston undergoes the ultimate horror of human disintegration, self-betrayal, intimately private as this experience may be, it is also the natural and inevitable consequence of all the other betrayals that constitute the system of totalitarianism.

II

Critical assessment of the climactic scene in Room 101 springs from the same two basically irreconcilable schools of opinion that inform attitudes to the book as a whole. Critics concentrating on the political parable tend to skim over this scene either by dismissing its importance or by admitting distaste for what they call the melodramatic or the theatricality of Grand Guignol,[16] which to some verges on the ridiculous.[17]

On the other hand, critics who examine the scene in terms of its psychological dimension usually follow the assumptions of Freudian depth psychology. They may find the scene crucial, but only as far as it reveals the particular nature of Winston's neurosis – paranoia, latent homosexuality, sado-masochistic tendencies[18] – all attributed to the Oedipal situation. What these psychological interpretations imply, and often explicitly state, is that Winston deliberately provokes his own punishment; that is, what happens to him in the Ministry of Love is just what he has been subconsciously craving for all along.[19]

There is no doubt that psychological scrutiny of this scene is essential to an understanding of the dramatic climax in the novel. But Freudian interpretations tend to have trouble reconciling their emphasis on Winston's (and ultimately on Orwell's) neurotic tendencies with the humanistic message of the political allegory. They fail to see that although Winston's ordeal in Room 101 unmistakably follows from his inner life, it is also the ordeal of Everyman, indeed of our common humanity in confrontation with the dehumanising forces of totalitarianism.

Yet it would be equally wrong by dismissing certain kinds of psychological interpretations to altogether dismiss the novel's psychological dimensions. Should the reader decide to act as a political analyst only, he would miss the complexity and power of this novel as it brings to focus the struggles of the inner man, struggles mapped out by Winston's memories, dreams, nightmares, the world of the subconscious. It is worth noting here that Michael Anderson's otherwise well-intentioned film version of *Nineteen Eighty-Four* suffers from this flaw: in a film it may even be inevitable to ignore the character's inner life. But as a result, when it comes to the scene in Room 101 – the climax in the film and in the novel – the film loses its intensity. Not having been exposed to Winston's nightmares, to his dream of the Golden Country, to the flashbacks of his past, the audience misses the very substance of Winston's psychodrama. Paradoxically, it is by concentrating on the political message exclusively that the director loses the focus and the vitality of that political message. The central thesis of Orwell's humanistic warning is that the most dangerous threat facing us in a totalitarian system is the inevitable loss of the individual's inner world, and, what is more, that this loss is irrecoverable.

Orwell acknowledges the far-reaching significance of the inner life, the world of the subconscious:

. . . the waking mind is not so different from the dreaming mind as it appears – or as we like to pretend that it appears . . . . The disordered, un-verbal world belonging to dreams is never quite absent from our minds, and if any calculation were possible I dare say it would be found that quite a half the volume of our waking thoughts were of this order. Certainly the dream-thoughts take a hand even when we are trying to think verbally, they influence the verbal thoughts, and it is largely they that

make our inner life valuable . . . . In a way this un-verbal part
of your mind is even the most important part, for it is the source
of nearly all *motives*.[20]

Although Orwell echoes much of the terminology and concern of
the Freudian critic here, this does not mean that he is in full
agreement with the Freudian assumptions or conclusions about
personality. We must realise that for Orwell self, personality, and
guilt assume a moral and ethical dimension. In effect, examining
Orwell's method of characterisation, one often gets a feeling that
he must have regarded even the subconscious as somehow morally
accountable. In Winston's case, for example, the 'dreaming mind'
is unmistakably a moral agent, performing much of the probing
search for the Truth hidden in the past. It is with the assistance of
the dreammind, that is through his dreams and nightmares, that
Winston succeeds in bringing to consciousness both his hopes and
fears, and succeeds in reaching self-understanding and moral
reintegration.

There is no doubt that Winston had carried the psychic burden
of guilt for almost thirty years and his recurring nightmares are
clearly expressions of a guilty conscience: somehow for the past
thirty years he had been thinking that he was responsible for his
mother's and sister's deaths. His guilt springs from a shameful
memory he had buried in his subconscious: the events immediately
preceding his mother's disappearance.

The first entry in Winston's diary is a record of irresistible
excitement and, at the same time, of his resistance, as the hidden
memory gradually comes to the surface. What he is trying to
describe is a scene from a war film he had just seen, in which a
Jewish mother holds a child, 'screaming with fright', in her arms.
In the face of inevitable disaster, she is shielding the child 'as if she
thought her arms could keep the bullets off him' (p 163).

In describing this scene, Winston becomes so agitated that he
is unable to express himself coherently: punctuation, sentence
structure disappear – he is breathless, eager to blurt it out. Still, as
the description approaches the forbidden, repressed memory, he
is unable to handle his mounting excitement:

> . . . *little boy screaming with fright and hiding his head between her*
> *breasts as if he was trying to burrow right into her and the woman*
> *putting her arms around him and comforting him although she was*

blue with fright herself . . . then the helicopter planted a 20 kilo bomb in among them terrific flash and the boat went all to matchwood. then there was a wonderful shot of a child's arm going up up up right up into the air . . . and there was a lot of applause from the party seats but a woman down in the prole part of the house suddenly started kicking up a fuss . . . until the police turned her turned out i dont suppose anything happened to her nobody cares what the proles say typical prole reaction they never –. (p. 163)

The entry is interrupted in mid-sentence because at this point Winston is still torn between the Party's sniggering, inhuman attitude to personal love and loyalty and an emotional reaction he cannot yet articulate.

The interrupted scene, however, will complete itself in Winston's subconscious mind, as if the dreaming mind had a will of its own, ready to 'take a hand' in the process already started. It is quite obvious that it was the protecting, shielding gesture of the mother's arm in the film which triggered Winston's excited reaction, and which now works its way further in the dreammind, in the form of a guiltdream, a nightmare.

Winston was dreaming of his mother.

. . . .

At this moment his mother was sitting in some place deep down beneath him with his young sister in her arms. He did not remember his sister at all, except as a tiny, feeble baby, always silent, with large, watchful eyes . . . . He was out in the light and air while they were being sucked down to death, and they were down there *because* he was up here. He knew it and they knew it, and he could see the knowledge in their faces . . . the knowledge that they must die in order that he might remain alive, and that this was part of the unavoidable order of things. (p. 181)

As the dreammind probes deeper and deeper into the submerged memory of the past, Winston comes to understand something about his guilt, and about the emotional and moral significance of the mother's protective gesture that he could not have articulated earlier:

The thing that now suddenly struck Winston was that his mother's death nearly thirty years ago had been tragic and sorrowful in a way that was no longer possible. Tragedy, he perceived, belonged to the ancient time . . . when there was still privacy, love and friendship. (p. 182)

It is quite clear, then, that the effort of articulating his thoughts in the diary leads to more profound levels of mental activity in the dreammind, which, in turn, leads to increasingly higher levels of understanding, pointing to the liberation of the suppressed memory and ultimately to the liberation of the self.

The subconscious wish for the liberation of the self is carried out simultaneously in the second of Winston's recurring dreams, the wishdream of the Golden Country. The importance of the sequence and the relationship of these two dreams has so far gone unnoticed:

All this he seemed to see in the large eyes of his mother and his sister, looking up at him through the green water, hundreds of fathoms down and still sinking.

Suddenly he was standing on short springy turf on a summer evening when the slanting rays of the sun gilded the ground . . . . In his waking thoughts he called it the Golden Country. (p. 182)

What is important here is that it is the wishdream that follows the nightmare and that it does so abruptly, that is, there is no gradual awakening, no transition between the two dreams. The facts that the nightmare is overtaken by the wishdream and that it is in violent contrast to it in terms of kinetic, colour and light images seem to me unmistakable signs of the dreamer's wish to escape, of what Orwell describes earlier in the book as 'the violent effort with which one wrenches one's head away from the pillow in a nightmare' (p. 169).

This 'violent effort', this deliberate 'wrenching away' is quite consistent. Whenever the Golden Country appears it manifests itself immediately after, and in sharp contrast to, a nightmare; it is also there when the dreamworld turns into the world of reality. When Julia and Winston agree to become lovers, they meet on a crowded public square to discuss the way to their secret meeting place. They can talk to each other only by pretending that they are watching the prisoners of war being led away to execution. Again, let's look at the juxtaposition, the relationship, between these two scenes:

With hands locked together, invisible among the press of bodies, they stared steadily in front of them, and instead of the eyes of the girl, the eyes of the aged prisoner gazed mournfully at Winston out of nests of hair.

Winston picked his way up the lane through dappled light and shade, stepping into pools of gold wherever the boughs parted. (p. 257)

As the drab, ominous urban scene is juxtaposed with the golden-green pastoral landscape, we experience the same sharp contrast, the same effect of a violent 'wrenching away': Winston is trying to tear himself away from the nightmare world created by Big Brother.

Then, with a slow 'shock of recognition' (p. 262) Winston realises that the scene is the fulfilment of his wishdream, as though it was the dreammind that had prepared him to find the Golden Country in reality.

Julia's role in the real scene is quite close to the fulfilment of Winston's dream in which 'With what seemed a single movement she tore off her clothes and flung them disdainfully aside' (p. 182).

And, yes! it was almost as in his dream. Almost as swiftly as he had imagined it, she had torn her clothes off, and when she flung them aside it was with the same magnificent gesture by which a whole civilisation seemed to be annihilated. (p. 264)

However, Orwell also shows the subtle difference between dream and reality. Although Julia and Winston's sexual encounter is a step toward liberation, at the moment of their first embrace they are still full of negative and primarily political emotions: 'Their embrace had been a battle, the climax a victory. It was a blow struck against the Party' (p. 265). Only through their repeated meetings in the room over the antique shop will their sexual-political conspiracy become a truly human commitment of personal love and loyalty. At this stage of their growth the glass paperweight will temporarily absorb the Golden Country, becoming their hope for a self-contained world together. Yet once it becomes the centre of the lovers' world in miniature, the glass paperweight suddenly expands to contain their whole Cosmos (what John Donne would have described as making the lovers' world an 'everywhere'). Appropriately, Winston comes to solve the puzzle of his personal existence after a dream in which he experiences a breakthrough, in and through the glass paperweight:

> It was a vast, luminous dream in which his whole life seemed to stretch out before him like a landscape on a summer evening after rain. It had all occurred inside the glass paperweight, but the surface of the glass was the dome of the sky, and inside the dome everything was flooded with clear soft light in which one could see into interminable distances. (pp. 294–5)

In Julia's healing, liberating presence Winston no longer resists the shameful, painful scene he had repressed for over thirty years. He recalls the last time he saw his mother and sister before they disappeared, after the starving family had been issued a small chocolate ration. He also recalls his selfishness in taking all the chocolate and fleeing for the door. This dream itself, and the discussion of its significance mark the climactic moment of Winston's growth and development because it makes him recognise the source of his guilt. 'Do you know' he asks, turning to Julia, 'that until this moment I believed I had murdered my mother?'

The searching, probing work of the 'unverbal dreammind' has been successful in bringing the suppressed memory to the surface and in relieving Winston from his bondage to the past. What liberates him from his previous nightmares is his recognition that he had not murdered his mother, although he had acted selfishly and betrayed her love for him. He also recognises that there is a way to redeem himself for that childhood betrayal: through his loyalty to Julia. And determining that for the future 'the object was not to stay alive but to stay human', he keeps dreaming about the Golden Country, about a world of the lovers' escape from the nightmare world of Oceania.

This dream of the Golden Country persists even after his arrest and through most of the long period of his torture and systematic degradation in the Ministry of Love. There is a point, for example, after he has been rendered intellectually harmless (he admitted that $2 + 2 = 5$), when he has a nightmare vision of becoming swallowed up by the big eyes, of becoming part of the brainwomb behind Big Brother's hypnotic eyes. 'Suddenly he floated out of his seat, dived into the eyes and was swallowed up . . . . The man in the white coat . . . was looking only at the dials' (p. 368).

Yet once more, without waking out of this nightmare, the

dreammind wrests itself away from being swallowed up. Winston wrenches himself away; he escapes, to the Golden Country, and with a hysterical sense of relief:

> He was rolling down a mighty corridor, a kilometre wide, full of glorious, golden light, roaring with laughter and shouting confessions at the top of his voice. (pp. 368–9)

But the dream of liberation and escape has undergone a significant change by now. The original Golden Country was Paradise because it was two lovers' world in Nature, apart from society. In the recent version of the dream Julia is still present, but so are the guards, O'Brien, and Mr Charrington – Winston's torturers. Just as significant, the free, rolling countryside of the external landscape has shrunk, turned into a corridor, albeit still a 'kilometre wide'. The golden-green world of Nature has changed into the golden-white light of the interior: the dream landscape turned into the corridor *within* the Ministry of Love. By now Winston is a captive of Oceania even in his dreams.

Yet the dream of the Golden Country, in progressively diminishing fragments, will recur several more times before Winston's last degradation, the decisive final transformation: 'he was sitting among enormous *glorious, sunlit* ruins with his mother, with Julia, with O'Brien' (p. 396), and then in a 'flat desert *drenched with sunlight*' [my italics] (p. 405). There is no doubt that the dream is waning, flickering, fading away. But even in its very last reminder, the Golden Country signifies that Winston still seeks a shelter because he has retained the basic ingredients of his selfhood. In spite of his loss of intellectual integrity, loss of emotional vitality, and loss of hope for action (represented by the emptiness of the sunlit ruins and the barrenness of the sunlit desert), he has managed to preserve his humanity. He conjures up the image of Julia and she becomes a part of him, the focus of his inner self. Recognising that his feeling of oneness is proof that his 'inner heart is still inviolate', Winston experiences a sense of victory over his torturers. It is at this moment that O'Brien chooses to take up the challenge. Taking Winston to the 'place where there is no darkness anymore', O'Brien forces him to go beyond the 'wall of darkness', beyond the 'last boundaries of the self, of the inner heart'.

Winston is made to enter Room 101.

III

To appreciate fully Orwell's unique achievement of combining credible psychology with the vision of political allegory, we should examine the following questions: why in Room 101 does the Party require from Winston that he offer up Julia as human sacrifice to be devoured by the starved rats in their cage? And why are the rats the inevitable choice for Winston's final humiliation and annihilation?

Answers to these questions spring from the fact that the scene in Room 101 is, in effect, the re-enactment of a previous crisis; it relates to that significant 'memory that he [Winston] must have deliberately pushed out of his consciousness over many years' (p. 295).

After his breakthrough dream in the glass paperweight, Winston comes to remember and relive this scene in detail:

> In the end his mother broke off three-quarters of the chocolate and gave it to Winston, giving the other quarter to his sister . . . . Winston stood watching her for a moment. Then with a sudden swift spring he had snatched the piece of chocolate out of his sister's hand and was fleeing for the door . . . . Even now he was thinking about the thing, he did not know what it was, that was on the point of happening . . . . His mother drew her arm round the child and pressed its face against her breast. Something in the gesture told him that his sister was dying. He turned and fled down the stairs, with the chocolate growing sticky in his hand. He never saw his mother again . . . . After he had devoured the chocolate . . . . (p. 297)

We see why Winston has been haunted by the mother's protecting, shielding gesture for so many years. It is her gesture of sacrificial love that haunts him because he feels that he had betrayed it. And as his mother had actually disappeared after this critical scene, the child Winston developed what he would today call 'survivor's guilt', making him feel, incorrectly, responsible for her death.

Neither the reader nor Julia have any difficulty finding an acceptable excuse for the child Winston's behaviour. Yet Winston himself feels that in his childhood crisis something about his deepest self was revealed. His recurring nightmares indicate that his horror of the 'dreadful thing beyond the wall of darkness' relates to something he finds 'unendurable, something too dreadful to be faced' about himself. The horror must relate to the self, since 'in the dream his deepest feeling was always one of self-deception, because he did in fact *know* what was behind the wall of darkness'. He feels that if he had enough courage, 'with a deadly effort, like wrenching a piece out of his own brain, he could even have dragged the thing into the open' (p. 281).

In its omniscience the Inner Party is aware of the breaking point of the protective walls of self, the specific kind of shame a particular individual can no longer tolerate. Consequently, O'Brien will shed light on the indescribable 'horror, which altered nothing . . . [yet had to] lie embedded in future time' (p. 245). When O'Brien completes Winston's thoughts it is as if he were dragging to light the 'dreadful thing' Winston had been unable to face: 'It was the rats that were on the other side of the wall' (p. 404). O'Brien has good reason for assuming that there is something in the hungry murderous beast crouching beyond the walls of darkness that Winston finds 'unendurable'. 'The rat . . . although a rodent, is carnivorous' (p. 405), O'Brien reminds us. When it is starved, it changes its nature, devouring, destroying anything.

The humiliation of hunger is a strong motif throughout the novel. Starved, the child Winston and his companions are reduced to scavenging beasts:

He remembered . . . above all, the fact that there was never enough to eat. He remembered long afternoons spent with other boys in scrounging round dustbins and rubbish heaps, picking out the ribs of cabbage leaves, potato peelings, sometimes even scraps of stale breadcrust from which they carefully scraped away the cinders . . . . (p. 295)

Hunger as a device for breaking down the personality is well known to the Inner party. As Winston enters the Ministry of Love, he gets a hint about the kind of fate Room 101 holds for different individuals by seeing two victims being dragged in there: a man with a 'tormented, skull-like face' who in full view of the other prisoners 'was dying of starvation' and a 'chinless man' who offers his last crust of bread to the starving one (p. 361). To punish this act of rebellion, the guard 'let free a frightful blow . . . full in the chinless man's mouth' (p. 362) – the part of the face already shattered and therefore the most vulnerable. One can assume that in Room 101 the man with the skull-like face will also be subjected to the suffering he is most vulnerable to: his gnawing and unbearable hunger.

Both the chinless man and the one with the skull-like face are appropriate characters in the naturalistic description of the torture chambers. Just as important, they represent facets of Winston's own personality: they are externalisations of his own unbearable hunger, of the 'chinless' weakness of his own broken will, and the resulting loss of face.

The scene between the chinless man and the starving man is significant in yet another way: it foreshadows the kind of supreme sacrifice expected from Winston in the end. The starved man's 'eyes seemed filled with a murderous, unappeasable hatred of somebody or something' (p. 361); he is willing to denounce, to betray anyone, beginning with the chinless man, his benefactor, including his young children, and he is giving them up to the most cruel forms of death imaginable. That starvation induces 'murderous, unappeasable hatred' is hinted at again when in Room 101 we see that 'the rats were fighting; they were trying to get at each other through the partition' in the ratcage (p. 405). In their insane hunger the rats are ready to devour each other, destroying their own species.

Let us now take a closer look at Winston's personal phobia of the rats. When Julia describes how the rats 'attack children . . . . In some of these streets a woman daren't leave a baby alone for two minutes . . . . And the nasty thing is that the brutes always – ' (p. 281). Winston finds the story so unbearable that he begs her not to finish the sentence. Once more, the sentence will be completed for Winston by O'Brien in the Ministry of Love: 'In some streets a woman dare not leave her baby alone in the house, ... They also attack sick and dying people. They show astonishing intelligence in knowing when a human being is helpless' (p. 405).

Through the repeated flashbacks we know that when the child Winston 'snatched' away that last piece of chocolate, his baby sister was dying and that his mother was also sick and helpless. As demonstrated by the episode he repressed in his memory for thirty years, all characteristics of the rats Winston is repelled by apply to Winston himself. His childhood crisis haunts him because he senses that in the ultimate trial the walls of personality melt away and he will turn into what he is most ashamed of.

Various psychological interpretations have related Winston's phobia of rats to Freud's study of the Ratman's case.[21] In this famous case study the source of the grown man's phobia is traced back to the child's Oedipal hatred of the father, and to his ensuing fear that he will be castrated by the rats as punishment.

There are, however, fundamental differences between Freud's and Orwell's handling of this phobia. It should be recognised that Freud describes the child's original offence as having taken place in the Oedipal situation, at the subconscious level in early childhood, that is, before the awakening of moral awareness. Young Winston's offence, on the other hand, is not related to the Oedipal drama. It takes place when he is between ten and twelve, and contrary to Freud's interpretation, young Winston's original offence is already a moral drama. He is tested through his feelings of love and loyalty to the only people who love him.

It is significant that his mother had already given him most of the chocolate willingly. 'Snatching away' and 'devouring' the rest, Winston allows his hunger, like uncontrollable fear or pain, to overpower the self until he becomes nothing but the living need to satisfy hunger. It is as if he were saying, 'I don't care whether you live or die: my hunger is unendurable, stronger than my love for you'. Going even further, devouring the food of the starving, he symbolically devours them alive. This symbolic act destroys something in Winston, and his sense of guilt literally 'gnaws' at him for nearly thirty years.

There is a moral and psychological paradox here essential to the understanding of the Orwellian definition of guilt, moral will, subconscious, and self: Winston feels guilty because he *did* have a concept of love, loyalty and self-sacrifice which he was forced to deny in the moment of crisis. As he describes the scene to Julia, he realises that although he could not have caused his mother's death – it was the Party that had vaporised her – he was nonetheless guilty: in the moment of crisis he willed her death.

Just as important, he realises that with Julia he has a new chance to forge another emotional and spiritual bond based on loyalty, devotion, and the mutual willingness for sacrifice. To liberate himself from the past and expiate the guilt, this is his second chance. By entering the world of adult love, he can redeem his childhood fall. Hence the first nightmare (in which his mother and sister sink to their death so that he may survive) is followed immediately by the dream of liberation. The lost Paradise of childhood can be redeemed by entering Paradise with Julia in the Golden Country.

Julia is not much of a character in her own right.[22] We don't even know her last name. Neither do we know a great deal about her inner life, the limits of her personality, the nature of *her* Room 101. What we do known about her is that she brings back to Winston the almost forgotten smells and tastes of real chocolate (p. 261), 'real sugar', 'real coffee' (p. 277–8), the sensual, emotional 'reality' of a world he had once known as a child through his mother's love.

Julia, then, allows Winston to return to this love but in a new form, with a new hope. The glass paperweight, emblem of their life together, enforces this almost magical connection between past and future, because the mysterious pink coral, the memento of the past, is also like a rosebud. It is an embryo, a small but distinct hope that their two loves may have a chance for futurity. 'How small it always was!' (p. 350) thinks Winston regretfully when the Thought Police shatter the glass paperweight 'on the hearth-stone' of what could have been their home, and 'the fragment of coral, a tiny crinkle of pink like a sugar rosebud from a cake, rolled across on the mat' (p. 350). And, instead of heralding the birth of their child, Julia's convulsions of pain (she was doubling up 'like a pocket ruler' and was 'thrashing about on the floor', (p. 350) anticipate Winston's grotesque trauma in the Ministry of Love.

There is no doubt that Julia shows some of the characteristics of the nurturing, sheltering mother. Not only does she bring coffee, sugar, and chocolate to their meetings, she also covers Winston with her limbs when he is frightened by the rats in their room. Yet her gesture of love is uniquely her own. Her repeatedly 'magnificent gesture by which a whole civilisation seemed to be annihilated' (p. 264) bespeaks *liberation* rather than protection. In its 'carelessness', the 'splendid movement of the arm' (p. 183) offers Winston liberation from sexual and political anxiety: in its 'grace' (p. 183) it offers Winston a chance for the liberation of the self, for acting out the original test again. In spite of all his humiliations in the Ministry, as long as he is able to stay loyal to her, Winston feels that he is still human, he is still himself, and that the 'dreadful thing which had lain embedded in the future had somehow been skipped over' (p. 369). Should he, however, fail in his second chance, he would no longer have the excuse of the child's immaturity or insufficient control over the self: the 'dreaful thing' he is forced to face in Room 101 is final, irreversible destruction.

Murray Sperber is right in pointing out that Winston's phobia of the rats takes the form of a 'body destruction phantasy'.[23] Yet I believe this fantasy here is quite independent from Freud's concept of the fear of castration. Winston's deep fear of mutilation by the rats refers to the 'wrenching a piece out of his own brain' (p. 281), an image more characteristic of lobotomy than sexual mutilation. Thus, ultimately the body destruction fantasy points to the fear of mental, moral, spiritual destruction.

What is at stake in Room 101 is not Winston's potency or manhood. It is his loss of face. The rats' cage is mask-like. They will devour his face from within. And it is not the Oedipal sexual offence that he is guilty of. He is guilty of denying the fundamental values of the private self. In his selfish and uncontrollable hunger he denied his mother and tore himself away from the primary bond of belonging, loyalty, and love. Now, in his uncontrollable fear of the rats, he re-enacts this first act of betrayal: he offers up the body of the only person he loves, as a surrogate for his own. When he screams, 'Do it to Julia', he offers her as a human sacrifice to the hungry rats. Once again, symbolically, he devours the one he loves.

In Room 101 he can no longer stay 'in front of' the wall of darkness: he is forced to get over to 'the other side' (p. 281). And as the walls of the private self are being destroyed, he feels that he is falling 'through the floor, through the walls of the building, through the earth, through the oceans, through the atmosphere, into outer space, into the gulfs between the stars – always away, away, away from the rats' (pp. 406–7). The irony is, of course, that having broken through the walls of darkness, he can no longer get away. Exposed to the cage of 'starving brutes' (p. 405) in Room 101, Winston hears *himself* become 'insane, a screaming animal' (p. 406). By allowing himself to be degraded to the level of the starved rats, he has become what he had been most afraid of. O'Brien did successfully conclude his experiment: the 'inner heart' of loyalty and self-sacrifice is only sentimental illusion. Ultimately man is nothing but a beast, and like a beast, he can be degraded until he is deprived of his will, until he becomes an instrument in the hands of the Party.

At this point we should realise that Orwell's strategies lead to conclusions fundamentally different from those of the Freudian critic. The starved rats, just like the child Winston, were themselves the victims of the Party's brutality. Ultimately the real face behind the mask-like cage of the rats is the face of Big Brother himself. It is Big Brother who turns his subjects into ferocious, hate-filled beings like himself, forcing them to act out the ritual of his own prime betrayal as human sacrifice. Winston's own final and crucial act of betrayal is some kind of horrible *imitatio dei*: in the moment he betrays his loved one, he becomes one with the godhead, acting out the inevitable yet horrible mystery, the loving union between victim and victimiser.

In effect, all the citizens of Oceania are kept in their cage, systematically starved, deprived of food, love, sexual and emotional satisfaction, so that the Party may channel all their pent-up energy into the hysterical quest for new victims, leading to the equally hysterical worship of their leader. All the people of Oceania become instruments in the hands of the Party, ready to denounce one another in order to assure their own survival. Yet there is a tragic irony in this process: as the victim's last bond of personal loyalty is broken, he has become the agent of his own enslavement, and ultimately that of his own extinction.

Room 101 is the dramatic centre of the novel because it both repeats and reverses two previous crises. It is the reversal of the breakthrough scene in which Winston liberates himself from the long repressed guilt by pledging loyalty to Julia: 'only feelings matter. If they could make me stop loving you – that would be the real betrayal' (p. 300). It is also the re-enactment of his childhood crisis. Forced to re-visit the crucial trial of his childhood, in Room 101 Winston fails again. The failure destroys his hard-won liberation, the maturity of his selfhood, and pushes him into another, far more terrifying infancy. The private self is enslaved, wiped out by the collective self. He becomes the image of his Maker, the prodigal son returning to the 'loving breast' (p. 416) of his parent.

Politically, Winston's capitulation was pre-ordained by the dynamic of totalitarianism. Thus, a sense of personal responsibility, guilt, or shame would be quite out of order. Yet the moral paradox here puts Orwell in a category quite distinct from both the Freudian critic and the critic studying the novel only in terms of the political spectrum. For thirty years Winston's sense of guilt has been a burden, but it also served as a reminder that he still had a sense of personal loyalty and could feel shame. In fact, it was this mysterious sense of guilt or shame that made him start his search for the Truth in the past, the search which led ultimately to moral regeneration.

Significantly, once he repeats his act of betrayal, he no longer carries the burden of guilt. Of course, he is also free of his sense of humanity, of the basic moral attitudes defining the private self. Once reborn, united with the collective self of Oceania, he is no longer capable of regret or guilt because he has no further claim to a private conscience.

Room 101 is a climactic scene in the novel, bringing together all the betrayals in a series of symbolic reversals. Visually, '101' suggests two parts of the self, face-to-face through zero: reduced to nothingness through fear and shame, Winston faces the rats in himself.

The number '101' also suggests repetition after a reversal: repeating the childhood trial, Winston reverts to another state of childhood.

In yet another visual allusion, '101' suggests links of a chain, that is, not only one, but a whole series of continuous, repeated reversals. Room 101 is at the heart of the novel because it is the centre of the mythical, the political, and psychological drama of betrayal. It is here that any victim is turned victimiser, by giving up, betraying, his bond of private loyalty. Paradoxically, it is precisely at this point that he will be finally trapped, 'chained' to become a true victim, willing to stay in the cage forever.

Ironically, it is by adjusting to the norm of the majority that Winston has now become, finally, insane. Having joined in the collective insanity imposed upon the population by Big Brother, Winston now willingly joins the other rats in their cage.

To see the effect of this psychic devastation, that is, the changes between private and collective self, we should take a last quick look at Winston's inner world, a look at his dreamcountry after his 'rebirth' in the Ministry of Love.

In the last scene of the novel Winston is sitting in the Chestnut Café, the haunt of other released traitors and thought criminals.

He had grown fatter since they released him, and had regained his old colour – indeed more than regained it. His features had thickened, the skin on nose and cheekbones was coarsely red, even the bald scalp was too deep a pink. (p. 408)

Guzzling his Victory gin and belching occasionally, with his bald pink scalp and thickened, expressionless features, he is like a grotesque reminder of a newborn infant (or a well-fed rat?). Then, we hear, suddenly; 'Uncalled, a memory floated into his mind. He saw a candlelit room . . .' (p. 414). In a reverie he recalls his home before his childhood crisis, the last happy moments before his mother and sister had disappeared. But according to the Party, there could have been no happiness in the past, especially not in the private bond between parent and child. As a result, the new-born Winston who would no longer acknowledge any private bond, dismisses the happy scene as a 'false memory' (p. 415).

And now, as he wrenches himself away from the memory of private happiness, the loudspeaker announces Big Brother's newest victory. Winston undergoes the communal experience of the hysterical hatred of the freshly appointed enemy, followed by the ecstatic worship of the leader. Then, in the midst of this communal ecstasy, we catch a last glimpse of Winston's familiar dream. In this final reverie he sees himself

> walking down the white-tiled corridor, with the feeling of walking in sunlight, and an armed guard at his back. The long-hoped-for bullet was entering his brain. (p. 416)

The earlier change from the golden-green landscape to the golden-white interior should remind us that in this sun-flooded white-tiled corridor we caught yet another glimpse of the diminishing Golden Country. But what happened to the originally wide and free landscape? Once it had been swallowed up by the corridor in the Ministry of Love (pp. 368–9), it had kept on shrinking and shrinking. But there is something else, still unexpected in the form and the sequence of these last two dreams. What we would call the 'good dream' appears first and Winston rejects it, while what we would call the 'bad dream' comes after, and now this is the one he craves. What is more, the Golden Country has undergone a total reversal.

Originally the wishdream of the Golden Country represented Winston's violent effort to wrench himself away from the nightmare – first to find freedom away from Oceania, then to rescue whatever was left of the inner self, within. By the end of the novel Winston is totally enslaved: nothing remains of the former self to compel him to get away or seek shelter. He dismissed his past as a 'false memory' and wishes to return to the torture chamber. Not only does he accept: he anticipates and celebrates the bullet in the back. It is the nightmare world of Oceania that had taken the place of his dream of Paradise.

It is only at the moment when Winston comes to celebrate the latest victory that his conversion has become complete: 'He had won the victory over himself. He loved Big Brother' (p. 416). To celebrate this victory is to celebrate a world born out of the madness of hatred, to celebrate the bullet in the back of the head. It is by giving up the private world of memories, of dreams and nightmares, that he is submerged in the collective insanity of Oceania, drowned by the waves of madness and self-destruction.

It is characteristic of Orwell's definition of the self that Winston is subjected to a series of tests leading towards his final disintegration. It is as if Orwell had set a series of rigorous examinations to define the indispensable ingredients, the last boundaries of our humanity. Are these fundamental ingredients to be found in the definition of the man of reason, 'I think, therefore I am'? But Winston remains human after his intelligence has surrendered to the Party. Is it, then, the romantic definition of 'I feel, therefore I am'? But Winston is still human after his inner world is reduced to the barrenness of a desert. Winston's breakdown becomes total only when he loses his ability to dream: in *Nineteen Eighty-Four* Orwell's final definition of our humanity seems to be 'I dream, therefore I am'.

Changes in Winston's character are indeed inseparable from changes in his dreamlife. As a matter of fact, one could actually delineate the structure of the plot simply by concentrating on the dream sequence. Parts I and II outline the rising action of Winston's search for self, for psychic liberation. To liberate himself from his nightmare the dreamer reaches out to the wishdream of the Golden Country. Eventually he is able to translate the wishdream to reality, and then he is also able to rid himself of his nightmares. Part III describes descent, the systematic breakdown of the self in the Ministry of Love. The gradual diminishing of the landscape of the Golden Country is tantamount to the gradual diminishing of Winston as a human being. Finally, after the climactic scene in Room 101, the dream emerges once more, but now it takes an entirely new form, assuming a significance diametrically opposite to that of the original wishdream.

After the climactic scene in Room 101 the structural movement spells out a line reminiscent of the double action of tragedy. Yet there is a significant difference here. In tragedy the descending movement of material loss is often simultaneous with the ascending movement of spiritual gain, a new light, a new insight being born out of the loss.

In *Nineteen Eighty-Four* the relationship between ascending and descending movements is the reverse. The material gain of survival, the undeniable gain of life, is equivalent to the loss of the human spirit which would make life worthwhile. It is precisely in this 'gain' of survival and adjustment after the walls of the private self had melted away that we must recognise that unspeakable 'horror' that had lain embedded in the future all along – a future inevitable and irreversible for any free human being once Big Brother assumes control over the world and over the psyche.

Having been forced to betray himself – as everyone else must in Room 101 – the last man of Europe has survived but he is no longer human: he is mutilated, lobotomised, he is no longer able even to dream, even to wish for an escape.

The psychological dimension of the novel does not contradict but gives vital support to the political allegory and is indispensable to the humanistic warning: since totalitarianism is built on a series of self-perpetuating lies, and on the unstoppable 'chain-reaction' of betrayals in the political arena, it also leads to the irreversible disintegration of the inner self, to the irrecoverable loss of our humanity.

4

False Freedom and Orwell's Faust-Book *Nineteen Eighty-Four*

Gerald A. Morgan

I

Orwell the novelist is best known as the man who writes on human hopes for life on this planet under the rule of Man, and gives them a bad report. Men ruled in the name of Man, he says, are robbed of freedom and human decency.

He grapples with the main problem of his age, that of a human ban on human suffering. It is a problem raised by the Enlightenment and by Auguste Comte's regime of Science, which were to have ended the human suffering allowed by rule in the name of God. At least, that was the hope offered by Rousseau and Voltaire, and again by Comte, and again by Marx, and again by Nietzsche who gave out news of the death of God. The age of Man might have gone splendidly, if it had not carried men to the Great War of 1914–1918 between empires with divine *and* human sanction for commercial reach, military aggression and quite astonishing slaughter.

Orwell came on the scene, as a schoolboy at Eton, during the Great War which marked a new Spring tide of human suffering. T. S. Eliot surveyed the wasteland, picking over the heap of broken images. George Bernard Shaw declared that nothing else than disaster could have been expected. The State ruled in the name of Man could only wreck itself, given the greed, the incompetence, the infantile vanity of Man in his present stage of evolution, with his horrendous technology. Shaw declared, in *Back to Methuselah*, that intelligent young men among the Great War survivors would

77

be looking afresh for a religion.[1] In this he was right, but not as he hoped.

What Shaw had in mind, for the rule of men in the name of Man, was a 'creative evolution' into a new kind of man fit for the huge task. Of course the idea of creative evolution was not new; it had formed the nineteen centuries of the Christian era, as G. K. Chesterton pointed out in *The Everlasting Man*.[2] But evolution by Man for Man, in the style of Nietzsche, was new still; perhaps, as implied by Shaw, it had not had a fair chance. Perhaps, as some thought, the Great War was a fluke, the last lash of a rule in the name of God. Hence, instead of creative evolution, the new religion sought by young men was often a type of mystical politics, a Platonist replay of the Levellers and the Reign of Saints known to Cromwell: politics pursued with devout zeal and with armed clashes of dogma.

In this way it came about that poets and authors, such as Thomas Mann, declared that human destiny must be read in political terms.[3] Some folks saw in Soviet Russia, where the undivine sanction of Man was applied with most enthusiasm, the brightest political message from the future. It was favoured more than the dark theme from Nazi Germany, which harked back to the ancient gods of race. The poet Yeats, a senator of Ireland, replied to Thomas Mann with his poem 'Politics,' demurring from a total human concern with such form of destiny. But in the same year began the war which destroyed Nazi Germany. It was war on a new scale, by which history's Great War was levelled as a mere serial World War I; with a toll of fifty million deaths in six years, World War II marked a new apex of human suffering. It also ushered in the Atomic threat of even greater pain.

The war marked a spectacular failure for the human regulation which was to have banished human suffering, and had instead intensified human misery past all remembering. It also led to some change of mind about human regulation on the Soviet plan, so that the brightest political message from the future had now become the worst. The human regulation of humans was exposed as a menace, and the most overtly human regulation was denounced as the most inhuman.

It could now be surmised that rule in the name of Man inclines toward bad regulation, without alternative. Mere humanity becomes its own antithesis. If God is a non-starter, the age of human regulation must progress by its own logic from misery to horror. In his novel *Doctor Faustus* about demonic seizure in the German tradition,[4] Thomas Mann reproved the Nazi venture among the old gods. It befell George Orwell to write the Faust-book from the future, whereby human regulation evokes its own god of power, in a chronicle full of dread.

II

Eric Blair was a reluctant prophet, like a Jonah bringing no good luck to the messmates in Burma, to the vagrants in England, or to the comrades in Spain. For all his stern temper, it can hardly be said that he wanted to bear the message of doom to socialists at the moment of their English triumph. In fact his whole life may be seen as an effort to be quite ordinary for his class in his generation: that is, to be an anti-bourgeois seeker and teacher of social justice. On one level his dystopian novel may be seen as a normal sequel to his other comments on a world which no-one thought satisfactory; the difference was in the shift from reportage to fantasy, but even this was quite ordinary in the pattern of dystopias established since 1846 – almost since the advent of the scientific regime of Auguste Comte, which had so quickly produced its own antithesis in French fiction.[5] A century of dystopians, from Emile Souvestre and Giraudeau to Robida to Butler to Kolney to Zamyatin, furnished the framework of *Nineteen Eighty-Four*. But by none of his ordinary ways could Eric Blair avoid imparting a deeper message, like a man designated for this in the world which shaped him as he strove to give it shape.

Even Blair's impulse to shed his class and breed, by becoming George Orwell, was quite ordinary in the religion of his time. His effort belonged with the new ascetical mode, which in a later phase filled Benedictine abbeys with veterans of 1945, but which in the 1920s moved Lawrence of Arabia to call himself a 'lay monk' and Private Shaw.[6] It moved Rudolf Hess to find a 'holy order' in the Nazi circle,[7] years before Hitler was named warden of the Holy Grail (Wagner politicised, so to say).[8] It moved Joseph Goebbels to embrace altruism and the working-class in his novel *Michael* (1929), where he sketches out the rebel plan[9] for 'Smith' or Orwell's *Nineteen Eighty-Four*. This, of course, was before Goebbels became Hitler's director of Newspeak; it was in the time when

Orwell himself embraced 'Lady Poverty' in something like Franciscan style,[10] and might have gone in any direction, but chose Fascism as the target for words and bullets. The Roman poet Lauro de Bosis, prompted by Bernard Shaw, wrote anti-fascist pamphlets and showered them from the sky above Rome, until the Duce's aircraft chased him into the sea where he drowned.[11] Orwell fought the Fascists in Spain, and got away to denounce the Communists. Ferruccio Parri won renown as 'a saint' of socialism,[12] as a Partisan leader, then as Premier of Italy for a half-year in 1945. Who knows what Orwell might have done, had he found a creed? But the bullet-wound from Spain confined him to the modest part of setting up the barricades for individual freedom; it was in his hermitage on a remote Gaelic island, that he suddenly composed a writ of doom for the new politics, the finish of what Spengler had called the Faustian Age.[13]

III

It may be that Orwell was designated prophet in his time because he was a loser. He would rather have been a teacher of the common man, somewhat as the *narodniki* who had gone among the humble folk of Tsarist Russia to spread the light, before the catastrophes of Great War and Revolution and Stalin. Comparison with those intellectuals on pilgrimage to the people, exchanging new lamps for old, offering Western liberties in place of ikons, is clinched by the Russian frame of *Nineteen Eighty-Four*. The dystopia of English socialism is very like the Russian novel *We* by Yevgeny Zamyatin.[14] The plots are almost the same: in each there is personal revolt against a dehumanised State, a self-assertion through sex and archaism, then betrayal and counter-betrayal and total conversion to the State. The appeal of Zamyatin's novel is more intellectual, as befits Russia; the appeal of Orwell's novel is more sentimental, as befits England. The protagonist of the Russian novel is a scientist, like its author, and the protagonist of the English novel is a man of letters, like its author. The all-powerful State in the novels is obviously nearer of attainment by Zamyatin's Russia than by Orwell's England, but the actual difference of degree makes no difference in fiction, since Orwell has no valid remedy to propose. The defender of liberty has no defence.

Comparison of the two novels would seem to show a marked inferiority of Orwell's, regarding both the tone and the audience addressed, as though the traditions of art in Russia were older and stronger than those in England. Each novel shows revolt by way of wilful decadence, which in Zamyatin's tale is betokened by the music of Scriabin and ironic allusions to the suffering God of Dostoevsky; the decadence in Orwell's tale means a life scarcely less grubby than official routine, and a wish by Smith that he could give everyone syphilis (p. 264). (Here is an echo from Orwell's first novel *Burmese Days*: corruption and filth are the main defence against Utopias.[15]) Zamyatin's novel is a scientific notation of lively intelligence by the nameless D-503; Orwell's novel is a diary of self-pity within a chronicle of woes for the heroically-named Winston Smith. Zamyatin heightens the Dostoevskian tension of freedom and happiness, with dilemmas of imagination versus entropy which brighten Soviet science-fiction to this day (for example in novels by the Strugatskys).[16] Orwell implies that William Morris was all right, and he bequeathes three bogies to Western folklore. Big Brother is modelled on the Well-doer in Zamyatin. Newspeak was displayed in Evelyn Waugh's 1938 novel *Scoop*, a satire on newspapers and politics.[17] Doublethink has been reported by various ex-communists, for instance Arthur Koestler.[18]

It might be said that Orwell's novel is a long brooding on these bogies, without any English means of driving them away. What England has is the statue of the old dictator Cromwell; the Cockney crowd in the slums; the pervasive squalor extended from Orwell's other fictions, and the old Christian song about bells and saints. These things are scarcely the sinews of war for liberating Airstrip One.

Yet these things are symbolic of a novel told in reverse. The character of most interest is O'Brien the inquisitor for Ingsoc; but Orwell has told the tale entirely from the point of view of Winston Smith, a feeble respondent to O'Brien's actions. Some people have said that Orwell was no artist, and Orwell seems to have confirmed this when he said that all literature has to be political.[19] Yet the inversion of his tale argues a knowing art; it may suggest a wilful or unconscious design in telling a tale as badly as it could be told, with some purpose unformed or undeclared.

The suggestion is there at the outset of the novel. Contrasting the general squalor of London in 1984 are the gleaming towers of the Ministries of Truth, Peace, Love and Plenty. Readers are encouraged to think of these titles as lies: here is honest George Orwell digging out the truth of things. The titles can prompt recollection of a joke actually made in Parliament by Winston Churchill when a Labour Party minister was shifted: since there was no coal when Mr Shinwell was Minister of Fuel, we may hope for peace now that he is Minister of War.[20] In Orwell's novel, the joke embodied in concrete bears three slogans coined by the Party and repeated on the money of the land. These also are presented as lies, although two are clearly paradoxes.

The slogan 'War is Peace' can be verified in several ways; for instance, by Bismarck's internal and external politics; for instance, by psychology, which also confirms the slogan 'Freedom is Slavery'. Here are compound equivocations, or, more precisely, analogical terms which depend for meaning on a wide range of possible keys. Stone walls do not a prison make. There is great peace in the single-mindedness of battle. Freedom without order is slavery to self-will. Common wisdom has many sayings to verify the slogans, but their paradoxical import is greatest in mystical writings, whether of the Russian or the English tradition. There is no way of saying some things, within the limits of politics; a sense of proportioned being may be hard to convey in plain words except by paradox, such as Dostoevsky uses, or the English author of *The Cloud of Unknowing* who fixes the true self exactly and nowhere.[21] The folk listening to a *starets* in Russia would know this, until the new ascetical *narodniki* came to enlighten them; the ancient English folk idealised by William Morris would know this, perhaps the people of Smith's Golden Country of oranges and lemons in *Nineteen Eighty-Four*, though it may be that the Middle English spirit had shrunk away before Orwell *narodnik* sat in school with the lords of empire.

Yet writers on politics need to be schooled in paradox, if only to understand the proportioned analogies of human existence and freedom. As Hugh Kenner has noted, paradox describes what analogy explains;[22] in the case of the slogans what is expressed is the relation of peace and freedom to other human conditions, so well understood in the age of the Magna Charta and the Golden Bull of Hungary.[23] John of Salisbury, who was present at the political murder of Thomas à Becket in the cathedral at Canterbury, states proportion in this way, in his *Policraticus*:

> Liberty means judging everything freely in accordance with one's individual judgement . . . . Nothing but virtue is more splendid than liberty . . . men should die, if the need arose, for

the sake of virtue. . . . But virtue can never be fully attained without liberty, and the absence of liberty proves that virtue in its full perfection is wanting. Therefore a man is free in proportion to the measure of his virtues, and the extent to which he is free determines what his virtues can accomplish; . . . it is the vices alone which bring about slavery.[24]

This is in stark contrast to Winston Smith's assertion of freedom by corruption. The same author might be looking across eight centuries to the prospect of *Nineteen Eighty-Four*, when he adds:

If iniquity and injustice, banishing charity, had not brought about tyranny, firm concord and perpetual peace would have possessed the peoples of the earth forever.[25]

In this view, it can be seen that freedom is a proportioned analogue of virtue, and that both are analogues of peaceful order.[26] The loss of perception of 'the bounds and correspondences of nature',[27] as when the analogical order of freedom is reduced to univocal vice or tyranny, signifies a mental disorder which can be projected either as Orwell's Airstrip One or as Hell in the terms of Gower's *Confessio Amantis* or Chaucer's *Canterbury Tales*.

Evidently it is in echoes of a healthier England stirring Orwell's nostalgia (Chaucer is named in *Nineteen Eighty-Four*), that the paradoxical slogans have their meaning. The novel is a parable of inverted order, a pathology of the new politics of which the third slogan is a symptom: 'Ignorance is Strength'. This could be a charming whimsy, as by the French wit Pierre Daninos: 'The English are sometimes ignorant; but their strength lies in not knowing it'.[28] In Orwell's context, however, the slogan is a mocking contradiction of Francis Bacon's fallacy 'Knowledge is Power' which cancelled Chaucer's era and John of Salisbury's; a fallacy which leads to the totalitarian fallacy that power is truth. Bacon is at the pivot where human order is inverted, the time of Marlowe's *Doctor Faustus*.

The three slogans 'Freedom is Slavery', 'War is Peace', 'Ignorance is Strength', would seem in various ways to be out of place in a novel of modern politics, unless their full resonance is meant to be known, as it were by a writing behind the writing. As they can be known, the inscriptions convey a mystical politics absorbing religion with everything else into a univocal tyranny. This is suggested by the fact that Orwell's novel, like Zamyatin's is an extended parody of religion, complete with ritual, hierarchy, heretics, inquisition, recantation, reclamation.

It is in the plot of *Nineteen Eighty-Four*, unfolding behind the paradoxical slogans, that a genius flares out behind Orwell's journalistic rule of plain workmanship. Orwell never claimed or admitted genius, even after the success of *Animal Farm*, yet there can be no doubt of his access to some collective unconscious or some inspiration, which carries his last novel far beyond a clumsy rehearsal of politics. There is a comic note which cancels his gloomy forecast, to prove him a prophet in truth. It can be seen in this way. Zamyatin's novel is a straightforward tale of revolt, capture and lobotomy. Orwell's novel, on a Party-structure like Zamyatin's, is a highly artful rewriting of Christopher Marlowe's farce, *The Tragical History of Doctor Faustus*.

In Orwell's version, the paradoxical slogans are the analogue of Jerome's Bible rejected by Faustus. The secret diary of Smith is the 'damned book'; O'Brien is Mephistopheles who has always known the mind of Faustus; the compact of revolt is sealed in red wine (instead of blood) with a toast to the fallen leader and 'primal traitor', Emmanuel, surnamed Goldstein; the book of spells brought from Hell for Faustus is Goldstein's banned book given to Smith; the pageant of Deadly Sins for Faustus embodies Smith's lust for corruption, while the succubus Helena who sucks the soul out of Faustus is played for Smith by deceitful Julia from the Anti-Sex League.

Orwell's deep revision touches four elements in Marlowe's play: the reversal of reason by Faustus; the equivocal Heaven defied by Faustus; the function of the Old Man, and the function of Mephistopheles. In Marlowe's play, Faustus flees Aristotle for the shallow logic of Ramus, where he starts a series of fallacies by which the sequel and the whole play is made a farce. Orwell spreads the fallacies of Smith all through his tale. Faustus wants to use Hell's power against a Heaven which seems *a priori* to have decreed his end in Hell. Smith joins the Goldstein brotherhood to oppose Hell, only to find that the brotherhood is a device of Hell, the aboriginal place of deception. Marlowe's Old Man tries to take Faustus with him to Heaven. Orwell's benign antiquarian, pointing Smith to the Golden Country, is a police official who traps Smith with Julia. Mephistopheles at no time hides his purpose from Faustus; but O'Brien serves the power called Big Brother while pretending to side secretly with Smith against the power. One implication of these revisions is emphasised by Orwell. Big Brother is a secular projection of God, inverted for politics; quite literally, *diabolus*. Smith learns to love Big Brother. Hell is by common consent the realm of inversion, where white can only be received as black; O'Brien could be at any place and say with Mephistopheles, 'Why this is Hell; nor am I out of it'. Smith is in the same case after a purgatory at the hands of O'Brien, when, in Orwell's words, his soul is 'white as snow' (p. 416).

IV

The reader of *Nineteen Eighty-Four* is not invited to pity O'Brien, but cannot do otherwise. The Argus of the Inner Party, the Grand Inquisitor of Airstrip One, is in a desperate case. He is hemmed in by the paradox of power.

O'Brien's work is negation; and human power, which negates itself like lust in its own attainment, must pall faster under the law of diminishing returns, when it is power aimed at negation. O'Brien could slaughter the entire Party on which he depends, without himself ceasing to shrink. His only satisfaction is to explain power, secretly, to the squirming Smiths, whose mental pain is not less than his own; but what he explains is a sort of childish nihilism. (The will-to-power, after all, is best observed in a baby in a cradle.) O'Brien's plight is declared in the titles of the Ministries of Love, Truth, Peace, Plenty; by O'Brien's negation these good things negate each other and are denied to O'Brien.

Desperate O'Brien is the chief jailbird of the fearsome but ludicrous power which he wields in the name of Big Brother who may or may not exist. The logical reduction of Newspeak must cancel Big Brother in any case. O'Brien is prisoner of nothing. With all his privilege and mockery, he is merely the highest human loser in a naughty world.

O'Brien is haunted by the absent Absolute whose titles grace the shining ziggurats of the new Babylon, the Ministries of Truth and Love. 'God is power', says O'Brien, declaring himself the priest of power (p. 387). But his god has power only to do harm: to make pain enough to change the human mind, which must think all reality confined in the historical present. This god forbids love and truth, knowing neither. Orwell's brilliance might be noted here, in his depiction of Lucifer more thoroughgoing than Marlowe's ever was; but it could be objected that Orwell's time offers more knowledge of inversion than Marlowe's did.

O'Brien, by his want of love, is cut off from humanity and the timeless present, is parted from truth, unable to know any guarantor of what is in his own mind. For all thought, O'Brien confronts the Great Deceiver imagined by René Descartes in his Méditations;[29] but while Descartes strove to outreach the Deceiver by inventing modern science (and was mocked for this by the Devil in Dostoevsky's Karamazov tale[30]), O'Brien serves the Great Deceiver and will destroy science by the linguistic science of Newspeak (even as science destroys the objects of science at Hiroshima). O'Brien cannot do other than to negate things by their own action, or negate minds by their own consent. His own choice of negative power throws him into nothingness, adrift from the human clamberers, as it were, on the cliff of eternity. These he cannot reach, except by deceitfully negating his negation in false friendship; nor can he harm them, except through their deceptive self-regard.

Ecce Homo, as Nietzsche might say, whose will-to-power led him to the mental asylum and to a musical rôle in Thomas Mann's novel of modern collapse, *Doctor Faustus*.[31] Here is O'Brien, his eyes aglint with that insanity added by Orwell, which is not merely one of those frivolous touches by which Orwell hides from himself the depth of his portrayal. Here is Winston Smith, wriggling his ego in the name of truth, lacking only the strength of O'Brien to share O'Brien's plight. Here is Julia, the little law unto herself, the vestal whose insistent lechery serves O'Brien and Smith to make unity in misery; is this the face that lights the rule of men by Man?

In Winston Smith, named by oxymoron like George Orwell, the author shows again his genius. Marlowe solipsised an audience, who soared with Faustus and fell in his fallacies. Orwell has evidently solipsised a host of readers, who throb too painfully with Smith to note his want of wit. Smith is somewhat less than *l'homme moyen sensuel*, in a situation which calls for a great deal more; he is not ready to die for Julia, or for liberty, or for anything else. He blends an intellectual contempt for the Proles with a 'mystical reverence' for them (p. 347), in the way set forth by Dr Goebbels for the Nazi era;[32] the very model of mystical politics, by which Smith would combine the addled brains of Party members and the vacuous resilience of Proles, to form a power to displace power.

Quite suitably it is at this point of Smith's mental process that O'Brien with stunning swiftness drops the genuine mask of sympathy, to make physical arrest of Smith who is already his mental prisoner. The sympathy, of course, is deceptive precisely because it is genuine feeling.

Smith is a partial obverse of O'Brien; he is a soft centre of feelings and mathematics, a Cartesian ego waiting to be hollowed out by O'Brien's nothingness, all the more easily since God, revered by Descartes, is denied by Smith (p. 392). Torture merely speeds up the voiding of Smith, whose every tendril of self-concern is hooked in the State of watchfulness. He has already agreed with O'Brien: 'We are the dead' (pp. 308, 348); 'We shall meet in the place where there is no darkness' (p. 177). The agreement is renewed in pain, unbearable feeling, in the place where of course the light is artificial, like the truth relied on by Smith for identity.

Unlike O'Brien, Smith has no thirst for absolutes. He is a vestige of the quondam new man, by political pilgrims misconceived. As an atheist astray from the flock of Russian and other nihilists,[33] he ought to be replacing God with Smith, but is no competition for Big Brother. He should aver with Sartre, that he is condemned to freedom;[34] but he would not survive the smile of O'Brien. His time in the crowded cell enlightens him, as would a night in jail with the nameless resister of a Utopian State in Graham Greene's novel *The Power and the Glory* where the loser wins although killed, like the Old Man in Marlowe's *Faustus*. But as Bernard Shaw pointed out, 'unambitious men are cowards when they have no religion', their lot is to be 'ruled by the childish . . . and the blackguards'.[35]

Smith rests his selfhood, his freedom as man, on an impossible triad. He believes in history as autonomous truth; he believes in 'the secret doctrine that two plus two make four' (p. 348); he believes, like Keats the Romantic poet, in the holiness of the heart's affections.[36] O'Brien snaps these straws with a malignant ease, as well he might. History cannot but be a shifting belief in the supposed meaning of supposed evidence for the autobiography of mankind. What we actually know, if we do, is of the instant present, which we cannot record while acting. Feeling is only nondefinition, in which a selfhood is moved like seaweed adrift. Number alone might help Smith, as a guarantee of metaphysical order and hence of liberty, in the world of Gower and John of Salisbury;[37] but in a world shaped by Descartes and Berkeley with unreal permutations of perception, the language of number may be not merely secret but idiot. Number, feeling and history cancel each other, as is demonstrated in Zamyatin's *We*. Thus, although Smith's mind is contained within O'Brien's, perhaps this is only because Smith has never been schooled to think. One ray of light falls on to his mind, making him ask why the birds and the Proles break out in song; but it soon fades. Feeling is his *métier*. When the novel starts he is feeling sorry for himself; then by easy stages the feeling is made part, and he with it, of the metaphysical self-hatred to which O'Brien is condemned.

V

Orwell's choice of Marlowe for a model is so apt, while unexpected, that it clamours genius. Marlowe and Orwell are masters in the same vein of atrocious comedy, working on the *reductio ad absurdum* of the cult of Man. It is the same vein worked by Jonathan Swift, in whose perfect black humour the fourth voyage of Gulliver shows us the lampshades of human skin at Belsen concentration-camp. The comic progress from Marlowe to Swift to Orwell is logical and constant, keeping pace with the shift of mystical *élan* from theology to utopian politics.

The fallacies of Faustus make Marlowe a comic dramatist, even if 'Hell is discovered' onstage in his parody of inverted faith. As Faustus is a dolt who follows an imbecile logic, so Smith is a boor who follows an imbecile metaphysics; it is normal in human thought for the one sort to produce the other, with dire effect on culture and politics. Smith's triad fails utterly to ward off O'Brien, being flawed in much the same way as the triads of Hegel, which germinate Fascism, or those of Marx, which germinate Communism; no-one need look for freedom or rational politics in a philosophy riddled with false analogies (that is, with metaphors) or with double-talk about the negation of negation. The fallacies of Smith and O'Brien bring the comic touch to Orwell's parody of mystical politics, even though human dirt and spite (and Goldstein the understudy Lucifer) are heaped on so lavishly by Orwell.

It can be seen that Orwell's Faust-book is a fiction, exposing itself as a fiction, about the cult of Man germinating those fallacies of power which are both catastrophic and comic: dreadful in the suffering they entail, ludicrous in their unreason. It can be seen also that Orwell in the garb of 'common man' plumbs the depth of metaphysics, when he exposes nihilism as a fiction. The reluctant prophet is famed for the image in his Faust-book, projected by O'Brien's *néantisme* of power: a boot stamping on a human face forever (p. 390). He gives us silliness in concrete form, nadir of the cult of abstract Man. It reminds us that, in merely human reference, there is no 'forever'; also that any human talk of negation has reference only to fancy. No 'nothingness' can exist in fact for us to talk about. Plainly the fictional O'Brien's voracious negation is a rhetor's dialectical toy, no more real than a self-created mortal man. Sometimes among actual human beings there could be one who let himself will negation of his own kind or other kinds of being; but such act of will can only degrade the self in him, while the cosmos could do without him if it had to.

We are led by Orwell's Faust-book to a faith beyond politics but needful for sane politics; not to Shaw's creative evolution but to religion, for instance Christianity, such as Orwell's book nowhere avows (parody is preachment enough). We are made aware that, as there is no real human negation allowed in the cosmos, so there is no action solely 'human' allowed to the self; self-sufficient existence is what we mortals cannot claim, as comedy reminds us always and as tragedy proclaims. Only by metaphor (that is, by false analogy) can we claim to create or destroy anything existent, in a world of matter we have not made; that is to say, only by a fiction. The process of fiction itself is the means by which we learn also, in Orwell's Faust-book, that the rule of man by Man is only a metaphor, not a particularly useful or happy one for mankind.

Thus there is in Orwell's book hardly any celebration of the real, and scant happiness or joy where Chaucer is merely a distant name. Yet O'Brien and Smith, however compelling they be as fictions, are fictions of negation which prove its fiction, though they be pressed with Hellish intensity. Even Lucifer requires existence not caused by Lucifer, before he can work his will for negation; and O'Brien must suppose a good bootmaker, before a man's boot can stamp on a man's face 'forever' in Orwell's *reductio ad absurdum*. The metaphor of Orwell's fable is marked off by the fact that there is no good person in it, whereas the Gulags and prison-States, allowed by vice in the real world, cannot keep out virtue.

It is plain that the rascals of Utopia have not yet seized our planet. In the actual year 1984, World War III has been staved off for nearly 40 years, and alternatives to the tyranny of Man, be it communist or capitalist by name, can be seen. There is promise of freedom and justice in the recovery of the way of thought which generated Chaucer's poetry and John of Salisbury's *Policraticus* (where, as noted above, freedom is a proportioned analogue of virtue). This way of thought, long abandoned for the mystical dialectics of Descartes, Kant, Hegel and such, is now rediscovered after the mechanistic thought of Descartes has failed the men of science. Recapture of the analogical mode of thought (which understands *Policraticus* as well as the paradoxical slogans of Airstrip One) speeds along at the Case Systems Research Centre in USA (1960), the General Systems Theory Group at Odessa (1966), and the World Organisation of General Systems and Cybernetics (1970).[38] Further, a Pope from out of the Soviet empire is heard round the world speaking of politics as the dignity of persons, guaranteed by love of the God-Man.

In itself the wave of conferences on Orwell in 1984 suffices to disprove his political forecast. His linguistic forecast holds good, insofar as Newspeak, the fallacy of epithet, belongs to a civilisation's fall. But the symbolic value of Orwell's Faust-book will stand. It seems to teach us that political thought cannot work in a vacuum; politics must be keyed to metaphysics by the analogical mode of thought (as in *Policraticus* or the Magna Charta), else it will fall by mystical and ambiguous religion of politics towards a monolithic tyranny.

To the foregoing an objection may be raised: Orwell never wrote on metaphysics. But we all imply our metaphysics in our acts and works; in Orwell's tale the fingers of O'Brien, held up to Smith's face, embody the basic metaphysical question of existential actuality, which Smith is unfitted to answer. Man found at his best is a citizen of the analogical universe, where freedom is proportioned to virtue – to what Orwell in his way conceives as common decency, when he writes a fable of Faustian politics and virtue's fall.

Part Two
Language and Politics

5

Words, Deeds and Things: Orwell's Quarrel with Language

Paul Delany

'He pushed the door open and entered the room. A yellow beam of sunlight, filtering through the muslin curtains, slanted onto the table, where a matchbox, half open, lay beside the inkpot. With his right hand in his pocket he moved across to the window. Down in the street a tortoiseshell cat was chasing a dead leaf' (*CE*, I, 2). For fifteen years the young George Orwell kept up this kind of silent commentary on his daily activities, as if he were simultaneously living his life and writing it. He passed it off as a 'common habit of children and adolescents'; but the habit started around the time he went to prep school, and it sounds like a classic obsessive symptom – a defence against the fear and loneliness that any child would feel on being sent away from home at the age of eight. The commentary is an endless spell that protects him from the hostile elements of St Cyprian's. Language runs parallel to reality; perhaps, by sympathetic magic, it may actually control external objects or make them better.

However, an opposite explanation is possible. The dangerous element may be language itself, rather than everyday objects and actions. Orwell's 'meticulous[ly] descriptive' incantations are a way of keeping words safely tethered to things, for he has already realised that world and word are separate powers. If unity and order are to be preserved, either world or word must rule; but he is still in doubt about which will hold the upper hand.

Orwell tells another exemplary story about actions being 'doubled' by words. In his early weeks at St Cyprian's he was sent up to 'Sambo', the headmaster, for wetting his bed. 'It was part of the punishment of reporting yourself', he recalls, 'that you had to proclaim your offence with your own lips. When I had said my say, he read me a short but pompous lecture, then seized me by the scruff of the neck, twisted me over and began beating me with the riding-crop. He had a habit of continuing his lecture while he flogged you, and I remember the words "you dir-ty lit-tle boy" keeping time with the blows'. Orwell left the study and foolishly boasted, while Sambo's wife 'Flip' was in earshot, that it didn't hurt. 'How dare you say a thing like that?' she burst out. 'Do you think that is a proper thing to say? go in and REPORT YOURSELF AGAIN!' A second beating duly followed, this time so violent that Sambo broke his riding crop. '"Look what you've made me do!" he said furiously, holding up the broken crop' (*CE*, IV, 333). We know the proverb about sticks and stones, but in this case it is the words that break the stick.

When Wittgenstein remarked that 'Words are deeds' he was giving only the second half of an imaginary exchange. 'Deeds, not words', says the proverb; words *are* deeds, the philosopher retorts. Sambo makes little Eric re-enact his wetting the bed in words, and then beats him for them. The confession is not a foreword to punishment, but *part* of the punishment. Then Eric is flogged again for his statement that the first flogging didn't hurt; this is rightly interpreted by Sambo as a gesture of defiance, regardless of whether it is a true description or not.

In 'Such, Such Were The Joys' we are constantly reminded that Sambo and Flip dominate their unfortunate charges *rhetorically*, by their strategic use of threats, praise or sarcasm. Only as a last resort do they use the rod to prove that others must speak as Sambo and Flip dictate. St Cyprian's taught Orwell to fear language in the mouths of rulers, and even to bear a life-long grudge against language's very existence. His famous claim that 'Good prose is like a window pane' (*CE*, I, 7) proposes that mental activity should be oriented towards objects, about which we 'think wordlessly' (*CE*, IV, 138). Language turns into demonic possession in his image of the orator whose spectacles, reflecting the light, turn him into a robot, programmed to emit an endless stream of words, words, words. 'The worst thing one can do with words', Orwell warns us, 'is to surrender to them' (*CE*, IV, 138).

But 'surrender' can mean either submission or seduction; this was another of the lessons of St Cyprian's. Cyril Connolly's memoir of the school shows that the more sensitive boys were conversant with two separate languages. One was everyday English, the other the language of poetry – 'the romantic escape [and] the purple patch'. On Saturday nights, young Cyril liked to put on the gramophone and read aloud a lyrical passage about sea-birds emerging at twilight to flit among the waves:

> The combination of the music with this passage was intoxicating. The two blended into an experience of isolation and flight which induced the sacred shiver. The classroom disappeared, I was alone on the dark seas, there was a hush, a religious moment of suspense, and then the visitation – the Manx shearwaters appeared, held their high carnival, and vanished. At length the schoolroom where each boy sat by his desk, his few possessions inside, his chartered ink channels on top, returned to focus. This experience, which I repeated every Saturday, like a drug, was typical of the period.[1]

Connolly and Orwell wrote poetry of their own, too; they would compare efforts and then 'separate feeling ashamed of each other'. Connolly purged this shame in adulthood through sarcasm, much of it self-directed, Orwell by insisting that his language be unadorned. In youth he passionately admired Dowson's 'Cynara', and he never gave up the *fin-de-siècle* notion that poetry was verbal music. 'The thought contained in a poem is always simple', he wrote in 'The Prevention of Literature'; 'what the poet is saying – that is, what his poem "means" if translated into prose – is relatively unimportant even to himself' (*CE*, IV, 67). 'Politics and the English Language' dismisses the whole aesthetic dimension of writing in a sentence: 'I have not here been considering the literary use of language', Orwell notes, 'but merely language as an instrument for expressing and not for concealing or preventing thought' (*CE*, IV, 139).

Orwell's suspicion of literary language has stirred debate on whether he is an artist in prose or only a talented pamphleteer. I wish to argue here that he was almost as suspicious of *ordinary* language – though for different reasons. The whole point of 'Politics and the English Language' is that ordinary language is not ordinary but exceptional, an ideal that can be achieved only by strenuous discipline. *Everyday* language is sick and becoming sicker; the 'window pane' of true ordinary language has been altogether darkened and distorted. Modern politics are bad because of the corruption of language, Orwell argues; but he also argues, paradoxically, that if language were good – that is, transparent – it would become politically insignificant. He proposes to refine and improve language, in order that language should no longer matter.

Orwell's argument rests on three premises, two of which I can only mention in passing. The first is that English has been suffering a gradual decline. Most linguists agree that such a diagnosis makes little sense. Literature has its ups and downs, evidently; but the language as a whole, in its everyday use, must always be adequate to the work required of it. His second concern is that language can now be deliberately engineered for political ends; here I would only note that, if one follows Saussure, changing language through an act of individual will is much harder than Orwell imagines in *Nineteen Eighty-Four*.

The third argument, central to Orwell's whole intellectual project, is that there has been a global shift towards 'abstraction' in language use. 'The object' is disappearing behind a cloud of verbiage; more and more, the argument goes, the *word* has usurped the authority of the *thing*. My first response to this claim is that, for someone so concerned with language, Orwell was sadly reluctant to think systematically about it. 'Language is something all-too-familiar to us', observed Nietzsche, 'therefore it needs a philosopher to be struck by it'.[2] Orwell was struck by it, even obsessed by it, but as a pragmatist rather than a philosopher. Continually worrying at the issue, he tried to pin down the essence of language in memorable phrases. But his formulas, when examined closely, have a way of turning against their own premises.

The first article of Orwell's creed, for example, is that meaning is founded on things rather than words. If one wants to write good English, he says, one should 'put off using words as long as possible and get one's meaning as clear as one can through pictures or sensations' (*CE*, IV, 138–9). *Gulliver's Travels* was a favourite book of his, but he seems to have missed the joke of the Grand Academy of Lagado's scheme 'for entirely abolishing all words whatsoever'. Those engaged on this project carry around with them 'such things as [are] necessary to express the particular business they are to discourse on'. 'Another great advantage proposed by this invention', Swift continues, 'was that it would serve as an universal language to be understood in all civilised nations, whose goods and utensils are generally of the same kind'. If language were just a collection of names, then its authority would indeed derive from the objects it refers to. Meaning would originate in the object, and language would serve only to disseminate it.[3] Orwell is not a total objectivist since he concedes that language does, in practice, generate its own meanings. However, he sees this fertility or potency in language as an *abuse*: a usurpation of the powers that properly should reside only in things.

Orwell imagines the ultimate abuse of language in Newspeak, consciously designed 'to make all other modes of thought impossible. It was intended that when Newspeak had been adopted once and for all and Oldspeak forgotten, a heretical thought – that is, a thought diverging from the principles of Ingsoc – should be literally unthinkable, at least so far as thought is dependent on words'. Is Newspeak then the last word in abstraction? On the contrary: its construction out of standard English requires the elimination of abstract concepts, such as 'free', and also the 'reduction of vocabulary . . . as an end in itself' (*Nineteen Eighty-Four*, p. 418). In the case of Newspeak, then, Orwell tacitly admits that abstract terms may represent important values in language. Words like 'democracy' are often exploited, but should they therefore be purged from the language altogether? If we drop 'murder' and 'execute', while retaining only 'kill', will the quality of our thought be the better for it? In some crucial ways, the engineers of Newspeak seem to be faithful disciples of 'Politics and the English Language'.

Even if Newspeak became the only language of Oceania, the triumph of Ingsoc would require something more: a fixed correspondence between words and things. Yet one of the most important objects in the book, Winston's paperweight, shows that this correspondence cannot be assumed. Winston imagines that the central piece of coral is himself and Julia, while the glass that encloses it suggests an invisible concept – private life – that shields us from the state. To Mr Charrington, however, the paperweight is simply a piece of bait, enticing those who are inclined to crimethink. When Winston and Julia are arrested it is promptly smashed by the Thought Police. The same object may be precious or contemptible, pragmatic or symbolic, depending on who is looking at it. A similar point underlies the old Prole's demand for a pint of beer, rather than the official half-litre. He prefers the smaller quantity, it is true, but he also has a sentimental attachment to the *idea* of the old pint. If objects have a variable semiotic value, then they can be just as subversive as words. Big Brother may indeed abolish many objects – this is one aim of his spartan regime – but the idea that objects might do nothing but serve the ruling ideology is truly fantastic.

Even if objects were stable elements, they could not reliably govern their verbal equivalents. The same entity may be called – with momentous consequences – a piece of earth, or a piece of property.[4] The meaning of the entity may be placed in the words used to name it or (my own preference) in the situation prevailing when the words are uttered. But Orwell's epistemology tries to entrench the meaning in the actual soil.

Why does Orwell return so persistently to the idea that truth lies in objects? Apparently because he so fears the alternative: that, as O'Brien says when interrogating Winston, 'Reality exists in the human mind, and nowhere else' (p. 374). Winston tries vaguely to remember the arguments against this view, but O'Brien easily over-rules him:

> This is not solipsism. Collective solipsism, if you like. But that is a different thing: in fact, the opposite thing . . . . The real power, the power we have to fight for night and day, is not power over things, but over men. (p. 389)

When Winston falls back on the one thing he really believes in, it is not any object but simply 'the spirit of Man'. This sounds like one of those fatuous abstractions that Orwell often warns us against, and Winston's clutching at it may be taken as proof that O'Brien has broken his capacity to argue back. But does Orwell reserve a better answer for himself? In fact, the debate between O'Brien and Winston has been fought out before, between Dorothy and Mr Warburton in *A Clergyman's Daughter*. After her pilgrimage through the lower depths of London, Dorothy came to understand 'the truism that all real happenings are in the mind':

> 'Things change in your mind', she repeated.
> 'I've lost my faith . . . .'
> 'A few months ago, all of a sudden, it seemed as if my whole mind had changed. Everything that I'd believed in till then – everything – seemed suddenly meaningless and almost silly. God – what I'd meant by God – immortal life, Heaven and Hell – everything. It had all gone. And it wasn't that I'd reasoned it out; it just happened to me.'[5]

The debate between Dorothy and Warburton is central to Orwell's quarrel with language. Her loss of faith has changed her whole perceptual system. As she looks out from the train at the sights of the English spring, she finds everything 'a little emptier, a little poorer'. 'How *can* one enjoy anything when all the meaning's been taken out of it?' she laments to Warburton, who is a cheerfully amoral hedonist. 'What do you want with a meaning?' he retorts. 'When I eat my dinner I don't do it to the greater glory of God; I do it because I enjoy it. The world's full of amusing things – books, pictures, wine, travel, friends – everything. I've never seen any meaning in it at all, and I don't want to see one.'[6]

Dorothy sees that they don't, as it were, 'speak the same language'. Warburton 'was quite incapable of realizing how a mind naturally pious must recoil from a world discovered to be meaningless'. Still less can Warburton understand her resolve to go back to her father's village and immerse herself in parish work, acting exactly as if her loss of faith had never happened. Warburton can only see in this 'a sort of mental gangrene . . . . You tell me that you've got rid of these ridiculous beliefs that were stuffed into you from your cradle upwards, and yet you're taking an attitude to life which is simply meaningless without these beliefs.'[7]

Who does Orwell side with: Dorothy, who hankers after her lost belief, or Warburton, the literal-minded hedonist? In a review of Cyril Connolly's *The Rock Pool*, Orwell speaks of the three ways of escaping the dreariness of 'modern mechanised life': 'One is religion, another is unending work, the third is the kind of sluttish antinomianism – lying in bed till four in the afternoon, drinking Pernod – that Mr Connolly seems to admire' (*CE*, I, 226). The first answer is Dorothy's, the third Warburton's, the second perhaps Orwell's own self-counsel of despair. The *real* answer, he says, is 'to be a normal decent person and yet to be fully alive'. By decent, however, he typically also means unthinking. His idea of a virginal language is the counterpart to his longing for an unproblematic relation between experience and ideology:

The fact is that Socialism, *in the form in which it is now presented*, appeals chiefly to unsatisfactory or even inhuman types. On the one hand you have the warm-hearted unthinking Socialist, the typical working-class Socialist, who only wants to abolish poverty and does not always grasp what this implies. On the other hand, you have the intellectual, book-trained Socialist . . . all that dreary tribe of high-minded women and sandal-wearers and bearded fruit-juice drinkers who come flocking towards the smell of 'progress' like bluebottles to a dead cat.[8]

Orwell hates sandals and fruit juice because they are the visible stigmata of the disease of thought. His philistinism, left over from prep school and the colonial police, is too often mistaken for intellectual vigour.

The limitations of Orwell's stance are clearly exposed in *Nineteen Eighty-Four*. The strongest opposition to Big Brother *should* be a spontaneous hatred of his tyranny by 'normal decent persons'. But those who are naively instinctive – the proles – have no political consciousness; while those who know what the fight is about have been alienated from their instincts:

> In the old days, [Winston] thought, a man looked at a girl's body and saw that it was desirable, and that was the end of the story. But you could not have pure love or pure lust nowadays. No emotion was pure, because everything was mixed up with fear and hatred. Their embrace had been a battle, the climax a victory. It was a blow struck against the Party. It was a political act. (p. 265)

Winston's 'myth of immediacy' may be traced back to D. H. Lawrence (a considerable influence on Orwell). To speak of the 'purity' of lust – in the old days – is to make the naked body into a kind of 'supreme object': one that has a single and compelling meaning that precedes interpretation. Although no actual words are spoken, the lovemaking of Julia and Winston has been contaminated by language. It has been made into a narrative, invaded by abstract terms like 'victory', its animal nature subdued to the political culture of Ingsoc.

But can sex, or any other human activity, ever be insulated from the play of interpretations – which is to say, from language and everything that our use of language drags along with it? In his review of Winwood Reade's *The Martyrdom of Man*, Orwell recognises the problems of positivist history:

> If one were obliged to write a history of the world, would it be better to record the true facts, so far as one could discover them, or would it be better simply to make the whole thing up? The

answer is not so self-evident as it appears . . . . A history constructed imaginatively would never be right about any single event, but it might come nearer to essential truth than a mere compilation of names and dates in which no one statement was demonstrably untrue. (*CE*, IV, 116–17)

Even if Winston could make contact with 'the events themselves', instead of labouring at his textual assembly line in the Ministry of Truth, he could not take it for granted that things were as they seemed, or that all the facts pointed in a single direction.

We may still admire Winston's passion for truth or, behind it, Orwell's own hatred of totalitarianism. What we must question, however, is the wish that these passions could be satisfied *outside of* language, in a more solid realm where things remain faithful to themselves. 'It is the powerful who made the names of things into law', remarked Nietzsche.[9] In our own time, Orwell has become precisely one of these men of power: the creator of Newspeak, doublethink, Big Brother; the origin of 'Orwellian', a double-sided term meaning either truth in the raw or truth turned upside down. The oldest trick in rhetoric is to deny that one is using any. Like Mark Antony before him, Orwell mounts the pulpit as a 'plain blunt man' who will deliver things in their native simplicity and honour; but within his 'objective' discourse we encounter, at every turn, signs that the external world, too, is a text.

6

Bentham and Basic English: The 'Pious Founders' of Newspeak

Mary Jo Morris

The Appendix on 'The Principles of Newspeak' in George Orwell's *Nineteen Eighty-Four* explains that the language is engineered in such a way that

> a heretical thought . . . should be literally unthinkable, as least so far as thought is dependent on words. (p. 417)

The anonymous speaker of the Appendix confirms what Symes, the Newspeak expert, says to Winston Smith in the novel proper:

> Don't you see that the whole aim of Newspeak is to narrow the range of thought? In the end we shall make thoughtcrime literally impossible because there will be no words in which to express it. (p. 201)

Just as Orwell's portrayal of Oceania exaggerates and criticises tendencies in contemporary politics, so Newspeak constitutes his reply to the language schemes popular from the 1920s to the 1940s, in particular to Basic English, the brainchild of the authors of *The Meaning of Meaning*, C. K. Ogden and I. A. Richards.

Unlike Esperanto, the best known of the artificial languages, Basic English is a simplified version of a natural language, and in this fact resides its greatest practical advantage over other language projects. In the *Manchester Evening News*, Orwell argues that the artificial language Interglossa, which was developed by Lancelot Hogben, has little chance of becoming universal when Basic is already comprehensible to two or three hundred million people.[1] Orwell makes mention of Basic several times in his essays. In its

favour he says that it can help restore clarity to English by acting
'as a sort of corrective to the oratory of statesmen and publicists'
(*CE*, III, 244). Elsewhere, he labels Basic 'a very simple pidgin
dialect' (*CE*, III, 41). An acknowledged source of *Nineteen Eighty-
Four*, H. G. Wells's optimistic scientific fantasy *The Shape of Things
to Come*, projects a future in which Basic English has become the
lingua franca of the world. While Orwell was broadcasting to India
during the Second World War, C. K. Ogden's chief assistant, Miss
Leonora Lockhart, gave a talk *on* Basic English *in* Basic English for
his programme. Although Orwell was interested in Basic, and
although he thought that a universal medium of communication
would be conducive to international peace, he was wary, as he
says in his review of Hogben's *Interglossa*, of 'the sinister way in
which several living languages are being used for imperialist
purposes'.[2] Memoranda between C. K. Ogden and Miss Lockhart
indicate that Ogden at least regarded this statement as a direct
criticism of Basic.[3]

Orwell's ambivalence towards Basic is well, but briefly, described
in John Atkins's *George Orwell: A Literary Study*:

> When Basic English was being canvassed as a possible inter-
> national language Orwell gave the idea his sympathy . . . . But
> it would be possible to purify the language without resorting to
> Basic. It was purity and simplification he desired . . . .
>
> Perhaps the reason why his sympathy with Basic English
> never developed into overt support was because he feared that
> Basic might be the forerunner of the manipulative language that
> he illustrated in *Nineteen Eighty-Four*.[4]

As Basic gained ascendancy over its competitors, Orwell became
suspicious of it, eventually so suspicious that he transformed it
into the totalitarian language, Newspeak.

In his article 'Basic English and Its Applications',[5] I. A. Richards
says that Ogden conceived the notion of devising a 'basic English'
while they were writing the fifth chapter of *The Meaning of Meaning*.
One of the key passages of that chapter reads as follows:

> *language, though often spoken of as a medium of communication, is
> best regarded as an instrument*; and all instruments are extensions,
> or refinements, of our sense-organs. The telescope, the tele-
> phone, the microscope, the microphone, and the galvanometer

are, like the monocle or the eye itself, capable of distorting . . . .
In photography it is not uncommon for effects due to the
processes of manipulation to be mistaken by amateurs for features
of the objects depicted . . . . In a similar fashion language is
full of elements with no representative or symbolic function, due
solely to its manipulation; these are similarly misinterpreted or
exploited by metaphysicians and their friends so as greatly to
exercise one another – and such of the laity as are prepared to
listen to them.

The fictitious entities thus introduced by language form a special
variety of what are called fictions. [my italics][6]

The immediate inspiration for both this passage and Basic English
was Ogden's work on Jeremy Bentham's theory of fictions; from
that work, Richards says, '[w]hat resulted was the wordlist of 850
words and, *more important*, the ordered system which restricted
their uses and idioms to a limited range'.[7] Ogden and Bentham
alike concentrate, not upon the ability of language to express
thought, but upon its ability to distort or control thought.

By 1933, Basic was being taught by Richards and others in China
with the support of the Rockefeller Foundation. It was also taught
in Latin America, Burma, India, and many European countries. In
the United States, it was considered useful for people wanting
naturalisation and for foreign sales people. Radio corporations
asked for trained Basic speakers as broadcasters, and telephone
companies thought that instructions in Basic would increase the
use of phones. Basic was supported by a number of prominent
men of letters, among them H. G. Wells, Julian Huxley, and George
Bernard Shaw, who at one time had decided to leave a sizeable
portion of his estate to an institute for the propagation of Basic.
Among the works of literature translated into Basic were Poe's *The
Gold Bug* (or, in Basic, *The Gold Insect*), *Gulliver's Travels* (which, in
the original, contains a devastating satire of language projects),
and the New Testament in 1000 words. William Empson used
Basic as a critical tool in his essay 'Basic English and Wordsworth';[8]
by trying to translate poetry into Basic, he claims, a reader begins
to understand the difference between complex and simple thought.
At Harvard University, a special committee was set up to examine
and develop the principles of Basic. In England during the second
world war, Winston Churchill appointed a committee of Ministers
to study the possible value of Basic as propaganda.

From very early stages in its development onwards, Basic was proposed as an international language. During the second world war, it was quite commonly regarded as part of the war effort, as a method of attaining linguistic unity against a common enemy. In an article entitled 'Eight Hundred and Fifty Words to Unite a World', L. H. Robbins claims that the voice of freedom speaks Basic: 'Today there are said to be secret classes in Basic in every land beneath the Nazi heel'.[9] Charges of linguistic or cultural imperialism were regularly levelled at the language project, and were just as regularly dismissed by Basic's defenders, who argued that the practical benefits of the scheme to new speakers of English rendered its political undertones negligible. However, even Richards, whose polemical defences usually stressed the usefulness and efficiency of the method, occasionally indicates the political potency of Basic:

there is a widespread feeling . . . that the maintenance of what may be called the English-speaking outlook in political and moral traditions requires an English-speaking people, a democracy which is linguistically united.[10]

Ultimately, Basic is to be regarded as a linguistic extension of the British Empire. Its main asset, as Ogden and many others claimed, was that 'some form of English [was] already the national or administrative medium of over 500,000,000 people'.[11] Faced with the military and economic decline of the empire, many Englishmen regarded Basic as a means of retaining ideological power internationally. Winston Churchill's speech about Basic, delivered at Harvard in 1943, concludes:

Such plans offer far better prizes than taking away other people's provinces or land, or grinding them down in exploitation. The empires of the future are the empires of the mind.[12]

Churchill's remark brought Basic a great deal of notoriety, and aggravated the suspicions of its critics, among them Orwell. Oceania, with its Thought Police and thoughtcrime, is an empire of the mind, and its language an only slightly disguised exaggeration of Basic.

Basic English is a version of English consisting of a vocabulary of 850 words, only 18 of which are verbs. Ogden decided upon 850 words because (a) that is the number that can be legibly printed on the back of a single sheet of notepaper, and (b) the number represents what one person, with hard work, can learn in a month. The method of teaching the language stresses the visual. All the words are visible to the student at one glance. Ogden devised what he called a Panopticon, a sentence-builder consisting of concentric circles of cardboard on which words are printed so that, no matter how the circles are manipulated, the words appear in a grammatically coherent order. Thus, the student can *see* how an English sentence is constructed. The system relies heavily on nouns; Ogden says that 'one important advantage of any system which stresses the noun is the assistance to be derived from the pictorial method, and particularly from the pictorial dictionary'.[13] In other words, Basic is taught by sight to the almost complete exclusion of other senses.

The reliance of Basic upon the visual is derived from Jeremy Bentham's similar dependence. Bentham's thought, including his thought on language, seems to be motivated at all times by a drive for security, particularly security from 'fictitious entities', those invisible and impalpable beings that are given existence by language. Indeed, his fear of these fictitious entities was almost pathological. Even during Bentham's old age, his servants had only to dress up as apparitions in order to free themselves from their master's presence; Jeremy would flee the house in terror at the sight of a ghost. Bentham blames his fear of ghosts on his childhood governesses, who spoke of ghosts as if they were real in order to frighten the boy into obedience. Ghosts are fictions; they have no existence apart from language. For Bentham, the central evil of fictions – of certain words and of ghosts alike – is that they deceitfully act upon the mind as if they were real. Bentham did not appreciate the tyranny of bodiless words over his psyche. Hence, the cornerstone of his language is the noun – preferably the concrete noun that names a real, visible thing.

Verbs do not name things; rather they give linguistic expression to the fact that things can change. They denote processes. Not surprisingly, Bentham expresses a prejudice against verbs:

> I use a verbal substantive where others use a verb. A verb slips through your fingers like an eel – it is evanescent: it cannot be made the subject of a predication – for example, I say 'to give

motion' instead of *to move*. The word *motion* can thus be the subject of consideration and predication.[14]

In an ideal language, Bentham intimates, all nouns would be in the nominative case, subjects of sentences. His anxious desire that things stay passive or subject, that they stay put, prompts him to perform complicated manoeuvres in order to diminish the importance of verbs:

> In the physical world, in the order of approach to real existence, next to *matter* comes *motion*. But motion itself is spoken of as if it were *matter* . . . .
>
> A *ball* – the ball called *the earth* – is said to be *in* motion. By this word *in*, what is it that is signified? *Answer*: What is signified is that *motion* is a receptacle, *i.e.*, a hollow substance; and that in this hollow substance, the ball called the earth is lodged.[15]

The reduction of 'moving' to a relation of one immobile thing, the hollow substance, to another immobile thing, the ball, to Bentham, has the satisfying effect of making movement completely static.

Basic employs Bentham's strategy of minimising verbs. One doesn't think in Basic, for instance; one 'has a thought'. The implication is that reality is an attribute solely of concrete things; verbs do not express *real* processes, but rather the static, spatial relations between material things with measurable dimensions. Fictions, among which we must evidently place verbs, 'owe their existence entirely to language'.[16] Although Bentham concedes that such fictions are necessary and that without them 'the language of man could not have risen above the language of brutes',[17] his animosity towards them underlies his entire theory: 'fiction has never been more or less than lying, for the purpose of extortion and usurpation'.[18] Ogden follows in his master's footsteps, railing as vigorously against 'Word-magic' as Bentham does against fictions.

At roughly the time when he began writing about language, Bentham was working on a scheme of prison reform. He devised a model prison which he called the Panopticon, the term Ogden chooses for the name of his sentence-builder. Bentham's Panopticon is a circular building with cells lining the walls; in the centre of the building is a watchtower from which the warden is able to observe all the cells without himself moving. The inspector is concealed from the prisoners:

> the essence of it consists, then, in the centrality of the inspector's situation, combined with the well-known and most effectual contrivances for *seeing without being seen*.[19]

Bentham suggests that the cells be 'bugged':

> a small tin tube might reach from each cell to the inspector's lodge . . . . By means of this implement the slightest whisper of the one might be heard by the other, especially if he had proper notice to apply his ear to the tube.[20]

The Panopticon's effectiveness depends upon constant surveillance and monitoring of prisoners' activities.

Bentham, infatuated with the simplicity and serviceability of his scheme, thinks that the architectural plan of the Panopticon is applicable

> to all establishments whatsoever, in which . . . a number of persons are meant to be kept under inspection. No matter how different, or even opposite the purpose: whether it be that of *punishing the incorrigible, guarding the insane, reforming the vicious, confining the suspected, employing the idle, maintaining the helpless, curing the sick, instructing the willing,* in any branch of industry, or *training the rising race* in the path of education.[21]

When Winston Smith agrees that two and two make whatever the Party wishes in *Nineteen Eighty-Four* (p. 382), he loses the ability to interpret and name the evidence of his senses; the Party destroys the foundations of empirical thought. In light of this scene, Bentham's speculations on the possible uses of the Panopticon become very sinister indeed. Although no evidence exists that Orwell knew the works of Bentham well, Winston's discovery of the Party's control of reality ominously echoes the Father of Utilitarianism. Bentham submits that a Panoptical orphanage would present

> a rare field for discovery in metaphysics: a science which, now for the first time, may be put to the test of experiment, like any

other. Books, conversation, sensible objects, everything might be given. The genealogy of each observable idea might be traced through all its degrees with the utmost nicety . . . . Two and two might here be less than four, or the moon might be made of green cheese; if any pious founder chose to have her of that material.[22]

Bentham's Panopticon is, it seems to me, simply a technologically inferior version of the prison-world of *Nineteen Eighty-Four*. Replace his inspector's station with the all-seeing telescreen and his tin tubs with microphones, remove the circular walls, and there it is: the totalitarian state of Orwell's imagining, where the very definition of reality is provided by the 'pious founder'.

Bentham's prison system and his language system function on similar principles. Both exploit the notion of display: what can be seen is not to be feared, what can be seen can be controlled. If language restricts itself to naming visible objects, it cannot breed invisible and insubordinate monsters. A prisoner under unfailing surveillance cannot challenge the authority of the inspector's eye. The confining of prisoners to monitored cells deprives them of the ability to act; just so, the diminution of the role of verbs deprives language as much as possible of the ability to express action. In both schemes, Bentham's aim is to achieve power over the visible. At the same time, he defines the real as the visible so that, in the end, what is seen can be manipulated without reference to any moral or physical reality outside the system. As O'Brien says, 'I tell you, Winston, that reality is not external' (p. 374).

In the third book of *Gulliver's Travels*, Jonathan Swift satirises noun-dominated languages. There, the professors of the Grand Academy are busy contriving languages that, ultimately, serve the interests of the tyrannical Laputans who rule from their flying island. Orwell writes of this book that

mixed up with much fooling, there is a perception that one of the aims of totalitarianism is not merely to make sure that people will think the right thoughts, but actually to make them *less conscious*. (*CE*, IV, 251)

The first project Gulliver encounters in the school of languages aims to shorten Discourse by cutting Polysyllables into one, and leaving out Verbs and Participles; because in Reality all things imaginable are but Nouns.[23]

The second of the schemes is one

for entirely abolishing all Words whatsoever: . . . since Words are only Names for *Things*, it would be more convenient for all Men to carry about them, such *Things* as were necessary to express the particular Business they are to discourse on.[24]

The people suffering under Laputan rule have been reduced to poverty; Gulliver says that he had never before seen 'a People whose Countenances and Habit expressed so much Misery and Want'.[25] The effect of 'thing-language' is to render their remaining possessions burdensome to them. When wealth of knowledge and richness of conversation depend upon the number of possessions one can cart on one's back, language becomes not only materialistic in the extreme, but also physically oppressive:

[the converser] must be obliged in Proportion to carry a greater Bundle of *Things* upon his Back, unless he can afford one or two strong Servants to attend him. I have often beheld two of those Sages almost sinking under the Weight of their Packs, like Pedlars among us.[26]

Swift's satire is directed largely against John Locke's study of language, in Book III of *An Essay Concerning Human Understanding*. However, it is an equally pertinent critique of Bentham's. Language that attempts to restrict itself to the naming of things loses its capacity to protest unjust rule or to defend such 'ghostly' principles as freedom or truth. In the process of freeing language from 'fictitious entities', Bentham shackles it to an onerous materialism.

Ogden's Basic English derives in virtually all its particulars from Bentham's proposed language. Both are the result of fear – in Ogden's case, the quite natural fear, widespread after the first world war of florid propagandistic language. Both Bentham and Ogden strive for an 'objective' language incapable of exploiting injudicious emotional prejudices. Basic's 850 words are chosen to encourage a morally neutral, descriptive use of language. Kenneth Burke criticises this, what he calls, 'semantic ideal':

Above all, it fosters, sometimes explicitly, sometimes by implication, the notion that one may comprehensively discuss human and social events in a nonmoral vocabulary and that perception itself is a nonmoral act.[27]

In Burke's view, if such an 'objective' language asserts itself as an ideal, even in the effort to expose political lies, it propagates a greater lie, that the dealings of human beings with each other can be adequately expressed without moral reference.

Newspeak is a specific parody of Basic in many respects. First of all, both are reductive languages. The aim of Newspeak is to reduce language to the barest minimum number of words; Basic claims that its 850 words are sufficient to express most ideas. Both make extensive use of the principle of substitution, so that the addition of prefixes and suffices to root words eliminates the need for other words expressing opposites or nuances of meaning. In Basic, all comparatives and superlatives are formed with 'more' and 'most'; in Newspeak, with 'plus' and 'doubleplus'. Bentham prefers verbal substantives to verbs; Basic reduces verbs to a minimum of 18; Newspeak is dominated by noun-verbs such as 'goodthing' and 'crimething'. In *Learning Basic English*, I. A. Richards advises:

> *Do* use any combination of words to form compounds if their meanings are clear from the separate words . . . ; postcard, overseer, beeswax, upside-down, looking-glass, good-looking, left-handed, etc.[28]

The words in the Newspeak 'B' vocabulary are, without exception, compound words like 'prolefeed' and 'joycamp'. In Basic, the word 'will' may not express the idea of purpose; in Newspeak, 'the *shall, should* tenses had been dropped, all their uses being covered by *will* and *would*' (p. 420).

The Newspeak 'A' vocabulary corresponds to the core vocabulary of 850 words in Basic: it consists of the 'words needed for the business of everyday life' (p. 418). Just as Basic restricts the meanings of words – it is not possible to make puns within the limitations of Basic – the words of the Newspeak 'A' list are

rigidly defined. All ambiguities and shades of meaning had been purged out of them . . . . It would have been quite impossible to use the A vocabulary for literary purposes or philosophical discussions. (p. 418)

To compare Richards' translation of a single sentence from Coleridge's *Biographia Literaria* with its original reveals a similar inadequacy on the part of Basic. Coleridge's sentence reads, 'The poet, described in ideal perfection, brings the whole soul of man into activity'. The Basic version reads:

The *poet*, if we may say what the best the wisest of *poets* does and though, in fact, no writer of verse may ever come up to such a level, (a) puts every power of man's mind to work, (b) makes all the parts of a man's mind awake and conscious, (c) makes a man become all that at his best he is able to be.[29]

Basic is constructed in such a way that metaphysical 'Word-magic' can be translated only into circumlocutions; ideal perfections and souls have no place in an objective language.

Newspeak's 'C' vocabulary is 'supplementary to the others and consist[s] entirely of scientific and technical terms' (p. 426). Basic, too, supplies supplementary and specialised vocabularies for biology, business, agriculture and, tellingly, for the reading of poetry and the Bible. The emotional, morally charged vocabulary that Basic excludes appears in Newspeak's 'B' vocabulary. In the 'B' vocabulary, all words are axiological; the use of the word is required to assent to its implicit moral and emotional evaluation of what it names. Thus, Newspeak achieves linguistic control over the otherwise uncontrolled and potentially subversive emotions.

Basic English was an overtly political movement in that its advocates saw it as a means of promoting international understanding and of preserving English ideals in the world. Its opponents regarded it as an instrument of linguistic imperialism. With Newspeak, Orwell exposes the deeper political implications of Basic. What Basic does at the most fundamental level is to stress the technological aspects of language; it is the reification of *The Meaning of Meaning*'s contention that language is 'best regarded as an instrument'. Technology is in and of itself ideologically neutral. Orwell's critique of Basic is not directed at the motives of its originators. Even if those motives are benign, and even if Basic English is immune from the germs of totalitarianism we find in the work of Bentham, Orwell's point is well taken: such a technique, no matter what ideology it supports, tends to make people 'less conscious'. The technological ideal of Basic can lead to Newspeak, truly the prison-house of language.

7

Orwell and the Language: Speaking the Truth in *Homage to Catalonia*

John Ferns

Any use of language is the chance to say something of our own –
which is the same as the chance to achieve sincerity . . . . By
using language we simultaneously express our individuality and
our connection with humanity: we imitate and use the language
of others because that allows us to be ourselves.

Ian Robinson, 'D. H. Lawrence and English Prose'.

To write in plain, vigorous language one has to think fearlessly,
and if one thinks fearlessly one cannot be politically orthodox.

George Orwell, 'The Prevention of Literature'.

Reviewing *Inside The Whale* in *Scrutiny* in September 1940, Q. D.
Leavis referred to *Homage to Catalonia* as 'valuable' and 'impressive'.
She described Orwell's role in the Spanish War as that of a 'critic-
participator', but what impressed her most about Orwell was this:
'the great thing is, he has a special kind of honesty, he corrects
any astigmatic tendency in himself because in literature as in
politics he has taken up a stand which gives him freedom'.[1]
Whether or not Orwell read this review, he was thinking through
similar matters several months later in 'Literature and Totalitarianism' which appeared in *The Listener* on 19 June 1941. There he
wrote:

The whole of modern European literature – I am speaking of the
literature of the past four hundred years – is built on the concept
of intellectual honesty, or, if you like to put it that way, on
Shakespeare's maxim, 'To thine own self be true'. The first thing

114

that we ask of a writer is that he shall not tell lies, that he shall
say what he really thinks, what he really feels. The worst thing
we can say about a work of art is that it is insincere . . . . Modern
literature is essentially an individual thing. It is either the truthful
expression of what one man thinks and feels, or it is nothing
. . . . Totalitarianism has abolished freedom of thought to an
extent unheard of in any previous age . . . . It declares itself
infallible, and at the same time it attacks the very concept of
objective truth . . . . writing of any consequence can only be
produced when a man *feels* the truth of what he is saying;
without that, the creative impulse is lacking.[2]

The same thoughts and feelings about truthfulness, the importance
of objective truth and the need to feel the truth are pressed home
by Orwell equally forcibly in 'The Prevention of Literature' five
years later.

Bill Hart's essay 'Speaking the Truth' can help us to understand
what Orwell achieves in *Homage to Catalonia* (1938) because Hart
shows us convincingly that speaking the truth is not merely a
matter of stating facts. Truth is something that must be thought
and felt; truth is difficult to speak and involves us in finding
appropriate language in which to speak. All of these matters
concern George Orwell in *Homage to Catalonia*. Hart writes in
criticism of Christopher Williams' book *What is Truth?*:

But he [Christopher Williams] hasn't got the only thing which
counts in the end – the sense of how difficult it is in anything
important to arrive at the truth of whatever it is you have to say.
And that goes together with him not having any proper sense
of why truth matters, that's to say, of why truth matters to *him*
. . . . It's hardly surprising in the circumstances that the kind of
truth speaking he has in mind is nothing too demanding. It
answers pretty well to the responsible journalist's conception of
'sticking to the facts'. But nothing beyond.

For Bill Hart the sort of 'truth speaking' that matters is 'that in
which a man is called upon to delve deeply into himself, which
requires character and imagination'. He continues:

It's where speaking the truth presents a difficulty, where the
truth you're reaching after isn't anything cut and dried, and

where it matters most to get it right, that speaking the truth is thrown into relief, that it comes closest to being itself . . . speaking the truth and finding your own voice amount to the same thing. It's only in your own voice that you *can* speak the truth . . . . If I am to be speaking truthfully, in the fullest sense, it's not enough for me to say 'what I believe' – I have to say what I *know* . . . if it wasn't the whole of you engaged in what you're saying, then you wouldn't be speaking the truth.[3]

The pertinence of Hart's account of speaking the truth to *Homage to Catalonia* can be readily shown. It needs showing particularly since the criticism that Orwell is somehow not speaking the truth has been given fresh currency as recently as 1984 in Stephen Wadham's quotations from the late Victor Gollancz in *Remembering Orwell*. Over against Orwell's achievement in *Homage to Catalonia* we are asked to put the following by Victor Gollancz: 'I should have thought that his literary honesty was impeccable: I mean, I doubt whether he ever used words for mere effect, and so on and so forth. His intellectual honesty is another matter. I should not myself have said that his intellectual honesty was impeccable. I hope you won't think I'm being stupidly paradoxical . . . . '[4] Unfortunately these remarks are 'stupidly paradoxical', since on what acceptable grounds can we separate 'literary' and 'intellectual' honesty?

What is necessary, now, is to discuss the nature and importance of *Homage to Catalonia* particularly in terms of Orwell's handling of language in his effort to speak the truth. Only through sincerity does Orwell achieve honesty. Critical discussion of Orwell's language, therefore, will help us determine his success in speaking the truth. We can begin profitably with his presentation of him meeting with the Italian soldier on the first page of the book:

> In the Lenin Barracks in Barcelona, the day before I joined the militia, I saw an Italian militiaman standing in front of the officers' table.
>
> He was a tough-looking youth of twenty-five or six, with reddish-yellow hair and powerful shoulders. His peaked leather cap was pulled fiercely over one eye. He was standing in profile to me, his chin on his breast, gazing with a puzzled frown at a map which one of the officers had open on the table. Something in his face deeply moved me. It was the face of a man who

would commit murder and throw away his life for a friend – the kind of face you would expect in an Anarchist, though as likely as not he was a Communist. There were both candour and ferocity in it; also the pathetic reverence that illiterate people have for their supposed superiors. Obviously he could not make head or tail of the map; obviously he regarded map-reading as a stupendous intellectual feat. I hardly know why, but I have seldom seen anyone – any man, I mean – to whom I have taken such an immediate liking. While they were talking round the table some remarks brought it out that I was a foreigner. The Italian raised his head and said quickly:

'*Italiano*? '

I answered in my bad Spanish: '*No, Inglés. Y tù*? '

'*Italiano.*'

As we went out he stepped across the room and gripped my hand very hard. Queer, the affection you can feel for a stranger! It was as though his spirit and mine had momentarily succeeded in bridging the gulf of language and tradition and meeting in utter intimacy. I hoped he liked me as well as I liked him. But I also knew that to retain my first impression of him I must not see him again; and needless to say I never did see him again. One was always making contacts of that kind in Spain.

I mention this Italian militiaman because he has stuck vividly in my memory. With his shabby uniform and fierce pathetic face he typifies for me the special atmosphere of that time. He is bound up with all my memories of that period of the war – the red flags in Barcelona, the gaunt trains full of shabby soldiers creeping to the front, the grey war-stricken towns farther up the line, the muddy, ice-cold trenches in the mountains.[5]

This is not Orwell at his best. There is more than a tinge here of adolescent hero worship and idealism. For a book which is finally so deep and true it begins badly. What is the 'something' in the Italian's face that moves Orwell so deeply? And isn't there an element of moral confusion in 'a man who would commit murder and throw away his life for a friend'? How does an Anarchist's face differ from the face of a Communist? Clearly we sympathise with the innocence of a man's 'pathetic reverence' for his 'supposed superiors'. But is this sufficient grounds for Orwell's 'immediate liking' ? 'Queer, the affection you can feel for a stranger!' is, in fact, embarrassingly self-revealing, while 'meeting in utter intimacy' sounds more like imitation Lawrence than genuine Orwell. Besides there is something uncomfortably like a schoolboy crush in 'I hope he liked me as well as I liked him' and 'But I also knew that to retain my first impression of him I must not see him again'. The Italian soldier's 'fierce pathetic face' typifies for Orwell 'the special atmosphere of that time' and this is the clue to the Italian soldier's eventually deeper importance and significance in *Homage to Catalonia*.

Even so, the embarrassingly sentimental and adolescent strain persists into the poem that celebrates the Italian soldier at the end of 'Looking Back On The Spanish War' of 1943, since what can Orwell possibly mean by:

> But oh! What peace I knew then
> In gazing on his battered face
> Purer than any woman's
>
> (p. 246)

which is just as problematic as 'Queer, the affection you can feel for a stranger!' Nevertheless, the poem is more impressive than the book's opening presentation of the Italian soldier and it is so precisely because it leaves the Italian soldier behind and deals with the larger human suffering of which the Italian soldier is representative. Indeed, before the poem Orwell admits that the Italian soldier is a symbol as much as anything else: 'He symbolizes for me the flower of the European working class' (p. 244). Orwell, it seems, at his best loves the Italian soldier for his naivety, for his innocence:

> For the flyblown words that make me spew
> Still in his ears were holy,
> And he was born knowing what I had learned
> Out of books and slowly.

Here we get closer to Orwell's sincere voice and so we believe him in the next stanza when he writes:

> The treacherous guns had told their tale
> And we both had bought it,
> But my gold brick was made of gold –
> Oh! who ever would have thought it?

There's an important thread here, for out of Orwell's capacity to efface himself and act for others grows a real sense of human value – the gold of the gold brick. This impulse to give and to sacrifice himself in a way, which we have to call Christian, Orwell transfers to his beloved Italian soldier:

> Good luck go with you, Italian soldier:
> But luck is not for the brave;
> What would the world give back to you?
> Always less than you gave.

The sense, then, of giving arrives at the point where *Homage to Catalonia* at its deepest and most valuable ends. Orwell reaches from individual suffering to the general human condition:

> For where is Manuel Gonzalez,
> And where is Pedro Aguilar,
> And where is Ramon Fenellosa?
> The earthworms know where they are.

At last, we discover what the 'something' is that Orwell saw in the Italian soldier's face and which it has taken the whole book to discover:

> But the thing that I saw in your face
> No power can disinherit:
> No bomb that ever burst
> Shatters the crystal spirit.
>
> (p. 247)

In celebrating the purity of spirit he imagines in the Italian soldier, George Orwell reveals his own. And what after all did the Italian militiaman symbolise for Orwell? Here we move towards the human centre of *Homage to Catalonia*'s meaning and value. At the end of 'Looking Back On The Spanish War', immediately before the poem, we find, expressed in the simple, colloquial language of 'shan'ts' and 'says', what Orwell spent his life struggling for:

The question is very simple. Shall people like the Italian soldier be allowed to live the decent, fully human life which is now technically achievable, or shan't they? Shall the common man be pushed back into the mud, or shall he not? I myself believe, perhaps on insufficient grounds, that the common man will win his fight sooner or later, but I want it to be sooner and not later – some time within the next hundred years, say, and not some time within the next ten thousand years. That was the real issue of the Spanish war, and of the last war, and perhaps of other wars yet to come. (p. 245)

Then, moving to the centre itself in a language unlike the overwrought language of the book's opening, Orwell reaches, with anger and conviction, the core of *Homage to Catalonia*'s human truth:

The damned impertinence of these politicians, priests, literary men, and what-not who lecture the working-class socialist for his materialism. All that the working man demands is what these others would consider the indispensable minimum without which human life cannot be lived at all. Enough to eat, freedom from the haunting terror of unemployment, the knowledge that your children will get a fair chance, a bath once a day, clean linen reasonably often, a roof that doesn't leak, and short enough working hours to leave you with a little energy when the day is done. Not one of those who preach against 'materialism' would consider life livable without those things. And how easily that minimum could be attained if we chose to set our minds to it for only twenty years! (pp. 244–5)

This, in essence, is what *Homage to Catalonia* is about.

But what are the factors that guarantee Orwell's sincerity in *Homage To Catalonia*, that, in Bill Hart's terms, convince us that Orwell writes not only what he 'believes' but also what he 'knows'? There are basically three elements here. First, Orwell is faithful to his experience; second, his lively self-irony acts as a further guarantor of his sincerity and sense of reality; and third, Orwell's capacity to reach through the political to the human world wins us over to his side against the *News Chronicle*'s and the *Daily Worker*'s false accounts of the war.

One of the book's most convincing passages occurs when Orwell recounts the night attack on the Fascist lines. Though Orwell's writing rarely achieves the range and vitality of Lawrence or

Dickens, and though his language is closer than theirs to Newspeak (revealing his and our implication in the modern dilemma he contemplates) here, nevertheless, he writes at his best:

> We crept onwards, always more slowly. I cannot convey to you the depth of my desire to get there. Just to get within bombing distance before they heard us! At such a time you have not even any fear, only a tremendous hopeless longing to get over the intervening ground. I have felt exactly the same thing when stalking a wild animal; the same agonised desire to get within range, the same dreamlike certainty that it is impossible. And how the distance stretched out! I knew the ground well, it was barely a hundred and fifty yards, and yet it seemed more like a mile. When you are creeping at that pace you are aware as an ant might be of the enormous variation in the ground; the splendid patch of smooth grass here, the evil patch of sticky mud there, the tall rustling reeds that have got to be avoided, the heap of stones that almost makes you give up hope because it seems impossible to get over it without noise. (p. 87)

We certainly feel here that Orwell is speaking in his own voice and that his communication of painful experience is genuine. Indeed, the subtle translation of expanded space into achingly extended time reveals his capacity to make a subtle art out of documentary writing. Such an account of experience guarantees and sustains the book's political argument.

Likewise, Orwell's self-irony reveals his growing self-awareness; it is not mere self-flagellation. The self-irony lights up the book and gives it both credibility and a necessary leaven of humour. Near the beginning he refers amusingly enough to 'my villainous Spanish' (p. 14) but when later the phrase recurs in the episode of Orwell bravely attempting to save Kopp, the ironic self-awareness lightens a more serious situation. His selfless action is described in a convincing and unselfconscious way: 'But it was obviously quicker and surer to go in person' (p. 209). Then, when he tries to explain Kopp's situation to the little officer, Orwell's lack of voice (the result of his throat wound) is exacerbated by 'my villainous Spanish which lapsed into French at every crisis' (p. 210). The self-irony helps to convince us of the genuinely selfless nature of Orwell's courage. Thus, the range of Orwell's irony is considerable throughout the book. Some further instances are worth noting.

The POUM dog, for example, is a virtually Dickensian character: 'One wretched brute that marched with us had had POUM branded on it in huge letters and slunk along as though conscious that there was something wrong with its appearance' (p. 21). Later, at the front Orwell writes, 'There were nights when it seemed to me that our position could be stormed by twenty Boy Scouts armed with airguns, or twenty Girl Guides armed with battledores, for that matter' (p. 28). On the night attack from which the earlier passage was taken we have this:

> To prevent us from shooting each other in the darkness white armlets would be worn. At that moment a messenger arrived to say that there were no white armlets. Out of the darkness a plaintive voice suggested: 'Couldn't we arrange for the Fascists to wear white armlets instead?' (p. 85)

Orwell's capacity to grasp the absurdity as well as the seriousness of the situation at the front makes us trust him because we feel that he had things in perspective – he is neither too solemn nor too flippant. The rightness of tone persuades us that he speaks in his own voice. As he had noted earlier, 'The real preoccupation of both armies was trying to keep warm' (p. 25). 'Often I used to gaze round the wintry landscape and marvel at the futility of it all', he writes (p. 26). Comically, he notes, 'the real weapon was not the rifle but the megaphone. Being unable to kill your enemy you shouted at him instead' (p. 42). Orwell's irony is a perfect antidote to the adolescent romanticism of, say, Hemingway's *For Whom the Bell Tolls*. It frames and focuses for us his sense of the meaning of his Spanish experience. Of this he writes, 'But it lasted long enough to have its effect upon anyone who experienced it. However much one cursed at the time, one realised afterwards that one had been in a community where hope was more normal than apathy or cynicism . . . . One had breathed the air of equality' (p. 102).

Even in the fighting in Barcelona which Orwell describes as 'one of the most unbearable periods of my whole life. I think few experiences could be more sickening, more disillusioning, or, finally, more nerve-racking than those evil days of street warfare' (p. 125), and when his bitterness breaks out as in his description of the fat Russian agent, 'it was the first time that I had seen a person whose profession was telling lies – unless one counts journalists' (p. 135), Orwell manages to retain his sense of humour. For example, when he has to smuggle guns, he says, 'Even a man as tall as I am cannot wear a long Mauser down his trouser-leg without discomfort. It was an intolerable job getting down the corkscrew staircase of the observatory with a completely rigid left leg' (p. 137). Even after he is shot through the throat on his return to the front and the hospital train turns out to be going to Tarragona rather than returning him to his wife in Barcelona, he writes, ' "Just like Spain!" I thought. But it was very Spanish, too, that they agreed to hold up the train while I sent another wire, and more Spanish still that the wire never got there' (p. 183). And about his wound itself: 'No one I met at this time – doctors, nurses, *practicantes*, or fellow-patients – failed to assure me that a man who is hit through the neck and survives it is the luckiest creature alive. I could not help thinking that it would be even luckier not to be hit at all' (pp. 185–6).

At the moral centre of *Homage to Catalonia* lies Orwell's account of the disillusioning street fighting in Barcelona and the suppression of the POUM. Here he is overridingly concerned to tell the truth and disabuse his readers of the lies of the *News Chronicle* and *Daily Worker*. It is probably not far from the truth to say that the six months in Spain in 1937 were the turning point in Orwell's life. Yet although he was politically disillusioned he remained optimistic about human nature:

> Curiously enough the whole experience has left me with not less but more belief in the decency of human beings. And I hope the account I have given is not too misleading. I believe that on such an issue as this no one is or can be completely truthful. It is difficult to be certain about anything except what you have seen with your own eyes, and consciously or unconsciously everyone writes as a partisan. (p. 220)

Here Orwell acknowledges the difficulty of speaking the truth and in acknowledging it he speaks it:

> I had come here to shoot at 'Fascists'; but a man who is holding up his trousers isn't a 'Fascist', he is visibly a fellow-creature, similar to yourself, and you don't feel like shooting at him. (p. 231)

Penetrating the political world, Orwell discovers the human world. It is a world that leads him beyond his belief in the Italian militiaman to his sense of the importance of the loyalty of the Arab youth whom he has come to know well. Significantly, Orwell's prose here is not tense with strained idealism but simple, natural and truthful:

> Could you feel towards somebody, and stick up for him in a quarrel, after you had been ignominiously searched in his presence for property you were supposed to have stolen from him? No, you couldn't; but you might if you had both been through some emotionally widening experience. (p. 233)

Orwell's increased grasp of and participation in the human world survives the political disillusionment he felt, a disillusionment that led directly to *Animal Farm* and *Nineteen Eighty-Four*:

> In Spain, for the first time, I saw newspaper reports which did not bear any relation to the facts, not even the relationship which is implied in an ordinary lie. (p. 234)

He continues:

> This kind of thing is frightening to me, because it often gives me the feeling that the very concept of objective truth is fading out of the world. After all, the chances are that those lies, or at any rate similar lies, will pass into history . . . what is peculiar to our age is the abandonment of the idea that history could be truthfully written. (pp. 235–6)
>   Nazi theory indeed specifically denies that such a thing as 'the truth' exists . . . . If the Leader says of such and such an event, 'It never happened' – well, it never happened. If he says that two and two are five – well, two and two are five. This prospect frightens me much more than bombs – and after our experiences of the last few years that is not a frivolous statement. (p. 236)

We are already in the world of *Animal Farm* and *Nineteen Eighty-Four*. *Homage to Catalonia* leads directly into those works.

Orwell insisted that 'however much you deny the truth, the truth goes on existing, as it were, behind your back' (p. 237). And the truth is that to attempt to argue a case for *Homage to Catalonia* as Orwell's best work would be exaggerated. *Animal Farm* is clearly one of the great allegories of modern literature, while *Nineteen Eighty-Four* in being Orwell's most successful novel is even more importantly a powerful prophecy of 1984. What needs to be said about *Homage to Catalonia*, at last, is that it prepares the ground for those works. Beside it Orwell's early novels and *Coming Up For Air* pale into insignificance, while *Road To Wigan Pier* appears detached and analytical. In *Homage to Catalonia* we return to the engagement and vitality of *Down and Out in Paris and London* but feel even more fully than we do there the force of Orwell's human presence. Indeed, it is here that we feel his human presence more fully than in any of his other extended works. His presence is human precisely in his concern to speak the truth. In *Homage to Catalonia* what is known is loved and in this respect Orwell reminds us of Wordsworth addressing Coleridge at the end of *The Prelude*:

> What we have loved,
> Others will love, and we will teach them how;
> Instruct them how the mind of man becomes
> A thousand times more beautiful than the earth
> On which he dwells . . . . [6]

George Orwell went to Spain to fight for common decency against fascism and he found decency in the Spanish people. But he also found something that went deeper than that. 'I have the most evil memories of Spain, but I have very few bad memories of Spaniards . . . . They have, there is no doubt, a generosity, a species of nobility, that do not really belong to the twentieth century' (p. 213). How do we know that Orwell is telling the truth? There is the simple sincerity of his language to support him and, if that is not enough, the moving episode of the two young Spanish soldiers who see him in the hospital and give him all their tobacco. Moving through politics to human nature, Orwell found a simple, sincere and flexible language in which to speak the truth.

8

Orwell's *Nineteen Eighty-Four* and Mao's Cultural Revolution

F. Quei Quo

Referring to Orwell's *Nineteen Eighty-Four*, Pierre Ryckmans, author of *Chinese Shadows*, stated that:

> Without even dreaming of Mao's China, Orwell succeeded in describing it, down to concrete details of daily life, with more truth and accuracy than most researchers who came back from Peking to tell us 'the real truth'.[1]

There were others who had similarly compared conditions in China in the days of the Great Proletariat Cultural Revolution with life under Ingsoc in Orwell's *Nineteen Eighty-Four*.[2] The similarities are undeniable, yet the fact remains that Mao and his associates did not have Orwell's *Nineteen Eighty-Four* as their drill manual in 1966 when the great upheaval in China was launched. As a matter of fact, it was only this year that I found Orwell's *Nineteen Eighty-Four* and Crick's book on Orwell in the Penguin shelf at the Beijing Friendship Store. Was there really that much similarity between the Big Brother and Chairman Mao, Goldstein and Liu Shaoqi/Lin Biao, Newspeak and the jargon of the Cultural Revolution, and the 'doublethink' and the ambiguities of 'revolutionary' and 'counter-revolutionary'?

In an article published late in 1966, George Kateb, like many of us who had no idea at that time that an Orwellian experiment had just begun in China, conceded the charge that the world of *Nineteen Eighty-Four* was unreal and its message unsound.[3] To claim *Nineteen Eighty-Four* nonetheless as a meaningful contribution to the study of politics Kateb wrote:

The system (of 1984) as a whole is endowed with a coherence that no system in the real world has ever had. Orwell asked himself the sociological question, What are the institutions required for a group of men in the modern world to wield absolute power? and the answer comes out in every detail, major and minor, of *1984*. In that respect the book is a *tour de force*, one of the most successful acts of political imagination ever made. Reading it, one is thereafter made sensitive to any happening in the world that resembles, even slightly, something in 1984: one is also equipped to examine dictatorships and oligarchies, past and present, with heightened understanding. One's perception of even normal politics is altered. 1984 is a splendid work in defense of freedom and equality. By predicting the future it may help to defeat its predictions; for that tactic to work, exaggeration is probably necessary. An image of pure evil must be presented, in order to sicken the decent man and make him more passionate in his attachment to the kinds of political good he still may be fortunate to enjoy.[4]

Events of the Cultural Revolution prove that Orwell's imagination was no exaggeration; it can and did happen! The Big Brother was not only omnipresent but also omnipotent in China. By early 1967, the portrait of Mao was everywhere and the little Red Book of *Quotations of Chairman Mao* was in every waving hand of the masses that gathered for all kinds of 'anti' campaigns. No speech was complete without quotations from the Red Book and no gatherings could end without shouting slogans demanding 'Down with' somebody or something, and roaring 'Long live' the Chairman. The cult of personality went as far as identifying all causes of success, ranging between winning a ping-pong tournament and launching the first missile, to the teaching of the Chairman. At the same time all kinds of capitalist crimes, counter-revolutionary thoughts and revisionist trends amongst the individuals were uncovered and made responsible for the incompleteness of the revolution.

In *Nineteen Eighty-Four* Winston wants to know the history of Oceania – the Revolution and the life before the Revolution. With the exception of an old drunk who faintly remembers the old days, there is nowhere he can find the truth. For 'Every record has been destroyed or falsified, every book has been rewritten, every picture has been re-painted, every statue and street and building has been

renamed, every date has been altered' (p. 290). In China the Red
Guards ransacked homes, buildings, temples and burnt tons of
books, documents and even furniture. They renamed streets,
buildings and sometimes even themselves.[5] Everything was
crowned with 'victory', as Orwell predicted, or turned 'red' as Mao
preferred: Victory cigarette, Victory Oilfield, Red Machine Factory,
Red Star Restaurant, and so on. In Shanghai and Beijing there
were two 'Writing Teams' manufacturing new historical stories
everyday. 'Lian Hsiao' and 'Ro Suding' were the pennames of Jian
Qing's literary gangs who rewrote a great portion of Chinese
history.[6] Good guys were transformed into bad guys and *vice-versa*.
Competent Imperial ministers became anti-revolutionaries and the
cruel Empresses were converted to great rulers of the dynasties.[7]
All this was the work of what Orwell would have readily recognised
as the Ministry of Truth!

The proliferation of a new jargon, a veritable Newspeak, made
an observer comment that 'the best glossaries of Maoist phraseology
are out-of-date a year after being printed'. Here are some examples:

Walking on two-legs: Mao's idea of applying both the modern and
pre-modern ways of production.

Three-Eight Working Style: the three phrases and eight characters
written by Mao to describe the working style to be adopted by
everyone; they are: political direction, simple and arduous
working style, flexible strategy and tactics, and 'united, tense,
stern and lively'.

Four Firsts: the priorities set by Lin Biao, namely, the human
factor first, political work first, ideological work first and living
ideas first.

Four Togetherness: the requirement that cadres eat, live, toil and
discuss with farmers or workers.

The list can go on *ad infinitum*. The Asian Research Centre in Hong
Kong had to append a nearly fifty-page Glossary for its readers in
its first volume on the Great Cultural Revolution published in
English in 1968.[8]

The terms in the Glossary were chillingly close to those in the 'B
vocabulary' of *Nineteen Eighty-Four*. A great many of them were
euphemisms, ideologically loaded, and were constructed deliberately for political purposes, just as Orwell defined them (pp. 420–
6). The frequent use of numbered abbreviations was perhaps

intended to conceal the discrepancy that might have existed between the ideographic Chinese language and the reality. The 'May 7th Cadre School' serves as the best example. All labour camps the cadres went to were called by that name. They could not by any stretch of the imagination be included in the traditional usage of the word 'school'. It was the hard labour required of every cadre by Mao's edict dated 7 May 1967.

Doublethink, according to Orwell, is 'the power of holding two contradictory beliefs in one's mind simultaneously, and accepting both of them' (p. 342). Indeed, it required more than 'doublethink' for one to survive through the Cultural Revolution without scars in one's mind. The man who wrote the handbook *How To Be a Good Communist*,[9] President of the State and for twenty years an acknowledged successor to Mao, disappeared in 1966. Liu Shaoqi was the Goldstein of China, accused of being a traitor, and an object of many hate-campaigns. The means of death in 1969 was never revealed. Lin Biao succeeded Liu to play the role of Goldstein. He rallied behind Mao in the purge of Liu, edited the *Quotations of Chairman Mao*, and was designated by Mao to be his successor. His succession was signed and sealed in the 1969 Constitution of the Communist Party of China. Then there came the uncovering of his plot against the B-52, a code-name Lin's son gave to the Chairman.[10] Lin died in a planecrash when he attempted to escape in 1971. The complete turnabout in the campaigns from 'pro to con' or *vice-versa* was rather frequent at all levels of leadership.

In 1966 Liang Heng was just twelve years of age. When the Cultural Revolution started he observed all the 'struggles' with excitement.[11] In Changsha, the provincial capital of Hunan, he was yearning to become a part of the Great Revolution. He recollects:

It seemed that everyday good people were exposed as evil ones lurking behind Revolutionary masks. Friendly people were hidden serpents, Revolutionaries became counter-revolution-aries, and officials who usually rode cars to meetings might actually be murderers. It was confusing because the changes came so fast, and we used to joke with each other saying 'They dug somebody else up today', meaning that, as the newspapers like to put it, 'The telescope of Chairman Mao Thought has been used to enlarge our enemies and reveal them in their original states'. Still, most people felt that the Cultural Revolution was a wonderful thing, because when our enemies were uncovered China would be much more secure. So I felt excited and happy, and wished I could do something to help.[12]

Little Liang learned to 'doublethink'. His father was a good party member who divorced his mother because of her 'rightist' connection. An attack on his father by the Red Guards did not discourage him from wanting to become one of them. He joined the Rebels, travelled to Beijing, took the New Long March, went to the countryside, became a factory worker, learnt the secret of 'eating Socialism', fell in love with girls, elected to go to college in the post-Cultural Revolution period, married his American English teacher in 1980 and now lives happily in the United States. His *Son of the Revolution* is the most revealing account of life in China during the decade of turmoil, and an unusual document in every way. In spite of the estimate that hundreds of thousands of people were victimised in the Cultural Revolution, still a large number of the Chinese population survived. But Liang Heng is one of the very few who succeeded in speaking of their own involvement in the Revolution. Nine out of ten Chinese one talks to nowadays would tell you that he or she was a victim. One wonders whatever could have happened to the millions who threw their stones at the 'rightists' at one time and spat on the 'leftists' later. Perhaps they all have evaporated in the logic of doublethink. Perhaps it all becomes explicable in Newspeak: THE VILLAIN IS THE VICTIM!

The xenophobia and ultra-puritanism of *Nineteen Eighty-Four* was there, too. During the Cultural Revolution foreign embassies in Beijing were attacked and the slogan 'be prepared for the war' was followed by the digging of underground shelters in the capital. Chairman Mao predicted in 1966 that China would be involved in a war with the United States *and* the Soviet Union within two years. In 1967 the Chinese Minister of Foreign Affairs spoke of the possibility of war against *either* the United States or the Soviet Union. However, these threats were all tied to domestic politics. An American invasion would mean the revival of capitalism and a war against the Soviet Union would mean a fight against the revisionists. The war fever ran so high that it became fashionable for women to have short haircuts and wear the faded combat jacket of the old Liberation Army.[13]

The Cultural Revolution turned to an anarchic civil war after 1968 when the army was called in to restore order. Mao's theory of contradiction and the idea of ceaseless struggle turned everybody against everybody else. A romantic revolutionary Mao certainly was, but rational administrator he was not. To distill his ideal 100%-proof pure communists out of the 800 million people, hundreds of thousands had to be 'vapourised' and still many more in their millions had to be thrown away as the lees of the process. Mao, the Big Brother personified, relied on Lin Biao, his O'Brien, for the operation of Cultural Revolution. Unfortunately, in this instance, O'Brien himself wanted to become Big Brother. After the uncovering of Lin Biao's plot, Mao's 'Inner Party' began to crumble. The 'Gang of Four' hung on to the coat-tail of 'Big Brother' who began to show his senility.

Perhaps it was the ensuing confusion that made every one in China a victim of the Cultural Revolution. Deng Xiaoping, one of the most hated revisionists, a Goldstein, was twice purged and twice resurrected or 'rehabilitated'. The well-known joke about three men in jail asking each other about the reason of their being jailed is an example of the 'ups and downs' in those days. According to the joke the first one told the other he was there because he supported Deng. The second one said he was there because he opposed Deng. So they decided to ask the third person why he was imprisoned. The third man raised his head and said: 'I am Deng Xiaoping'. A wall-poster appeared in Canton in 1973 depicting the great repression following the summer of 1968 as follows:

> All across the land, there were arrests everywhere, suppression everywhere, miscarriages of justice everywhere . . . . Now there was no law and no heaven. This was a rehearsal of social fascism in our country.[14]

So much for the similarities between life in the Oceania of *Nineteen Eighty-Four* and Mao's China in the late sixties. The behavioural similarities, however, conceal a fundamental difference between Orwell's political idea and Maoism. There is also a difference in the motivation and historical setting of the two dramas. First, just like Orwellian scholars who impute all kinds of motives to the writing of *Nineteen Eighty-Four*, the many analyses of China's Cultural Revolution speculate about the reason why Mao launched the campaign.[15] In contrast with Orwell who was 'sick and dispirited',[16] Mao in 1966 was still 'healthy and spirited'. At the age of seventy-three Mao swam for an hour in the Yangtze River

and commented: 'The current of the Yangtze is strong and there
are many waves, but if a person is not afraid to struggle he will
overcome all difficulties'.[17] The whole nation was impressed by
the Chairman's physical strength and was convinced of his determination to carry on the revolution. Perhaps herein lies the
difference between Orwell and Mao as builders of future worlds.
While Orwell very likely wrote Nineteen Eighty-Four as a warning
sounded by a disillusioned democratic socialist, Mao wrote his
scenario of Cultural Revolution out of his everlasting zeal for
revolution.

Although disagreement between Mao and some of his old
comrades was apparent by the mid-sixties, the Chairman was in
no danger of losing his stature. However, Mao found himself that
while he was personally enthroned as leader, his revolutionary
method was being less and less applied in the daily operation of
the state affairs. Things had become routinised. The party had
become an establishment in itself; it had become the government.
In 1959 Mao gave up the presidency of the state but retained the
party chairmanship. In 1966 he found himself surrounded by
comrades who were more concerned about stability than change.
Everything was slipping back to non-revolutionary norms and
'economism' was claiming priority.

To interpret the Cultural Revolution in terms of a power struggle
between Mao and his old comrades is an oversimplification of the
matter. A Dutch diplomat who observed the event close at hand
commented:

> The great difference between the Cultural Revolution and the
> Stalinist purges on the 1930s lies in the ideological aspect which
> in China played a principle role and in the Soviet Union a
> secondary one. Thus, in China, the active participation of the
> masses was made possible, whereas in the Soviet Union the
> purges were carried out by the secret police.[18]

The Cultural Revolution, from every information made available
later, was really a revolution. Mao inspired the Red Guards, the
workers and the masses to take the place of the party, the
government, and whatever other social organisations and institutions there were.

There are other differences as well. Orwell's Nineteen Eighty-Four
shows the Stalinist rule of terror by the secret police; but Mao's

Cultural Revolution was mob-rule caused by his fantasy of populism. Unlike Orwell's Oceania where the mass remained as 'proles' who were left 'corrupted', Mao's China pinned its hope in the unlimited wisdom of common folks. Interestingly enough, Mao and Winston, the latter probably speaking for Orwell, saw the same light. 'If there is hope', writes Winston, 'it lies in the proles' (p. 216), and repeats this again and again (pp. 227, 230). If only they could somehow become conscious of their strength they could overthrow the party – a task impossible from within. On what Winston bases his hope is not clear, for in Oceania no attempt is made to inspire the proles with any ideology.

Thus, Winston's hope faded away as it faced the dilemma that 'until they [the proles] become conscious they will never rebel, and until after they have rebelled they cannot become conscious' (p. 217). This is where Mao and Winston part ways. For Mao everything is 'from the masses to the masses'. In a speech at the fifth mass rally in Beijing, Lin Biao, then still Mao's confidant, said:

> Under the guidance of Chairman Mao's correct line, the broad revolutionary masses of our country have created the new experience of developing extensive democracy . . . the Party is fearlessly permitting the broad masses to use the media to free airing of views, big character posters, great debates and extensive contacts, to criticize and supervise the Party and Government leading institutions and leaders at all levels.[19]

If Orwell's political pessimism in *Nineteen Eighty-Four* is a reflection of the feebleness and vulnerability of intellectual conviction, Mao's optimism in the Cultural Revolution must be an expression of firmness and certainty based upon his revolutionary experience.

The difference in historical settings is rather obvious. The Oceania of *Nineteen Eighty-Four* is already a totalitarian society, or as Irving Howe puts it, 'might be called post totalitarian'. Exercise of power there, therefore, is to preserve the absolute rule of the Inner Party over all others. That absolute rule is to be perfected by control of mind, not merely of behaviour. The Cultural Revolution of Mao's China is a *prelude* to totalitarianism. Capturing of power by the mass was to destroy all practices and ways of life inconsistent with the Maoist ideology. Its ultimate goal was, as Hannah Arendt generalised for totalitarianism, 'to prove that its (the ideological) respective supersense has been right'.[20] In this instance, Mao wanted the Chinese reality to conform to his political and social fantasy. The way to totalitarianism and the preservation of totalitarianism, however, depended on the same process – 'a boot stamping on a human face'.

One might wonder if the problem with the Chinese Cultural Revolution was not the actual personal existence of Big Brother. In Oceania no-one ever knows whether Big Brother truly exists. He is a symbol, as is Goldstein. One represents the absolute good and truth, and the other, evil and falsehood. They are the embodiment of the Party and its Enemy. In China, it was all too real and too secular. The Chairman appeared in person. He had a wife, nephew and relatives who all wielded power in the system. Worst of all, Mao's O'Brien – Lin Biao – also wanted to supplant Big Brother. Thus, there was a succession problem in China, a problem that Orwell avoided. In China the sincere response by the masses to the call of Big Brother was met by too many human failures on the part of Big Brother himself. For a totalitarian system to function smoothly, a Big Brother needs many 'middle' and 'small' Brothers who would abide by, but never challenge, the hierarchy of power.

In this sense Orwell was a better political scientist for he knew the theory of organisation better than Mao. Mao wanted to rule directly over everybody, over everything and through all time. Where Mao failed most miserably was in his disregard of the need for professionalisation, especially in politics. In the midst of the Cultural Revolution a Western diplomat commented:

> Lin Piao and Mao Tse-tung were strangers to complex social structures. They feared any liberalisation and its accompanying social competition and complicated control methods and did not understand the demands of a modern economy. They did not understand the many-sidedness of society and the need of a bureaucracy. Their distaste expresses itself in a preoccupation with the common man, the one that can help himself, the eternal amateur . . . . Mao Tse-tung considered the Cultural Revolution necessary in order to restore the ideal of the common, proletarian man to its original glory.[21]

Mao defied the old Confucian teaching that in a society some must labour with the mind and be fed by those who labour with the body. When Mao made everyone labour with the mind, the Chinese economy collapsed.

Finally, the greatest contrast lies between the ending of the two dramas. In Orwell's *Nineteen Eighty-Four* the hope is kept alive through the mouth of Winston: 'It is impossible to found a civilisation on fear and hatred and cruelty. It would never endure . . . . It would have no vitality. It would disintegrate. It would commit suicide', says Winston (p. 391). And, finally, it is the spirit of man that Orwell hopes would defeat his own nightmare. Yet in the end Orwell makes his hero succumb to the old Imperial Chinese way of torture. In the Chinese Cultural Revolution, ironical as this may sound, the rebel used the modern Western 'Jet plane ride' to extort confession and self-criticism from their victims.[22] In China it took ten years before the proles rebelled; but they overwhelmingly did. On 26 March 1976, at the same Tiananmen Square, where Big Brother had commissioned millions of young people to fight for his vision in 1966, millions of them now returned to show their defiance. As a Western reporter put it, it was a 'display of the ability of the human spirit to withstand long years of totalitarian rule and emerge strengthened'.[23] The drama of *Nineteen Eighty-Four*, as it was enacted in China, ended with the final victory of Winston over O'Brien. The question, then, seems really to be one of the durability of human flesh, not human spirit.

Any comparison of Orwell's *Nineteen Eighty-Four* and Mao's Cultural Revolution suggests that control mechanisms designed by human beings against their fellow men are the same everywhere. It all entails attacks on human vulnerability along the lines of pain and pleasure. Orwell gave up on the proles from the outset, though with some reluctance. Mao abandoned the political professionals and turned to the proles. Winston Smith betrayed Orwell's hopes, as did Mao's proles by turning against him. They are all human beings of flesh and blood, but also possessing a soul. While individual flesh is mortal the soul of the collectivity transcends time. Had Orwell and Mao consulted each other they might have arrived at the simple political wisdom that you can fool some of the people some of the time but not all of the people all of the time. Totalitarianism cannot last forever as long as the human spirit exists, though it will triumph somewhere some of the time as long as our flesh is mortal.

Part Three
Literary Criticism

9

Orwell and Eliot: Politics, Poetry, Prose

Graham Good

At first sight, Orwell and Eliot would appear to have little to connect them, in background or outlook or anything else.[1] Eliot was an established poet, critic and publisher by the time Orwell knew him, and a declared conservative and Anglo-Catholic. Orwell was still a struggling novelist and journalist, and a committed social democrat. Nevertheless, there is an intriguing personal connection, mainly during the early 1940s, and also a literary and intellectual one. All of this was more important for Orwell than for Eliot, who was a figure of great symbolic significance for the younger writer though in complex and often contradictory ways. Orwell often focused on the same issues as Eliot, opposing, but also incorporating Eliot's ideas into his own thinking. After describing the circumstances of their friendship, this paper will compare their views on certain historical, cultural and literary matters (class vs. élite, poetry vs. prose, community vs. individual), ending with the implication of these ideas in their culminating imaginative visions, *Four Quartets* (1944) and *Nineteen Eighty-Four* (1949).

The personal relationship was basically sought by Orwell. He belonged to a generation whose sensibility had been partly formed by Eliot's early poetry, and Orwell's depiction of modern urban life has a typical *Waste Land* atmosphere to it. Indeed Orwell claimed to know by heart large parts of early Eliot without having ever consciously committed it to memory (*CE*, II, 273). The miseries of lower-class life shown in Orwell's novels have many analogues in Eliot: the pub scenes, the mimicking of working-class speech, the dreary commercialism and the degraded sex. Gordon Comstock, the failed poet of *Keep the Aspidistra Flying*, is like a Prufrock who is trying to become a T. S. Eliot; his major work, called *London*

Pleasures, is heavily derivative from Eliot in vision, if not in versification:

> Sharply the menacing wind sweeps over
> The bending poplars, newly bare,
> And the dark ribbons of the chimneys
> Veer downward; flicked by whips of air.
> Torn posters flutter . . .[2]

Comstock could also be seen as 'a young man carbuncular' (though perhaps not a seducer of typists) before he resigned from his job in an advertising agency. Orwell's heroes typically belong to the seedy shabby-genteel class seen by Eliot as the dreadful quintessence of modern mass society; but where *The Waste Land* sees it from above, or from a long cultural distance, Orwell's novel forces us to share its shut-in perspective.

Orwell, of course, had begun his literary career by wanting to share the conditions of the very lowest class of the big cities, and ironically it was precisely Eliot who rejected the record of this experience when a version of *Down and Out in Paris and London* was submitted to Faber for publication in 1932. This attempt to live *The Waste Land* in person at its most dehumanised level was too untidy for Eliot: 'it seems to me too loosely constructed, as the French and English episodes fall into two parts with very little to connect them'.[3] However, the rejection was courteous and even friendly in tone, and it did not prevent Orwell from once more seeking publication with Faber in 1944, twelve years later, with *Animal Farm*. This time Orwell got a much longer letter, perhaps because of his increased stature as a writer, or perhaps because the two now had a personal relationship. But the result was the same: a rejection. It has gone down in history as one of the great misjudgements of a masterpiece. But in some ways Orwell's submissions are harder to account for than Eliot's rejections. Bernard Crick points out that neither book would have seemed at all in keeping with Faber's reputation as a publishing house.[4] Orwell's actual publishers, Gollancz and then Warburg, were obviously much more suitable for the kind of work he was doing: why did he hanker after the conservative literary prestige of Faber, and the approval of its eminent conservative director?

The problem is compounded by Orwell's open if qualified hostility as a reviewer of Eliot's work (it is of course indicative of their respective positions in the publishing world that Eliot's rejections came *before* publication, Orwell's only *after*). He reviewed the first three of the *Four Quartets* in *Poetry London* for October–November 1942, and asserted that the failure of impact of the poems when compared to Eliot's earlier poetry was due to a lack of conviction in the religious faith he wanted to express. Orwell held that the despair of the earlier work was more deeply felt and more widely shared by readers at the time. Orwell makes the extraordinary suggestion that the *Quartets* would have been better if Eliot had been more intensely reactionary, instead of stopping halfway, in what Orwell termed 'negative Pétainism' (*CE*, II, 242) – surely a deliberately stinging classification in 1942. Orwell returned to the attack in 1948, with a review of *Notes Towards the Definition of Culture*, where he accused Eliot once again of halfheartedness, this time in his defence of class society. In both cases it was not so much Eliot's conservatism as his *dilution* of that conservatism which drew Orwell's mockery.

Despite these attacks, Orwell continued to court Eliot in other ways. As well as wanting Eliot to publish him, he wanted to publish Eliot, inviting him in a letter of 29 November 1943 to submit a poem or article to *Tribune*, of which Orwell had just become literary editor. Eliot did not take this up, but he had accepted an earlier invitation when Orwell was working for the BBC Indian Services, to read 'What the Thunder Said' from *The Waste Land* as part of a programme about Oriental influence on English literature. This was broadcast on 1 December 1942, and by 1944, the two were not only regularly exchanging letters, but lunching together occasionally. These meetings were not as frequent as Orwell wanted, and much of their correspondence of 1944 is taken up by Orwell proposing dates and Eliot rejecting them for later ones, since he was only in London several days a month and his lunchtimes tended to be booked well in advance.[5] Were these meetings the kind of 'dining with the opposition'[6] Eliot thought necessary for a healthy political culture? Perhaps out of a desire to find common ground with Orwell, Eliot seems to have implied a greater sympathy with the Left than one would have suspected. Pointing out in July 1944 in a letter to Rayner Heppenstall that Eliot had published in a British propaganda paper in Moscow, Orwell commented, 'To judge by his private conversation he has definitely changed some of his political views though he hasn't made any public pronouncement yet' (*CE*, III, 186). Though

Orwell's tone betrays a certain smugness at having inside information, Eliot's public views showed little sign of change except in the direction of greater conservatism. Yet clearly it did not prevent him showing sympathy *privately* to Orwell's outlook.

During this period, Orwell and Eliot were both publishing in the *Partisan Review* in the USA. Here two of Eliot's *Four Quartets* were first published, and later came two prose pieces: 'The Music of Poetry' (November–December 1942) and 'Notes Towards a Definition of Culture' (Spring 1944). The direction of this series of contributions, from poetry to criticism of poetry, to criticism of society, is interesting, and perhaps cushioned the shock for readers of finding a right-wing social philosophy in the pages of their left-wing journal. The latter essay, the germ of the eventual short book which Orwell reviewed in 1948, was given further prominence by a series of replies in the following issue (Summer 1944) by R. P. Blackmur, Clement Greenberg, William Phillips and I. A. Richards. Orwell probably followed the development of this controversy from the beginning, since his 'London Letter' was a regular feature in the magazine, including these two issues. At any rate, in a letter of 15 September 1944,[7] less than two months after Eliot's rejection of *Animal Farm*, Orwell reminded him of their being fellow-contributors to the *Partisan Review*. Perhaps the link in his mind was that if Eliot could publish in a Leftist journal like the *Partisan Review*, why should not a conservative publishing house have taken *Animal Farm*? One crossover would have justified another. This would also make more plausible Orwell's request for an Eliot poem or article for *Tribune*. But the *Partisan Review* had always prided itself on the independence of its literary features from the political side of the journal, and eventually it seemed to one of the editors, Dwight Macdonald, that the literary side was coming to predominate too much. His letter of resignation was published in the July–August 1943 issue, along with his stated intent to found a new, more political journal which would still include cultural concerns. Orwell's letter to Eliot referred to the *Partisan Review* in the course of drawing attention to this new journal, which was called *Politics* and which first appeared in February 1944 (it lasted until 1949). Eliot thanked Orwell for the information,[8] and evidently followed up on it, for the Preface to the book publication of *Notes Towards the Definition of Culture* (1948) contained a reference to an article in the first issue by Dwight Macdonald, entitled 'A Theory of Popular Culture'. This article, incidentally, inaugurated a regular series on 'Popular Culture', to which Orwell later contributed his study of popular crime fiction, 'Raffles and Miss Blandish' (November 1944). Eliot endorsed the Macdonald theory in an ambivalent way by describing it 'as the best *alternative* to my own that I have seen'.[9]

Why did Orwell recommend this magazine so particularly to Eliot, given that it was an offshoot *to the left* from the *Partisan Review*, already sufficiently opposed to Eliot's political position? We can understand Orwell's sympathy for 'dissent within dissent', since it reflected his own situation within the left, but what accounts for Eliot's interest and even partial sympathy? This question opens up the whole relationship of Orwell's and Eliot's views of society and culture, both of which were most fully articulated in the context of the Anglo-American debate of the 1940s on the subject of mass culture. Clement Greenberg was one of the originators of the debate with his 1939 essay 'Avant Garde and Kitsch': he reprinted it in his 1969 collection *Art and Culture*, followed by his review of the book publication of Eliot's *Notes Towards the Definition of Culture* (Greenberg had been one of the original respondents to Eliot's short early version in the *Partisan Review* in 1944). Greenberg's essential point in the earlier essay is that avant-garde art and kitsch are parallel and related phenomena, emerging at the same historical moment, when the industrial revolution uprooted aristocratic high culture and authentic folk culture. This created a rootless artistic community, which was thrown back on formal experiment as the only way to keep art developing, and an urbanised mass, who demanded an easy substitute for the folk art they had forgotten.

The Macdonald article which Eliot admired offered a variation on this basic theme. Macdonald saw a dangerous tendency for Popular Culture and High Culture to converge and mix: 'whereas Folk Art had its own special field, in which it was often excellent, Popular Culture is merely a vulgarised reflection of High Culture',[10] he asserted. In turn it polluted high culture, turning it into what he called Academicism, or 'Popular culture for the élite'. The only authentic high culture after that was the avant-garde, whose heyday was 1890–1930. Since 1930 the different cultures have tended to converge, Macdonald believed, into a more or less sophisticated universal kitsch. He ended by offering two political solutions; one was the reactionary one typified by Ortega y Gasset, which would be to rebuild the class walls and restore 'the old High

Culture – Folk Art compartmentation'. The socialist solution would be to produce a truly human culture (not a class culture) through mass education and democracy.

This second solution is, of course, the one attempted by western governments over the past forty years and only now being challenged or abandoned. The first solution is the one essentially advocated by Eliot, who would make as good an example of it as Ortega. Eliot could easily describe Macdonald's scheme as the best alternative to his since Macdonald had already set up the socialist and conservative answers as the main solutions available. But there is a further twist: Eliot could safely recommend Macdonald's essay because Macdonald's own argument through most of its length points more strongly to the reactionary solution than to the progressive one. Most of Macdonald's evidence is of the beneficial effect *for both levels* of a culture divided into levels. His examples of a single culture, without levels, are all bad. Hence his conclusion can only be a vague gesture in the direction of an unknown future: somehow the unified culture of socialism will be better than the converging cultures of capitalism in the 1930s.

Whether or not it was due to the influence of Macdonald's article, Eliot's emphasis on the healthy effect of the separation of levels of culture certainly increased between the 1944 *Partisan Review* version and the 1948 book version of his *Notes*. He stated in the latter, for example, 'What is important is a structure of society in which there will be, from "top" to "bottom", a continuous gradation of cultural levels'.[11] This structure excludes the notions of class interest and class struggle. Eliot's ideal classes are disinterested, thinking not of increasing their own development and power at the expense of others, but rather of making their distinctive contribution to the harmony and vitality of the whole. 'Each class has a function to maintain its general level of culture, not merely for its own benefit, but for the benefit of the whole society'.[12] Thus what he is offering, Eliot says, is not a defence of aristocracy as a separate class, but rather 'a plea on behalf of a form of society in which an aristocracy should have a peculiar and essential function'.[13] In other words, an aristocracy is needed not so much for its own good as for the good of the rest of us who are on lower, or as Eliot puts it, 'less conscious' grades of culture. Elsewhere, Eliot also recommended a vigorous working-class culture, and worried not only about the disappearance of the culture, but of the class itself. In his essay on Marie Lloyd (whom he called 'the expressive figure of the lower classes') he sees the middle class absorbing the classes above and below it: 'The lower class still exists; but perhaps it will not exist for long . . . . With the decay of the music-hall, with the encroachment of the cheap and rapid-breeding cinema, the lower classes will tend to drop into the same state of protoplasm as the bourgeoisie'.[14]

Orwell shared Eliot's concern about the degeneration of popular culture in the twentieth century. He noted the vestiges of a more authentic 'folk' culture: 'there is still an appreciable amount of folk poetry (nursery rhymes etc.) which is universally known and quoted, and forms part of the background of everyone's mind. There is also a handful of ancient songs and ballads which have never gone out of favour' (*CE*, II, 333). These popular forms he found authentic in that they are developed and transmitted communally, and in *Nineteen Eighty-Four* Winston Smith finds something reassuringly substantial in the 'Oranges and Lemons' rhyme, something quite alien to the Party slogans. Nevertheless, this culture is easily forgotten by its participants, and ignored or co-opted by the authorities. The machine-made 1984 hit song 'It was only a hopeless fancy' is just as popular as any traditional song ever was: the Party has succeeded in replacing folk culture with mass culture.

The Proles also seem quite content with the machine-produced fiction of the Ficdep (including the Pornosec where Julia works) and Orwell's novel seems to extend the pessimistic view of popular culture he expressed in his pioneering essays on boys' comics, obscene post cards and popular crime fiction – a kind of cultural equivalent of his 'down and out' tramping escapades. His analysis repeatedly stresses several points. First, mass culture is unbelievably unrealistic, and distracts people from what is going on around them. He speaks of 'the drugged millions to whom the world of the gangsters and the prize-ring is more "real", more "tough", than such things as wars, revolutions, earthquakes, famines and pestilences' (*CE*, III, 218). Secondly, much of it is unbelievably dated. Orwell writes of boys' stories published in the late 1930s: 'The clock has stopped at 1910. Britannia rules the waves, and no-one has heard of slumps, booms, unemployment, dictatorships, purges or concentration camps' (*CE*, I, 479). Thirdly, Orwell stresses the recent increase in brutality and cynicism in popular fiction, which he attributes to Americanisation. His example is James Hadley Chase's novel *No Orchids for Miss Blandish*

(1939) which he calls 'a day-dream appropriate to a totalitarian age' (*CE*, III, 223). That is to say it *does* belatedly reflect the new period, but only in a simplified and individualised form, which reproduces the new brutality, not in its realistic or actual forms in the political world, but in a fantasy form. For Orwell, mass culture has an anaesthetic effect on the senses and the conscience, and this aligns him with Eliot, who deplores the working man's turning from the music hall to the cinema, 'where his mind is lulled by continuous senseless music and continuous action too rapid for the brain to act upon',[15] a set of reactions perhaps closer to Eliot's own than to that of the average cinema-goer. The tradition of these remarks goes at least as far back as the 'savage torpor' Wordsworth saw in the audiences of the eighteenth-century melodrama.

But in Orwell's view it was not only mass culture which was becoming corrupted in the 1940s. The whole culture was succumbing to the same disease, the same weakening of morality and taste, but on different levels and in different ways. The universal disease to Orwell was power worship, but it had many different symptoms:

> People worship power in the form in which they are able to understand it. A twelve-year-old boy worships Jack Dempsey. An adolescent in a Glasgow slum worships Al Capone. An aspiring pupil at a business college worships Lord Nuffield. A *New Statesman* reader worships Stalin. There is a difference in intellectual maturity, but none in moral outlook. (*CE*, III, 223–4)

This structure is reminiscent of the many 'grades of consciousness' in Eliot's hierarchical culture. But of course Orwell is *against* class society whether corrupted or not, though he does not give much idea of what a classless society or culture might look like. We have comments such as 'where there is equality there can be sanity' (*Nineteen Eighty-Four*, p. 348) from Winston Smith, but Orwell's vision of actually existing society exaggerates differences of culture to a point where they become almost zoological. His imagination dwells so strongly on class differences that his commitment to abolishing them seems pale and theoretical by contrast. Certainly he was hard on any who shed their original class culture, like the proletarian intellectuals he attacks in *The Road to Wigan Pier*, whether they are 'the type who squirms into the middle class via the literary intelligentsia or the type who becomes a Labour MP or a high-up trade union official.'[16] Orwell's vision of the 'alien cultures' of England was as hierarchical as Eliot's, except that his evaluation of it was negative, and Eliot's positive.

The idea of an undifferentiated society appalled Eliot, for to him culture meant division: a society without class divisions would be a society without culture. But what Eliot saw coming in the 1940s was not an egalitarian society but an élitist one. In *Notes* he takes up Karl Mannheim's distinction between classes (hereditary) and élites (chosen from all ranks of society to organise and administer it). The specific question is the transmission of culture: Eliot argues that true culture can only be passed on by the family within a continuing class structure. The élite will not be able to transmit culture except through public education, which for Eliot is only a secondary and less valid way: he holds that a large part of culture is unconscious, and that education can only transmit what is conscious, and indeed only a part of that.

Orwell's review, surprisingly for a social democrat, begins by supporting Eliot's position. He *agrees* that élites will be less effective culturally than classes, and adds the following argument which he says Eliot missed: whereas classes change and develop because of the unevenness of hereditary transmission (the fluctuating abilities and opportunities from one generation to another), élites tend to ossify because they can perpetuate their mentality by choosing and training only the obedient and orthodox. Orwell here reverses the usual argument, that classes ossify *because* they are hereditary, and that élites are more vigorous *because* of the constant influx of new blood. His examples of ossified élites are the Catholic Church and the Communist Party (a favourite pairing of his). Also, we can see the reflection of his argument in the account of the Party given in Goldstein's *Book*:

> The Party is not a class in the old sense of the word. It does not aim at transmitting power to its own children, as such . . . . The essence of oligarchical rule is not father-to-son inheritance, but the persistence of a certain world-view and a certain way of life, imposed by the dead upon the living. A ruling group is a ruling group as long as it can nominate its successors. (*Nineteen Eighty-Four*, p. 338)

Orwell, then, agrees with Eliot's misgivings about élites. But the fear that they might be *worse* than the classes they replace does not lead him to *defend* the existence of class society, as Eliot does. Halfway through the review Orwell abruptly parts company with Eliot, after supporting his argument, or at least making large concessions to it. The turning point comes in the middle of a paragraph:

> Yet one continues to have, throughout his book, the feeling that there is something wrong, and that he himself is aware of it. The fact is that class privilege, like slavery, has somehow ceased to be defensible. (*CE*, IV, 456)

Incidentally, Orwell had accused Eliot of a similar offence before, of 'defending [Kipling] where he is not defensible' (*CE*, II, 184). It is characteristic of Orwell to wait until midway through his review before coming out with this absolutely fundamental objection. He follows it immediately with another familiar accusation: essentially that Eliot is half-hearted, that he lacks the courage of his own conservatism. He accuses Eliot of backing off his defence of the class structure by pretending that classes and élites can in some way be combined: the classes will perpetuate culture, but the élites will promote efficiency at the same time. Orwell asserts that Eliot has confused his argument for fear of seeming morally offensive.

But Eliot is concerned with the unity of cultures as well as its division. For him, the ideal unifying force binding the different social levels into a whole is religion. In the *Notes* he says that,

> there is an aspect in which we can see a religion as the *whole way of life* of a people, from birth to the grave, from morning to night and even in sleep, and that way of life is also its culture . . . . And then we have to face the strange idea that what is part of our culture is also part of our lived religion.[17]

For Orwell that 'totalizing' force within modern culture is power-worship, which he sees as having become a substitute for God-worship: 'God is Power' (*Nineteen Eighty-Four*, pp. 387, 398), as O'Brien states and Winston repeats. Essentially, Eliot is advocating a society divided by classes but united by religious belief; Orwell a society without class divisions, but diversified by different individual beliefs. Religion was not a desirable unifying force to him, and in fact he saw religion as having potentially the same effect as totalitarian ideology. Significantly, *Nineteen Eighty-Four* contains no analysis of the fate or possible survival of organised religion in Oceania. Winston shows no religious leanings except a vague interest in church bells. This is presumably because Orwell saw religious belief, as reflected in its institutions (like the Catholic Church) and period of dominance (like the Middle Ages), as being basically similar to totalitarianism, not a force against it, as it has become in some Communist countries. Winston sees empirical science as a much more potent challenge to totalitarianism, and in his arguments with O'Brien he has frequent recourse to it to back up his ideas. It is O'Brien who constantly refers to religion, as if recognising that his ideology should saturate the people's whole way of life as religion once had. Where Orwell's own loyalty was to the period he described as 'the Protestant centuries' (*CE*, IV, 60) between medieval Christendom and modern totalitarianism, O'Brien claims affinity with the middle ages, and reflects the Party's historical perspective, in which, 'the centuries of capitalism were held to have produced nothing of any value' (*Nineteen Eighty-Four*, p. 241).

Protestantism and capitalism for Orwell seem to have had mainly the negative virtues of not being Catholicism and Communism, that is, not interfering with the individual as much. Orwell always characterised Eliot, following the poet's lead, as an Anglo-Catholic, to associate him firmly with what he saw as Catholic anti-individualism. Eliot was Orwell's type of the intellectual fleeing into religion. As he put it in his review of the *Quartets*, 'Eliot's escape from individualism was into the Church' (*CE*, II, 240). Eliot had in fact exactly the opposite historical perspective to Orwell, in that his favoured period of literature ended where Orwell's began: in the seventeenth century. The rise of good prose for Orwell coincided with the fatal 'dissociation of sensibility' for Eliot; and the medieval period, as typified by Dante, was a kind of ideal for Eliot, but to Orwell was the nearest analogue to modern totalitarianism: the Church had the desire to enforce total orthodoxy but only limited means to do so. Communism was to Orwell a kind of fulfilment in the modern period of Catholicism in the middle ages: inquisition, torture, censorship and surveillance all reappeared, but now vastly enhanced by the power of technology. Orwell too turned to the past for positive values, but not to Eliot's 1300 (the age of Dante) or 1600 (the age of Shakespeare) but rather to 1900 or 1910. Why the nostalgia for the Edwardian period? It was not because freedom and equality were realised then (Orwell's own school reminiscences would be enough to destroy that notion), but because then it was still possible to *hope* that freedom and equality *might* be realised. Orwell was nostalgic for the age of optimism and progressivism, the age of Shaw and Wells – precisely the age which Eliot disliked the most, precisely the generation which he and the Modernists successfully set themselves to overthrow, and which he saw as the culmination of two centuries of Whiggery (Eliot manages to make this word sound like an obscenity).

Both Orwell and Eliot treated the period after 1914, and even more after 1930, as a new age, to rank in importance with the medieval period and Orwell's 'Protestant centuries'. Both viewed the new age with deep misgivings and were led to reflect on and evaluate the two previous eras in the new context. For Eliot the new age was the *outcome* of the Whiggish centuries, resulting in the desperate disarray of the twentieth century, in which one could only hope to hold on to the remnants of the class structure and religion and cultivate the literature of integrated ages. For Orwell, the new age was a *betrayal* of the Protestant centuries' hope for freedom and equality which, though never fulfilled, was kept alive by successive movements of idealists and reformers.

Orwell and Eliot thus have symmetrical but opposing views of history: they agree on the divisions, but disagree on the evaluations. And this holds true for their views of the literary aspect of this history: both agree, very broadly, that the age of poetry ended in the seventeenth century and was replaced by an age of prose, and both hint that the new age might offer new possibilities for poetry. In Eliot's view, Milton and Dryden aggravated the dissociation of thought and feeling, and then (in the capsule history from his essay on 'The Metaphysical Poets') 'Keats and Shelley died, and Tennyson and Browning ruminated'.[18] The twentieth century offered the possibility of renewing poetry by an emulation of poets like Donne and Dante, and by reviving verse drama. Orwell's literary history reads like an exact reversal of Eliot's, following the fortunes of prose instead of poetry as the key indicator of cultural health:

> prose literature almost disappeared during the only age of faith that Europe has ever enjoyed. Throughout the whole of the Middle Ages there was almost no imaginative prose literature and very little in the way of historical writing. (*CE*, IV, 66)

Then follows the age of 'good prose', and particularly of the novel, which enshrines Orwell's central values: 'The novel is practically a Protestant form of art; it is a product of the free mind, of the autonomous individual' (*CE*, I, 518). Finally comes the modern age, which Orwell presents as totalitarian or pre-totalitarian, and accordingly as poor in prose as the middle ages:

> It is probably not a coincidence that the best writers of the thirties have been poets. The atmosphere of orthodoxy is always damaging to prose . . . . No decade in the past hundred and fifty years has been so barren of imaginative prose as the nineteen-thirties. (*CE*, I, 518)

Orwell seems, incidentally, to condemn his own prose in that last statement. But a more general implication is that he is conducting a doomed but honourable rearguard action as a last representative of individualism in a new age of orthodoxy, a kind of 'last man in Europe' like Winston Smith. The poets would survive and perhaps even prosper under totalitarianism, as they had done in the middle ages. He asserts:

> the atmosphere of totalitarianism is deadly to any kind of prose writer, though a poet, at any rate a lyric poet, might possibly find it breathable. (*CE*, IV, 65)

The main reason is that:

> good verse, unlike good prose, is not necessarily an individual product . . . . Serious prose . . . has to be composed in solitude, whereas the excitement of being part of a group is actually an aid to certain kinds of versification . . . . Even in a society where liberty and individuality had been extinguished there would still be need either for patriotic songs and heroic ballads celebrating victories, or for elaborate exercises in flattery . . . . (*CE*, IV, 67–8)

Rather insultingly, Orwell attributes the survival power of poetry to a certain lack of political integrity, which in turn means a lack of individualism, and his rancour towards Auden and Spender and their pro-Communism is probably behind these comments. Orwell poses as a prose writer in an unpropitious time – a position not unlike Eliot's pose as a poet. For Orwell the age of prose was framed by two 'ages of poetry' where the preconditions of prose composition (freedom, individuality, privacy) were, or would be, absent.

This pattern of agreed structures and opposite evaluations continues if we move from comparing their non-fictional prose of the 1940s on social and cultural theory to comparing their major work of that decade in their respective creative genres: poetry for Eliot and fictional prose for Orwell. In *Four Quartets* and *Nineteen Eighty-Four*, questions of history, culture and belief are focused around the re-integration of an isolated individual. In Eliot the larger whole is variously the family (in the genealogical sense) the Church, and the Anglo-American and European cultural traditions, while in Orwell it is the Party, its ideology, and its Anglo-American empire, Oceania. But the 'self' of *Four Quartets* desires and seeks the re-integration, while Winston Smith, at least consciously, fears and defies it. Eliot's epigraph from Heraclitus points to the limitations of the individual mind: 'Although the Word (Logos) is common to all, most people live as if each of them had a private intelligence of his own.'[19] Clearly, this 'private intelligence' is precisely what Winston Smith sees as the source of all truth and value, and the basis of the personal independence he is striving to establish, in part through writing his diary, though it barely attains the level of what Orwell would call 'good prose'.

Winston's individualism is closely linked, as in Alan Sandison's succinct description of Orwell's beliefs, to empiricism:

the senses are inalienable, and in the reception of their independent and particular report of the natural world is proof of individuality.[20]

This is the core of the autonomous self defended by Orwell, but rejected by Eliot in *Four Quartets* in an unusually peremptory tone:

You are not here to verify,
Instruct yourself, or inform curiosity
Or carry report. You are here to kneel
Where prayer has been valid.[21]

The first sentence is practically a summary of Winston's doomed project: his need for verification before he believes anything, his curiosity about the facts and relics of the past, and his need through his diary to leave a report of his experience. To Eliot curiosity means an attachment to empirical time as well as space:

> Men's curiosity searches past and future
> And clings to that dimension.[22]

There could hardly be a better description of Winston Smith's consciousness, even including the hint of insecurity in the 'clinging' metaphor. In O'Brien's future vision of Oceania, naturally, 'there will be no curiosity, no enjoyment of the process of life' (*Nineteen Eighty-Four*, p. 390). For Winston, curiosity and the information it provides about real times and places are the foundation of the sense of self he is trying to develop and preserve. For Orwell, too, curiosity is perhaps the highest virtue, as the purest motivation for the free mind to encounter the objective world. But for Eliot, 'curiosity' is a level of consciousness that the saint, and occasionally the ordinary believer, can and should transcend.

Perhaps more than anything else, Winston's humanist sense of attachment to the world needs a clear sense of time: an ordered sequence from past through present to future within which events can be placed – remembered, enacted, or anticipated. Winston's heresy is to try to retrieve his own personal past, through memory, and to leave a record of the present for the future, through his diary. In a sense his project is both more subjective (more personal) and more objective (true to the actual facts) than the Party's 'collective solipsism', where communal belief obliterates private fact. The individuation of the self in the present depends on access to a personal past. Without this there are no attachments to the world beyond the present situation, and the detached self can then easily be merged into the collectivity of the Party. In Oceania there is nothing other than the present: the past and the future are mere projections of the present, constantly adapted to its needs.

> All history was a palimpsest, scraped clean and re-inscribed exactly as often as was necessary. (*Nineteen Eighty-Four*, p. 190)

> The past not only changed, but changed continuously. (p. 225)

The attachments of the self to the past are constantly being broken. As Winston puts it:

History has stopped. Nothing exists except an endless present in which the Party is always right. (p. 290)

Here we can trace almost verbal echoes of Eliot's ideas, such as his frequent emphasis on the 'presentness' of the past of a culture, and the right of the present to revalue that past. In 'Tradition and the Individual Talent', for example, he avers that 'the past should be altered by the present as much as the present is directed by the past'.[23] This incessant revision of the tradition, of course, does not extend to rewriting the texts as in Oceania, but does emphasise their reinterpretation and reconfiguration and so to that extent reminds us of *Nineteen Eighty-Four*: 'Who controls the past', ran the Party slogan, 'controls the future: who controls the present controls the past' (p. 186).

For Eliot, as for the Party, history can stop and be gathered around the present moment: 'History is now and England'.[24] For him, in a way which would have alarmed Winston Smith, history is not fixed: the past, individual or collective, can be altered, *is* incessantly altered, by the present:

> History may be servitude,
> History may be freedom. See, now they vanish,
> The faces and places, with the self which,
> as it could, loved them,
> To become renewed, transfigured in another pattern.[25]

This vanishing of the self, along with the attachments which formed it, is essentially the goal of Winston's re-education in the Ministry of Love.

The time-sense Winston tries to preserve and reconstruct is linear and secular, 'progressive' we might say: time as an irreversible sequence in which individual, social and human progress can be measured. Against this, *Four Quartets* has a fundamentally religious sense of time, which stresses patterning and repatterning, configuration and reconfiguration of the same set of elements, the unchanging constants of divine and human nature. Winston's time, with its stress on precise dates as measures of individual and social change, is the quantified time-sense developed in the bourgeois-liberal epoch from the seventeenth century onwards. Yet *Nineteen Eighty-Four* itself is predominantly structured not around that sense of time, but around the religious time-sense, like *Four Quartets*. In other words it has a mythic-religious or Modernist time-structure, rather than the linear progression typical of the bourgeois English novel from Defoe to (say) Arnold Bennett. Winston's open, developmental time is, we might say, *contained* by O'Brien's religious, preordained time.

This religious time-sense could be summed up in the opening words of 'East Coker': 'In my beginning is my end'.[26] They are an adaptation of the motto of Mary Stuart, which is quoted in its original form at the end of the poem: 'In my end is my beginning'. These quotations reinforce a sense of time as preordained, so that it can only unfold what is already virtually present, and not bring anything new. Significantly, this phrase was one of the few Orwell spontaneously remembered from *Four Quartets* (memorability was his main test of poetic quality), but he did not give Eliot credit for it, having recognised that it was a quotation. Orwell then went on to use an adapted form of it himself, and, like Eliot, to use it as a structuring principle. Almost exactly halfway through the book, when he has received the summons to O'Brien, Winston reflects:

> What was happening was only the working-out of a process that had started years ago . . . . He had accepted it. The end was contained in the beginning. (*Nineteen Eighty-Four*, p. 294)

Orwell's main modification of the quotation, the adding of 'contained', is echoed near the end when O'Brien tells Winston, 'It was all contained in that first act' (*Nineteen Eighty-Four*, p. 395). This idea of the first event containing the entire sequence, of the part containing the whole, provides a clue to the time structure of the novel. The 'Oranges and Lemons' rhyme and the 'place where there is no darkness' leitmotiv, are just two examples of Orwell's use of Modernist techniques to effect a 'religious' patterning of time, like that of the *Four Quartets*, which surrounds and undercuts Winston's secular, individual time.

It seems, then, as if Orwell's novel partly rejects Eliot's poetics of history, but partly incorporates it. Winston's 'prose' outlook is surrounded and finally silenced by the 'poetic' or religious reassurances in the novel, those which suggest affinities with Eliot. Orwell's world of autonomous individuals, distinct objects and verifiable facts, set within linear time and measurable space, is swallowed up. Apparently Orwell's values are based on the notion of *independence*, of discrete, freely-acting, autonomous entities while

Eliot's are based on *interdependence*, a view of the world in which divisions are only ramifications of an eventual total connectivity. Yet Orwell constantly shows the collapse of his own philosophy through his pessimistic view of history and through his defeated fictional heroes, such as Winston. Thus Orwell's viewpoint seems in various ways to be *contained* by Eliot's, more than simply opposed to it. Eliot's career in a literal sense contains Orwell's in that he was already a dominant figure in the 1920s through *The Waste Land*, and continued to be in the 1950s after Orwell's death. Eliot's history, too, seems to contain Orwell's, the medieval-modernist affinity framing the bourgeois centuries. Orwell's prose tradition of the eighteenth and nineteenth centuries was contained by Eliot's poetic one, from Dante or Donne to *Four Quartets*. The autonomous self and the prose which preserved it seemed to Orwell like an anomaly, a break in history soon to be covered over and perhaps obliterated permanently by the new collectivism. Individualism failed because of the emotional strain it involved, and because it could not answer death. In his review of the *Four Quartets* Orwell wrote: 'So long as man regards himself as an individual, his attitude towards death must be one of simple resentment' (*CE*, II, 238). Only a collective creed can assuage this feeling by giving the comforting assurance of some kind of afterlife, either in heaven or in a future society which will justify one's efforts in life. Orwell valued the 'attached' self, attached to the physical world through sensation, memory and record. But he could not provide this philosophy with a future, either in or beyond the world. His pessimism led him to incorporate in his work the opposite values to those he espoused. Orwell used ideas and techniques of Eliot's prose and poetry to dramatise the defeat of his own ideal: a society of free and equal individuals.

10

Orwell as Literary Critic: A Reassessment

Michael L. Ross

To the modern student of literature, Orwell's criticism must seem crude and rudimentary. Indeed, Orwell's essays about literature bear very little relationship to literary criticism as that term is now understood. Modern literary criticism . . . tends to concentrate upon given texts. Above all it is attentive to the words on the page and to the quality of mind and responsiveness to which the words attest. It is conducted by means of a set of verbal conventions that make for the neutralisation, sometimes even for the virtual extinction, of the personality of the critic. It is meticulous in its formulations even at the risk of becoming Alexandrian. With Orwell it is quite otherwise. There is no great reverence for the novel or poem as a thing in itself, nor is there much critical vocabulary. His essays seldom offer a new insight into a work.[1]

Keith Alldritt's assessment of Orwell as a literary critic will serve as a convenient point of departure for my own reassessment. It casts serious doubts on the validity of Orwell's entire critical performance, doubts that any serious defence of Orwell must attempt to resolve.

My purpose is not, however, to act as Orwell's over-anxious hagiographer. All I wish to do is to contest Alldritt's dismissive conclusion: 'There are then, let it be said, no claims to be made for Orwell as a literary critic'.[2] I will hardly, of course, be the first to have made substantial claims for Orwell's achievement as a critic. George Woodcock, as early as the 1960s, had already argued Orwell's cause eloquently: 'Once [Orwell's] bias is recognised the essays all have their value as criticism, in spite of their defiantly amateur quality; every one of them contains a whole series of

157

original and pointed statements about its subject, delivered in vivid and arresting language'.[3] More recently, Bernard Crick has affirmed that Orwell 'was capable of literary criticism of the highest order'.[4] Nevertheless, it is Alldritt's opinion that more closely voices the prevailing academic consensus. Few have challenged John Wain's judgement that Orwell was 'a literary critic who never bothered to learn his trade properly',[5] and that 'it isn't for "literary criticism", in the real sense, that one reads Orwell's essays on books'.[6]

Such dismissals prompt the questions: what is literary criticism 'in the real sense'? Who does or does not qualify as a bona-fide 'literary critic', and according to which criteria? The case against Orwell goes far beyond his own individual performance as critic. He tends to be judged as a *type* of critic, now out of favour, in the light of a model of 'real' criticism currently in favour. By today's standards, the critical pronouncements of a detached and systematic specialist will *ipso facto* be given more weight than those of a knock-about, politically-embroiled journalist and novelist. It would, of course, be misleading to assume that Orwell never does any of the things we today expect a 'real' literary critic to do. I hope to demonstrate in what follows that Orwell's criticism frequently is in fact 'attentive to the words on the page and to the quality of mind and responsiveness to which the words attest'. All the same, Woodcock is correct in pointing out Orwell's defiance of tendencies that were already starting to look fashionable in his own day – his disdain for 'cults of impersonality' and specialised 'critical vocabularies'.[7] Was Orwell staging a commendable rear-guard action, or was he merely lagging deplorably behind the vanguard? Before confronting that question, I would like to consider briefly the critical equipment with which Orwell was armed.

Orwell's judges have sometimes been reluctant to concede him the barest qualifications of a critic. According to Woodcock, 'Even [Orwell's] reading was limited . . . .'[8] Noting that 'except for those on Swift and Shakespeare none of the major literary essays deals with anything outside the Victorian and Edwardian periods', Alldritt concludes that 'the range, if not the depth, of Orwell's reading corresponds to what may be called Edwardian middle-class taste'.[9] Yet against this place Orwell's declaration: 'The writers I care most about and never grow tired of are Shakespeare, Swift, Fielding, Dickens, Charles Reade, Samuel Butler, Zola, Flaubert and, among modern writers, James Joyce, T. S. Eliot and D. H. Lawrence' (*CE*, II, 24). For an Edwardian, Orwell would appear to have had catholic tastes. The presence of two French novelists on Orwell's list emphasises his resistance to insularity, a shortcoming which provokes his most strenuous complaints against Victorian and Edwardian writing: 'The feeling you have with Joyce or Eliot, or even Lawrence, that they have got the whole of human history inside their heads and can look outwards from their own place and time towards Europe and the past, isn't to be found in Galsworthy or in any characteristic English writer in the period before 1914' (*CE*, II, 205). His admiration for Joseph Conrad, on whom he projected an extended study which his death interrupted, derives partly from Conrad's liberating contact as a 'transplanted Pole' with Continental trends: 'Conrad was one of those writers who in the present century civilised English literature and brought it back into contact with Europe, from which it had been almost severed for a hundred years' (*CE*, IV, 489). Such an attitude stands in refreshing contrast with the tendency of some English critics to regard the Continent and its literatures as a perplexing moral lapse on the part of the Creator.[10]

The supposed narrowness of Orwell's reading has, however, done less to make him the target for censure than the palpable eccentricity of his judgement. Witness this, from 'Lear, Tolstoy and the Fool'; 'Tolstoy is right in saying that *Lear* is not a very good play, as a play. It is too drawn-out and has too many characters and subplots. One wicked daughter would have been quite enough, and Edgar is a superfluous character, indeed it would probably be a better play if Gloucester and both his sons were eliminated' (*CE*, IV, 292). For John Wain, 'This innocent remark reveals, first, that [Orwell] cannot have taken the slightest trouble to read what other critics have said about the play, and secondly that, for all his acuteness, he was incapable of the sort of attentive, close study that we expect of a real literary critic'.[11] Nevertheless, flagrant though it may be, Orwell's casual misjudgement of Shakespeare in this single instance hardly clinches the case for his general incapacity as a critic. It would seem safer to base conclusions about Orwell's critical habits on his dealings with authors closer to him than Shakespeare, either in temperament or in time.

One such author was Jonathan Swift, and Orwell's celebrated essay on him, 'Politics and Literature', therefore provides a more apposite hunting-ground for critical crudenesses than the *King Lear* essay. The lapses one encounters in this instance prompt more seriously disturbing reservations about Orwell's basic critical approach. For all its brilliance, much of what Orwell says in the essay betrays a disconcerting failure to recognise Swift's satiric strategy for what it is, a failure deriving largely from Orwell's obstinate refusal to distinguish between a writer's personal concerns and the uses to which he puts his imagination. An example is his assertion: 'Swift was presumably impotent, and had an exaggerated horror of human dung: he also thought about it incessantly, as is evident throughout his works' (*CE*, IV, 217). It seems not to have occurred to Orwell that the frequency with which Swift mentions excrement might depend on its usefulness as a blunt symbolic device for deflating grandiose human pretensions, rather than on Swift's morbid obsession with chamber-pots. A similar type of reasoning underlies Orwell's general conclusion: 'Swift is a diseased writer. He remains permanently in a depressed mood which in most people is only intermittent, rather as though someone suffering from jaundice or the after-effects of influenza should have the energy to write books' (*CE*, IV, 222). The diagnosing of Swift's adroitly crafted satire as a symptom of chronic melancholia is the sort of manoeuvre which more recent criticism deserves applause for having abandoned. Ironically, Orwell's own fiction, above all *Nineteen Eighty-Four*, has itself all too frequently suffered from such glib amateur psychologising.

It is best to acknowledge, then, that Orwell's critical assumptions could in some instances be naive, and could sometimes lead him to read literary texts in an obtuse or facile manner. I must next turn to what is perhaps the most damaging charge that has been brought against Orwell as a critic: his alleged 'inability to recognise any real function or value in the practice of literary criticism'.[12] According to Woodcock, 'Not merely did Orwell reject evaluative criticism; he also doubted if there was any point in the formal analysis of writing'.[13] Evidence pointing to such ingrained scepticism abounds in the body of Orwell's writing. The attitude surfaces early in his career, and remains conspicuous in as late an essay as 'Writers and Leviathan': 'I often have the feeling that even at the best of times literary criticism is fraudulent, since in the absence of any accepted standards whatever . . . every literary judgement consists in trumping up a set of rules to justify an instinctive preference' (*CE*, IV, 408). Yet place against this the conclusion of Orwell's 1941 broadcast-talk 'The Meaning of a Poem', which contains a sensitive, careful analysis of Orwell's favourite short poem, Hopkins's 'Felix Randal': 'I have tried to analyse this poem as well as I can in a short period, but nothing I have said can explain, or explain away, the pleasure I take in it. That is finally inexplicable, and it is just because it *is* inexplicable that detailed criticism is worthwhile. Men of science can study the life-process of a flower, or they can split it up into its component elements, but any scientist will tell you that a flower does not become less wonderful, it becomes more wonderful, if you know all about it' (*CE*, II, 134).[14] If Orwell's doubts about the adequacy of interpretation are still clearly visible here, they only set in bolder relief his willingness in this instance to champion the cause of literary analysis, rather than scoff at it.

Point-blank self-contradictions come, of course, as no surprise to readers of Orwell. The value of literary interpretation is only one among a variety of topics on which his thinking was subject to spectacular trapeze-swings from one perch to another. But it would be shallow to view Orwell's swerves of opinion as arbitrary, eccentric quirks occurring in a historical vacuum. One needs to register Orwell's own sober recognition of how cultural and political pressures were acting so as to deform the contemporary critic's thinking. 'In the Europe of the last ten years', he complains in 'The Frontiers of Art and Propaganda', 'literary criticism of the older kind – criticism that is really judicious, scrupulous, fair-minded, treating a work of art as a thing of value in itself – has been next door to impossible' (*CE*, II, 123). The otherwise plausible objection that Orwell's criticism displays 'no great reverence for the novel or poem as a thing in itself' needs to be reassessed in the light of Orwell's own explicit misgivings.

Not only the enveloping political climate, but his private financial heavy weather made it harder for Orwell to produce 'judicious' and 'scrupulous' criticism of the sort he admired. 'I find this kind of semi-sociological literary criticism very interesting,' he writes wistfully in 1940 *à propos* of his essay on Dickens, '& I'd like to do a lot of other writers, but unfortunately there's no money in it' (*CE*, I, 528). Routine reviewing, though it did bring in needed money, was in Orwell's view no substitute for more serious criticism. In 1937 he reports to Jack Common that, apart from working on *Homage to Catalonia*, 'I am not doing anything except the usual hack-work of reviews which I don't count as writing' (*CE*, I, 289). Nine years later, in 'Confessions of a Book Reviewer', he poignantly defines the reviewer's essential activity as 'pouring his immortal spirit down the drain, half a pint at a time' (*CE*, IV, 183).

Yet Orwell's best reviews, far from being hack-work, reward attentive and repeated reading. He himself, in the early essay 'In Defence of the Novel', projects an ideal state of affairs in which reviewers would be, not the venal and harried hacks all too familiar to us, but rather 'people who really cared for the art of the novel (and that means, probably, neither highbrows nor lowbrows nor midbrows, but elastic-brows), people interested in technique and still more interested in discovering what a book is *about*' (*CE*, I, 254). A hindrance to serious reviewing is, he admits, the lack of distinction in the subject matter: 'To apply a decent standard to the ordinary run of novels is like weighing a flea on a spring-balance intended for elephants' (*CE*, I, 252). But his dismay at the average quality of the literature consumed by the English public adds urgency to his support for criticism as a legitimate and irreplaceable activity. In a piece dating from 1944, he maintains that the missions of the artist and the critic are not antithetical but rather complementary. 'We in this country have bad taste, as we have bad teeth, because of complex but discoverable social causes. It is a thing to be fought against, and an important part of the fight devolves on the artist and the critic. The artist fights it by preserving his integrity: the critic fights against it by educating the public' (*CE*, III, 260).

So far so good, but such a stand prompts a difficult question: what type of dentistry is the probing critic to use in repairing the public's taste-decay? Orwell on the whole rejected any purely aestheticist panacea. In 'The Frontiers of Art and Propaganda' he writes of the decade of the thirties:

> this period of ten years or so in which literature, even poetry, was mixed up with pamphleteering, did a great service to literary criticism, because it destroyed the illusion of pure aestheticism. It reminded us that propaganda in some form or other lurks in every book, that every work of art has a meaning and purpose – a political, social and religious purpose – that our aesthetic judgements are always coloured by our prejudices and beliefs. (*CE*, II, 126)

However, Orwell's cherished conviction that art furthers some programmatic design obviously complicates for him the critic's mission of improving the public's taste. Such a view is bound to intensify his suspicion that literary judgements merely rationalise the critic's 'instinctive preference', which may itself likely be tinged by his settled political or religious convictions. 'Educating the public' might well become tantamount to indoctrinating the public with the critic's pet dogmas, disguised in the sheep's clothing of 'literary values'. Woodcock claims that Orwell 'denied the possibility of any genuine evaluative criticism, and it was in this denial . . . that his deliberate identification with the plain unintellectual man was most strongly expressed';[15] but such reasoning oversimplifies the motives behind Orwell's distrust of evaluation. With his hypersensitivity to the subtle threads binding literary judgements to political and religious ideology, he was deprived of the robust confidence that another critic – say, an F. R. Leavis – might place in his own evaluative acts.

Under such circumstances, it was natural that Orwell should search for a measure of literary worth that was independent of the individual critic's egocentricity, and that he should frequently turn for such an impersonal measure to the verdict of posterity. 'There are no rules in novel writing', he says in his essay on Dickens, 'and for any work of art there is only one test worth bothering about – survival' (*CE*, I, 455). In practice, however, resorting to the Darwinian evidence of survival can too easily shade into an evasion of critical responsibility, either through disclaiming all individual preferences or through dissimulating them under augustly 'impersonal' robes. In 'Inside the Whale', for example, Orwell announces:

The first test of any work of art is survival, and it is a fact that a great deal that was written in the period 1910–30 has survived and looks like continuing to survive. One has only to think of *Ulysses*, *Of Human Bondage*, most of Lawrence's early work, especially his short stories, and virtually the whole of Eliot's poems up to about 1930, to wonder what is now being written that will wear so well. (*CE*, I, 510)

Can it be pure coincidence that the modern works in which Orwell detects the glow of 'survival' are precisely the ones for which he himself harboured a glowing personal enthusiasm? What the severely 'impersonal' test of survival really boils down to here is the question: 'Which books do I, George Orwell, after ten or twenty years still find myself reading?'

I do not wish to imply that the 'survival' criterion was invariably a mere cover for Orwell's zeal in promoting his own pet authors. I do wish to point out, however, that Orwell's individual judgements were far too importunate to be easily thrust into the background. In many instances, indeed, he thrusts them without the least embarrassment vigorously into the foreground. Witness this from the 1945 essay 'Notes on Nationalism': 'Chesterton's battle poems, such as "Lepanto" or "The Ballad of Saint Barbara", make "The Charge of the Light Brigade" read like a pacifist tract: they are perhaps the most tawdry bits of bombast to be found in our language' (*CE*, III, 366). In disclaiming evaluation and flourishing his banner of 'survival' Orwell could, as Woodcock notes, be blithely inconsistent: 'In dealing with contemporary writers Orwell in practice often ignored his rule, talking of "the best writers of our generation" . . . and discussing writers like Yeats and Eliot in tones which left no doubt at all that he considered them superior to, say, Kipling or Noyes.'[16] As a critic, then, Orwell was far indeed from lacking the will to discriminate; it was, rather, a philosophical dilemma that inhibited him from urging his preferences as law. He could accept neither of the two contending conceptions of criticism that dominated by turns the literary world of his time, as he perceived it. The first, the doctrine of 'art for art's sake', had prevailed in the twenties, when ' "art has nothing to do with morality" was the favourite slogan,' and when 'to admit that you liked or disliked a book because of its moral or religious tendency, even to admit noticing that it *had* a tendency, was too vulgar for words (*CE*, I, 257). The other conception gained predominance in the thirties: the belief of the 'good party man' that the rightness or wrongness of a writer's political views determined the worth of what he wrote. This dogma Orwell regarded as 'a half-conscious confusion of ideas which vitiates nearly all politico-literary criticism':

To dislike a writer's politics is one thing. To dislike him because he forces you to think is another, not necessarily incompatible with the first. But as soon as you start talking about 'good' and 'bad' writers you are tacitly appealing to literary tradition and thus dragging in a totally different set of values. For what is a 'good' writer? Was Shakespeare 'good'? Most people would agree that he was. Yet Shakespeare is, and perhaps was even by the standards of his own time, reactionary in tendency . . . . What, then, becomes of the notion that Eliot is disqualified, as it were, by being an Anglo-Catholic royalist who is given to quoting Latin? (*CE*, II, 292–3)

Orwell himself could not embrace the ivory-tower orthodoxy that excluded ideology as a literary province, but neither could he accept the orthodoxy of engagement that derived literary values uniquely from ideology.[17] There is consequently little basis for Alldritt's contention that 'Orwell is usually concerned with a writer's "position" and with the extent to which that position is coincident with his own . . . . For him a work of literature is something that can be reduced to a simple statement of outlook and something which is valuable in so far as it may serve as an objectification of his own outlook'.[18] In reality, Orwell's criticism seldom bears out what this implies: that Orwell saw a work of literature as reducible to an idea-capsule, and valued the work only in so far as the ideas contained in the capsule matched his own. Orwell's repeated advocacy of authors he considered 'reactionary' becomes inexplicable in terms of such an assumption. The distinction he makes in 'Writers and Leviathan' is much more to the point here: 'One's real reaction to a book, when one has a reaction at all, is usually "I like this book" or "I don't like it", and what follows is a rationalisation. But "I like this book" is not, I think, a non-literary reaction; the non-literary reaction is "This book is on my side, and therefore I must discover merits in it" (*CE*, IV, 408).

Orwell, then, was concerned with exploring specifically 'literary' as opposed to ideological preferences, but was unwilling to retreat into a purely aestheticist position. What he needed was to develop a mediating, integrated theory of his own, but he was not a sufficiently systematic thinker to embark confidently on such an undertaking. A statement dating from the last months of Orwell's life represents perhaps his closest approach to resolving the dilemma:

The more I see the more I doubt whether people ever really make aesthetic judgements at all. Everything is judged on political grounds which are then given an aesthetic disguise. When, for instance, Eliot can't see anything good in Shelley or

anything bad in Kipling, the real underlying reason must be that
the one is a radical and the other a conservative, of sorts. Yet
evidently one does have aesthetic reactions, especially as a lot
of art and even literature is politically neutral, and also certain
unmistakable standards do exist, e.g. Homer is better than Edgar
Wallace. Perhaps the way we should put it is: the more one is
aware of political bias the more one can be independent of it, &
the more one claims to be impartial the more one is biased. (*CE*,
IV, 504–5)

What this implies is the critic's obligation to strive to become in
the greatest possible measure ideologically self-acquainted, to
identify his own narrow, native bias and reach beyond it so as to
grasp the 'certain unmistakable standards' that Orwell here, for
once, acknowledges. Just which standards are unmistakable is,
however, a vexed question.

If he was always reluctant to allow the belief-content of a literary
work to determine the critical standards one applied to it, Orwell
was also unwilling to regard belief and literary effect as simply
unconnected. A passage from 'Inside the Whale' can serve to
illustrate how he attempted to define the connection:

there exist 'good' writers whose world-view would in *any* age
be recognised as false and silly. Edgar Allan Poe is an example.
Poe's outlook is at best a wild romanticism and at worst is not
far from being insane in the literal clinical sense. Why is it, then,
that stories like 'The Black Cat', 'The Tell-tale Heart', 'The Fall
of the House of Usher' and so forth, which might very nearly
have been written by a lunatic, do not convey a feeling of falsity?
Because they are true within a certain framework, they keep the
rules of their own peculiar world, like a Japanese picture. But it
appears that to write successfully about such a world you have
got to believe in it . . . . It seems therefore that for a creative
writer possession of the 'truth' is less important than emotional
sincerity. (*CE*, I, 523)

I have quoted this not for the light it throws on Poe – Orwell's
incautious eagerness to read an author's fiction in terms of his
presumed derangement is, once again, embarrassing – but rather
for the light it throws on two literary criteria to which Orwell has

frequent recourse: the criterion of internal consistency of vision, and the related criterion of 'emotional sincerity'.

Sincerity provided Orwell's most often-consulted touchstone for judging a literary work. 'The first thing that we ask of a writer is that he shall not tell lies, that he shall say what he really thinks, what he really feels,' he argues in 'Literature and Totalitarianism'. 'The worst thing we can say about a work of art is that it is insincere . . . . Modern literature is essentially an individual thing. It is either the truthful expression of what one man thinks and feels, or it is nothing' (*CE*, II, 134–5). 'Sincerity' is of course a notoriously elusive quality to define, as Orwell himself admits in 'Lear, Tolstoy and the Fool', where he classes 'sincere' as one of those 'vague terms . . . which can be interpreted in any way one chooses' (*CE*, IV, 290). The concept, nevertheless, signified enough for him to make it the basis for his case against the censorship of literature. As he writes in 'The Prevention of Literature':

> the imaginative writer is unfree when he has to falsify his subjective feelings, which from his point of view are facts. He may distort and caricature reality in order to make his meaning clearer, but he cannot misrepresent the scenery of his own mind: he cannot say with any conviction that he likes what he dislikes, or believes what he disbelieves. If he is forced to do so, the only result is that his creative faculties dry up. (*CE*, IV, 65)

In practice, sincerity was often closely linked for Orwell with the scrupulous documenting of uncomfortable fact. Of Smollett, for example, he notes that 'by simply ruling out "good" motives and showing no respect whatever for human dignity', that author 'often attains a truthfulness that more serious novelists have missed. He is willing to mention things which do happen in real life but are almost invariably kept out of fiction' (*CE*, III, 247). Orwell's somewhat extravagant enthusiasm for Henry Miller derives from his view of Miller as a later and more introspective Smollett. 'Why is it that these monstrous trivialities are so engrossing?' he asks in a review of Miller's *Black Spring*. 'Simply because the whole atmosphere is deeply familiar, because you have all the while the feeling that these things are happening to *you*. And you have this feeling because somebody has chosen to drop the Geneva language of the ordinary novel and drag the *real-politik* of the inner mind into the open' (*CE*, I, 496–7). A rare assurance in plying between the world of modern power politics and the world of personal feeling lies behind that Orwellian phrase, 'the *real-politik* of the inner mind'.

The quality of sincerity was for Orwell inseparable from the writer's endowment of first-hand experience. In 'Inside the Whale', he observes of the 'dominant writers of the thirties' that 'they can swallow totalitarianism *because* they have no experience of anything except liberalism' (*CE*, I, 516). Quoting a passage from Auden's poem 'Spain' containing the lines, 'Today the deliberate increase in the chances of death,/The conscious acceptance of guilt in the necessary murder', he comments:

> it could only be written by a person to whom murder is at most a *word*. Personally I would not speak so lightly of murder. It so happens that I have seen the bodies of numbers of murdered men – I don't mean killed in battle, I mean murdered. Therefore I have some conception of what murder means . . . Mr Auden's brand of amoralism is only possible if you are the kind of person who is always somewhere else when the trigger is pulled. (*CE*, I, 516)

As Keith Alldritt has justly said,

> Cited in isolation [Orwell's] words may seem pompous in a way that they do not in context. But they are a good example of Orwell's manner of scrutiny, of his own actual experience. And they exemplify his characteristic scorn of an intellectual community which is prone to ignore the reality that is known and felt and to become enmeshed in, and excited by, mere words.[19]

I would add that the sort of scrutiny that is rooted in personal experience seems eminently worthy of being included within the sphere of 'real' literary criticism. Orwell himself would have found impoverishing, perhaps even incomprehensible, the current 'isms' that mean to purge criticism of gross references to the critic's own experience, or indeed to external reality *tout court*.

But what impressed Orwell more than mere external, factual verisimilitude was a writer's authenticity in transmitting the inner life. It is for this reason that he was so stirred by James Joyce's accomplishment as a novelist:

[Joyce] dared – for it is a matter of *daring* just as much as of technique – to expose the imbecilities of the inner mind, and in doing so he discovered an America which was under everybody's nose. Here is a whole world of stuff which you have lived with since childhood, stuff which you supposed to be of its nature incommunicable, and somebody has managed to communicate it. The effect is to break down, at any rate momentarily, the solitude in which the human being lives. (*CE*, I, 495)

A prime virtue of the sort of authorial sincerity that dares to lay bare without shame the workings of the inner mind is its unique power to forge bonds between author and reader, man and man. Orwell's career can with little exaggeration be summed up as a life-long battle against human isolation, whose final and most appalling form is the regimented solipsism enforced by the authorities, and promulgated by their spokesman O'Brien, in *Nineteen Eighty-Four*.[20] For Orwell, a major function of literature is to break down that isolation, and a major function of criticism is to identify literary works that do so. It follows that the critic's role is also to condemn literary tendencies which reinforce the barriers of factitious and snobbish exclusiveness. Orwell's uneasiness with F. R. Leavis's stance in *The Great Tradition*, which in 1949 he reviewed in his last column for the *Observer*, is perfectly captured by the review's heading: 'Exclusive Club'.[21] 'One has the impression', Orwell comments, 'that what Dr. Leavis most wants to do is to induce in the reader a feeling of due reverence towards the "great" and of due irreverence towards everybody else. One should read, he seems to imply, with one eye always on the scale of values, like a wine-drinker reminding himself of the price per bottle at every sip'. Sectarian exclusiveness appealed to Orwell just as little in its religious form. In another late review, this one of Graham Greene's novel *The Heart of the Matter*, Orwell suggests that Greene 'appears to share the idea, which has been floating around ever since Baudelaire, that there is something rather *distingué* in being damned; Hell is a sort of high-class night club, entry to which is reserved for Catholics only, since the others, the non-Catholics, are too ignorant to be held guilty, like the beasts that perish' (*CE*, IV, 441).

Orwell's 1942 review of three of Eliot's *Four Quartets* is especially instructive for the way in which Orwell levels his criterion of sincerity against religious orthodoxy.[22] Comparing these late poems unfavourably with Eliot's earlier work, Orwell says: 'It is clear that something has departed, some kind of current has been switched off, the later verse does not _contain_ the earlier, even if it is claimed as an improvement upon it. I think one is justified in explaining this by a deterioration in Mr Eliot's subject matter' (CE, II, 237). What Orwell means by a 'deterioration in subject matter' turns out to be Eliot's relinquishment of an essentially sceptical world-view in favour of an Anglo-Catholic one. It seems natural to ask: Is Orwell not violating his own declared tenets here? Is he not using the idea-content of Eliot's poems in an embarrassingly literal fashion to determine their artistic worth?

I believe he is not. Ultimately, his standard of judgement in the review comes down not to ideological 'rightness' or 'wrongness', but to linguistic vibrancy – itself an offshoot of sincerity. The crux of his argument depends – here as so often in his criticism – on a comparison between quoted passages, in this instance between the closing lines of 'The Dry Salvages' and two stanzas from the much earlier 'Whispers of Immortality'. Orwell comments, 'I do not think it is questionable that the [passage from the earlier poem] is superior as verse, and also more intense in feeling' (CE, II, 238). Clearly, Orwell's judgement here proceeds from sensibility, not from ideology. He does not indulge his own religious scepticism at the expense of honesty in evaluation; rather, he brings in the 'deterioration in subject matter' _a posteriori_, to account for a perceived decline in poetic force. Once again, Orwell trusts that the sincerity of the writer's conviction will make itself felt in the intensity of his language, while tepid beliefs will trickle languidly into tepid verse.

Orwell's logic leads to the conclusion that Eliot, like any other poet, can write with energising sincerity only when he sets himself to express feelings belonging peculiarly to his own world and time. The early poems 'were an end-product, the last gasp of a cultural tradition, poems which spoke only for the cultivated third-generation _rentier_, for people able to feel and criticise but no longer able to act' (CE, II, 239). All the same, 'that was the price that had to be paid, at any rate at that time, for writing a poem worth reading. The mood of lassitude, irony, disbelief, disgust, and not the sort of beefy enthusiasm demanded by the Squires and Herberts, was what sensitive people actually felt'. As a result, '"Prufrock" is an expression of futility, but it is also a poem of wonderful vitality and power, culminating in a sort of rocket-burst in the closing stanzas' (*CE*, II, 239–40). Eliot's dilemma, then, is that conventional, outworn Christian belief is impotent to provide him with the vivid stimulus he had once derived from his bleak but timely unbelief. If it is obvious here that Orwell's assumptions are eminently debatable, it is equally obvious that they involve something more than a doctrinaire imposing of his own belief, or unbelief, on another writer's achievement.

Closely allied to sincerity, for its power to bridge human solitudes, is another of Orwell's critical touchstones: doubleness of perspective. Orwell observes:

The interest of [Henry Miller's] *Tropic of Cancer* was that it cast a kind of bridge across the frightful gulf which exists, in fiction, between the intellectual and the man-in-the-street . . . . Books about ordinary people behaving in an ordinary manner are extremely rare, because they can only be written by someone who is capable of standing both inside and outside the ordinary man, as Joyce for instance stands inside and outside Bloom; but this involves admitting that you yourself *are* an ordinary person for nine-tenths of the time, which is exactly what no intellectual ever wants to do. (*CE*, I, 230)

It is Charles Dickens's doubleness of vision that prompts Orwell to admire the treatment of characters like the Murdstones in *David Copperfield*: 'Dickens has been able to stand both inside and outside the child's mind, in such a way that the same scene can be wild burlesque or sinister reality, according to the age at which one reads it' (*CE*, I, 424). Dickens's excellence here derives from his genius as a builder of bridges between the child's sensibility and the adult's. Yet Dickens fails in his presentment of work, as Orwell explains to Humphry House, because his vision here remains single and external: 'when Dickens gives a detailed description of someone working, it is always someone seen from the outside and usually a burlesque (like Wemmick or Venus)' (*CE*, I, 531). Orwell applies his criterion of the double perspective impartially, not only to the fiction of a Dickens or a Joyce but also to a popular story like Nevil Shute's *Landfall*, praising Shute's treatment of his pilot-protagonist: 'He sees the young airman's point of view, because, presumably he has at some time shared his experiences. He can stand inside him as well as outside him and realise that he is heroic as well as childish, competent as well as silly' (*CE*, II, 45). Orwell's emphasis on duality of vision shades into an appetite for the paradoxical; it is perhaps not so surprising that he harboured a life-long admiration for Oscar Wilde.

I have been trying to show that some, if not all, of the assumptions Orwell brought to the task of literary criticism were, however debatable, far from simplistic. I will now turn to one more painfully naive-sounding assumption with which he has been attributed. 'For Orwell', according once again to Alldritt, 'content and style are easily separated . . . . The modern belief in the indissoluble fusion of language and meaning . . . has no place in Orwell's criticism'.[23] There are a number of statements scattered through Orwell's writings that lend credence to Alldritt's charge. In as late an essay as 'The Prevention of Literature' Orwell is still capable of discussing form, at least in poetry, as though it could be neatly dissociated from substance. Arguing that 'it is not certain whether the effects of totalitarianism upon verse need be so deadly as its effects on prose', he backs up this dubious supposition by explaining that

> what the poet is saying – that is, what his poem 'means' if translated into prose – is relatively unimportant even to himself. The thought contained in a poem is always simple, and is no more the primary purpose of the poem than the anecdote is the primary purpose of a picture. A poem is an arrangement of sounds and associations, as a painting is an arrangement of brush-marks. (*CE*, IV, 67)

But if Orwell on occasion voices what amounts to a glibly aestheticist theory, in what he says elsewhere he flagrantly parts company with his more simplistic theoretical self. An essay like 'The Meaning of a Poem' could be taken virtually as a point-blank rebuttal of the views advanced in 'The Prevention of Literature'. After demonstrating how, in 'Felix Randal', Hopkins 'by combination of sound and association . . . manages to lift an ordinary village death on to the plane of tragedy', Orwell continues:

> But that tragic effect cannot simply exist in the void, on the strength of a certain combination of syllables. One cannot regard a poem as simply a pattern of words on paper, like a sort of mosaic. This poem is moving because of its sound, its musical qualities, but it is also moving because of an emotional content

which could not be there if Hopkins's philosophy and beliefs were different from what they were. (*CE*, II, 132)

One could wish that the Orwell who was writing in 1946 had listened more attentively to the Orwell who spoke these words over the BBC in 1941.

At its best, Orwell's criticism is informed by the conviction, expressed in the essay 'New Words', that 'aesthetic and moral considerations are in any case inextricable' (*CE*, II, 4). His sensitivity to the *rapport* between style and meaning manifests itself conspicuously in regard to Joyce's *Ulysses*. 'Joyce actually is more of a "pure artist" than most writers', he acknowledges in 'Inside the Whale':

> But *Ulysses* could not have been written by someone who was merely dabbling with word-patterns; it is the product of a special vision of life, the vision of a Catholic who has lost his faith. What Joyce is saying is 'Here is life without God. Just look at it!' and his technical innovations, important though they are, are there primarily to serve this purpose. (*CE*, I, 508)

Years earlier, in a letter to Brenda Salkeld, Orwell had produced a more detailed analysis of the bearing of Joyce's experiments with style:

> When I first came on *Ulysses* it was some odd chapters in a review, and I happened to strike that passage where Gerty Macdowell is soliloquizing. It then seemed to me a sort of elephantine joke to write the whole passage in the style of the Heartsease library, but I now see that you could not possible display the interior of the girl's mind so well in any other way, except at much greater length. You will remember no doubt how well the horrid little narcissistic touches about her 'girlish treasures' and being 'lost in dreams' etc. were done. Similarly Bloom, Mrs B and Dedalus are all given styles of their own, to display the different qualities of their minds. (*CE*, I, 126)

If all this has by now become a commonplace of Joyce criticism, the point is that it was *not* such a commonplace in 1933. Orwell, though hardly a 'Joyce scholar', still shows an impressive independence of insight into sophisticated matters of stylistic innovation.

I will conclude by looking in some detail at one of Orwell's better-known longer pieces, his 1942 essay on Kipling. Although this essay has been called 'one of [Orwell's] most tentative and inconclusive',[24] I would argue that it displays Orwell's characteristic balance between flexibility and conclusiveness, and that it easily eclipses the essay to which it serves as a reply, T. S. Eliot's introduction to his *A Choice of Kipling's Verse* (1941). In the very structure of his essay, Eliot leaves himself more open than Orwell to the charge of separating concerns of content arbitrarily from concerns of style. The first of his two numbered sections is devoted almost exclusively to matters of technique and genre. Eliot first tries to classify Kipling's poems according to traditional 'type'; he then searches for appropriate 'poetic criteria' to apply to a poet as 'journalistic' as Kipling,[25] and goes on to enumerate the precedents that might have influenced Kipling, dwelling especially on the ballad tradition. The second section of Eliot's essay consists, by contrast, mainly of a discussion of Kipling's politics, which Eliot is not reluctant to explain or indeed to defend. He speaks of Kipling's depth of affection for India, and of his feeling for the reality of imperial rule and the responsibilities that it entails. He gives some account of Kipling's effort to cultivate, late in life, the 'historical imagination'. Only in his final pages does Eliot return to more strictly 'poetic' concerns, warning against too scrupulous an endeavour to distinguish between 'poetry' and mere 'verse' in Kipling's *oeuvre*. Nowhere in the essay does he make explicit connections between Kipling's hallmarks as a poet and either his political opinions or the social context within which those opinions took shape.

Orwell begins his essay in typical fashion by scrutinising Kipling's political beliefs, but then moves towards an encompassing judgement that combines the political with the aesthetic.[26] An example of Orwell's incisiveness about the bearing of political attitudes on literary effects is his comment on the power Kipling draws from his imperviousness to Liberal cant:

> We all live by robbing Asiatic coolies, and those of us who are 'enlightened' all maintain that those coolies ought to be set free; but our standard of living, and hence our 'enlightenment', demands that the robbery shall continue. A humanitarian is always a hypocrite, and Kipling's understanding of this is perhaps the central secret of his power to create telling phrases. It would be difficult to hit off the one-eyed pacifism of the

English in fewer words than in the phrase, 'making mock of uniforms that guard you while you sleep'. (*CE*, II, 187)

Orwell's anti-pacifist bias of the early war years is patent in this extract, and might be seized upon as evidence that his literary judgements are at bottom politically tendentious. Nevertheless, Orwell is far from using Kipling merely as a club with which to bludgeon liberal pieties. Where Eliot praises Kipling for reviving the ballad tradition, Orwell sees Kipling's peculiar way of handling the ballad as reflecting his own privileged social position: 'In the ancient ballads the lord and the peasant speak the same language. This is impossible to Kipling, who is looking down a distorting class perspective' (*CE*, II, 189).

Ironically, the novelist Orwell's comments on Kipling's use of language and of popular verse-forms turns out to be more to the point than the poet Eliot's. Discussing the origins of Kipling's popularity, Eliot observes: 'There is always a potential public for the ballad: but the social conditions of modern society make it difficult for the good ballad to be written. It is perhaps more difficult now than it was at the time when *Barrack-Room Ballads* were written: for Kipling had at least the inspiration and refreshment of the living music-hall.'[27] Orwell's estimate of such 'inspiration and refreshment' is amusingly at variance with Eliot's:

> The trouble is that whenever an aesthetic judgement on Kipling's work seems to be called for, Mr Eliot is too much on the defensive to be able to speak plainly. What he does not say, and what I think one ought to start by saying in any discussion of Kipling, is that most of Kipling's verse is so horribly vulgar that it gives one the same sensation as one gets from watching a third-rate music-hall performer recite 'The Pigtail of Wu Fang Fu' with the purple limelight on his face, *and yet* there is much of it that is capable of giving pleasure to people who know what poetry means. At his worst, and also at his most vital, in poems like 'Gunga Din' or 'Danny Deever', Kipling is almost a shameful pleasure, like the taste for cheap sweets that some people secretly carry into middle life. (*CE*, II, 193–4)

One might condemn the label Orwell coined for such verse – 'good bad poetry' – as itself an evasive compromise of critical judgement, 'a means', as Alldritt says, 'of justifying literary admirations which the critical intelligence cannot support'.[28] In practice, however, Orwell's 'good bad' category served him as a means of confronting an unpleasant but stubborn fact: the isolation of the English social and cultural élite, to which he belonged, from the general public and its tastes. 'It is no use pretending', he urges toward the end of the Kipling essay, 'that in an age like our own, "good" poetry can have any genuine popularity. It is, and must be, the cult of a very few people, the least tolerated of the arts . . . . Ours is a civilisation in which the very word "poetry" evokes a hostile snigger or, at best, the sort of frozen disgust that most people feel when they hear the word "God"' (*CE*, II, 194–5). Kipling's importance for Orwell (like that, on a higher level, of Dickens) lay partly in his power to survive as a kind of precious 'missing link', a cultural bridge between the connoisseur and the man in the street.

> The fact that such a thing as good bad poetry can exist is a sign of the emotional overlap between the intellectual and the ordinary man. The intellectual *is* different from the ordinary man, but only in certain sections of his personality, and even then not all the time. But what is the peculiarity of a good bad poem? A good bad poem is a graceful monument to the obvious. It records in memorable form . . . some emotion which very nearly every human being can share. (*CE*, II, 195)

Highly as Orwell may prize Kipling as a rare instance of cultural 'overlap', he does not allow that consideration to determine his final estimate of Kipling's literary standing. As the concluding comparison between Dickens and Tolstoy in his Dickens essay also shows, Orwell viewed universality of appeal as a valid criterion of artistic worth, but certainly not as the sole criterion. Similarly, his respect for the seriousness of some of Kipling's political attitudes does not prevent him from denying – unlike Eliot – 'that Kipling's view of life, as a whole, can be accepted or even forgiven by any civilised person' (*CE*, II, 184). Like any number of Orwell's essays, the one on Kipling demonstrates Orwell's almost Keatsian faculty for entertaining apparently conflicting ideas without severe strain or confusion.

Between 'negative capability' and sheer self-negation the line in Orwell's writings is sometimes bewilderingly thin. Yet much of the fascination of Orwell's criticism comes from his incurable habit of contending with himself: about the very possibility of literary interpretation, about its proper function, about the nature of literary values. In exploring the relations between fiction and reality, poetry and belief, the writer's ego and the world he imagines, Orwell tried out a variety of shifting positions. Some of these may look untenable today, but few of them were simply borrowed ready-made without receiving Orwell's searching scrutiny. We ourselves have scant cause to mimic the hero of Tennyson's 'Locksley Hall', counting our glorious gains while casting a patronising glance backward at the shade of George Orwell, left miles behind along the ringing grooves of changing critical fashion. Many of the fundamental issues that Orwell bravely and at times rashly engaged remain with us, however they may have been transformed by the years. To those issues Orwell brought a breadth of experience and – to use his own slippery term – a sincerity that would be difficult to match today. He expressed his literary opinions, right-headed and wrong-headed, in language that is forceful, lucid and unpretentious – qualities not notably conspicuous among us academic newspeakers of 1984 and *passim*. Orwell as a literary critic is perhaps almost a shameful pleasure, and I may be convicted of having carried a taste for cheap sweets into middle life. For all that, I would gladly exchange pounds of elaborately confectioned analysis by the most impeccably certified of professionals for the study of Conrad that another year or two of life might have enabled Orwell to place in our hands. Perhaps the most fitting way to end a discussion of Orwell as a critic is to recall the epigraph to *Coming Up for Air*: 'He's dead, but he won't lie down'.

Panel Discussion

Peter Buitenhuis

I am very happy to welcome these four speakers to the table: Michael Ross from McMaster University; Bernard Crick; Ian Slater, novelist, script-writer and author of the recent book on Orwell, *The Road to Airstrip One*, and George Feaver of the University of British Columbia, who raised some issues yesterday which can be fruitfully debated at this point.

The panel should address a number of questions that came up in the course of the last three days. The first has to do with the issue of Orwell's political affiliation, particularly in his last years. Was he a socialist or was he a liberal? Was he moving towards liberalism, or was he moving towards the right? Secondly, we should deal with the claim made yesterday that *Nineteen Eighty-Four* is a testament of despair. The third issue was raised by Bernard Crick this morning in relation to Ross's paper on Orwell as a literary critic. Is it to be taken for granted that the critic in the old sense has disappeared – that we will now be saddled with endless tomes of academic criticism and nothing else? Has the language of criticism become so mired in complexity and jargon as to exclude the layman from such intricacies? And lastly, another issue was raised this morning: if this conference is re-assessing Orwell, should we not also be re-assessing his earlier novels? Almost all the proposals we received and accepted for this conference were in fact concerned with *Nineteen Eighty-Four* and with the criticism. Very little was received in connection with the earlier fiction. Should we be concerned with this imbalance?

George Feaver

Maybe I should start, since we are privileged to have Bernard Crick in our midst, and this question arises out of his work. In a famous letter, Orwell writes: 'My recent novel [*Nineteen Eighty-Four*] is not intended as an attack on socialism or on the British Labour Party (of which I am a supporter) but as a show-up of the perversions to which a centralised economy is liable and which have already been partly realised in Communism and Fascism'. Now it seems to me that Bernard Crick's biography of Orwell is an especially important document in this connection. Julian Symonds says of Bernard's book: 'the work contains masses of material to be found nowhere else and is the biography that anybody interested in Orwell's life must consult . . . ; however little they agree with its approach, that will remain true.' As we are all aware, there has been very considerable debate over Orwell's literary remains: some contending that he is a neo-conservative – or would be if he were with us – and others that he is a socialist. It seems to me that he would nowadays be termed what he was in his life, a liberal/socialist in the British tradition. Bernard Crick's characterisation of Orwell as a democratic socialist is one by which Orwell imagines as an ideal end or ultimate aim a world in which there would be free equals. My characterisation of his beliefs would be that he desired not so much free equals as aspirations to an equality of liberty. I agree with Ian Slater's contention in his new book *Orwell: The Road to Airstrip One* that Orwell's pessimism is not defeatism. This is consistent with my characterisation of him as someone who was not a democratic socialist but a social democrat. I will stop there so as to get things going.

Bernard Crick

I know perfectly well that social democrat has become the name of a political party now in Britain, and Orwell's old friend Tosco Fyvel has claimed that if he were alive today Orwell would be a social democrat: Tosco is a social democrat. Malcolm Muggeridge is sure he would be a Christian if he were alive today and also an anti-Semite, which is rather strange. *Encounter* and the CIA and all that crowd were certain that he would be living in New York above the 10th floor somewhere. I think this is a silly controversy. The only scholarly thing to do is to locate somebody at their last known address. I think that if Orwell had lived he wouldn't have joined the social democratic party but would probably have stayed and fought it out within the Labour Party. When I was a student, social democrat meant someone influenced by the German revision-ist Marxist philosophy – they were to the left of those who called themselves democratic socialists. Now the thing is more or less turned round. I think you have got to take Orwell's socialism very seriously. Whether one says free equals or equality and freedom I think that is very much a political philosopher's matter of nuance; whether one is saying that you cannot have a free society without a substantial condition of equality or whether one says equality is also a moral end in itself. I think Orwell did believe it was a moral end in itself but never at the cost of sacrificing liberty: he was perfectly determined to try to balance the two.

We should also consider the other claim that has been made lately by Norman Podhoretz that Orwell was leaning towards the right, and if he had lived would have become a cold warrior. It seems to me that kind of stuff is really obsessive. To put Orwell in the camp of the cold war is in an odd way to distort the possibility that people could be militant, stalwart and brave anti-communists – he was as brave as to be an anti-communist in 1936 and onwards – and yet nonetheless not espouse the American camp. There are some European socialists who believe in a third force – whether it is an intellectual delusion or not – or at least who believe in keeping some separate identity. There was a lot of that sort of belief around in the 1940s and there is a lot around now.

Ian Slater

I would like to make a few comments with regard to the question about whether or not *Nineteen Eighty-Four* is a testament of despair in relation to an experience I had this year which I might share with you. Before I begin I would like to say that it seems to me a number of people forget that Orwell set Airstrip One in England because he felt that if that kind of totalitarianism could triumph in a country with a relatively long democratic tradition, it could triumph anywhere. I happen to think that is a point worth making, because recently I read in our local [Vancouver] press a rather long article comparing *Nineteen Eighty-Four* with Canadian politics and society. I was not convinced of any connection, and indeed the piece reminded me of Orwell's point that, while we must resist seeing the world in terms of black and white, not all countries are the same, and there is a great deal of difference between living in a country where you can be dragged out of bed at four in the morning without a police warrant and a country that requires police to knock on your door and at least issue you a warrant. It seems to me that is worth saying in terms of the temptation we have to second some of Orwell's views for our own society. That's not to say that there aren't some tendencies worth watching, but we should bear in mind the importance of degree.

That was driven home to me earlier this year when I was invited to a PEN conference in Bled, in northern Yugoslavia, for which Orwell was the theme. On arriving, I observed several things which reminded me of *Nineteen Eighty-Four*. Most of the eastern bloc countries had refused to attend: Romania, Hungary and a few others, Bulgaria, and, of course, Albania. I don't think anyone told Albania it was on. The man from Moscow did come after an initial refusal. One of the other eastern representatives who did attend mumbled something to me rather angrily that that is just like Moscow: they refuse and then they finally send someone just to check it out. At the beginning of the conference, after the obligatory anti-US barrage, we got down to business. The business was in the first place an attack by the Moscow representative on Orwell's innocence and naivety, which is about the worst thing a Russian can say to you. He also deeply resented the fact that, in *Animal Farm*, Orwell characterised all the Soviet people as pigs. That was of course immediately countered by a Yugoslav representative who said at some length that the pigs weren't the Russian people but were Stalin and his lieutenants. The Moscow man seemed a little nonplussed by this but carried on anyway. One noticed how deep the hatred of the Soviet system is. That is true whether they come from the Near or the Far Eastern bloc. The current Czechoslovakian joke was that someone asked a Czech if he had three wishes, what would they be? He said: 'My first wish would be that China would invade Czechoslovakia; my second wish is that China would invade Czechoslovakia, and my third wish is that China would invade Czechoslovakia.' Why would he want that? The reply was that the Chinese would have to cross Russia six times. So the depth of animosity was quite extraordinary. Later on, as we were touring the mountains around Bled, one of the eastern representatives kept mumbling to me. 'Where is he, that man from Moscow? Where's Big Brother?' The people from the eastern bloc were using *Nineteen Eighty-Four* as a very real description of their life both in the physical sense in the run-down nature of Oceania and also in the psychological sense.

Later I was invited to give an address at the Communist Youth

Palace in Belgrade, to speak at the University, to see a film of *Nineteen Eighty-Four* and join a panel discussion on the film. At lunch there was great excitement about the film, and I was told that there would be a tremendous fight for seats. So I turned up early, and indeed the theatre was jam packed. It was the première performance of *Nineteen Eighty-Four* – I don't mean the new one; I mean the old one. It was the first time it had been shown in Yugoslavia, and it was very well-translated. The line which got the best response – essentially a non-political line – was when Julia comes into the hide-away. Winston says, 'What have you got there?' She says, 'Open it and see'. He opens the package and smells it and says, 'Coffee, real coffee!' The theatre just about came apart because at that time Yugoslavia was going through that exact experience. Afterwards, at the panel discussion, the mood was so pessimistic that one felt constrained to try to add a little levity to the proceedings, so I read one of my favourite passages in an attempt to convey the fact that, while *Nineteen Eighty-Four* is dismal in its outlook, Orwell did talk about some hope in the future. If we had courage enough to fight against totalitarianism, it need not take us over. So I read the following passage from an essay of 1946:

At any rate spring is here, even in London, N.1, and they can't stop you enjoying it. This is a satisfying reflection. How many a time I have stood watching the toads mating or a pair of hares having a boxing match in the young corn, and thought of all the important persons who would stop me from enjoying this if they could. But luckily they can't. So as long as you are not actually ill, hungry, frightened or immured in a prison or a holiday camp, spring is still spring. The atom bombs are piling up in the factories, the police are prowling through the cities, the lies are streaming from loudspeakers, but the earth is still going round the sun, and neither the dictators nor the bureaucrats, deeply as they disapprove of the process, are able to prevent it.

Immediately as I ended that quote, one of the other panellists, a foreign editor from the Yugoslav journal *Nim*, turned to me and said: 'They're working on it.'

George Feaver

It seems to me there is a very understandable tendency to identify the world of *Nineteen Eighty-Four* with the Soviet satellite countries and the USSR itself. No doubt there is a great deal of truth in that but what worries me a bit is that it might lead to an attitude to some complacency on our part, as if to say, 'Just look at those poor devils living in the world of *Nineteen Eighty-Four* over there, while we are happily exempt. Orwell's prophecies have come true for them, but thank God not for us.' I'm just not convinced that that's an entirely legitimate way of looking at the world or that Orwell himself would necessarily have looked at it that way.

Ian Slater

That's quite true. That is why I began with remembering that he mentioned Airstrip One as being England, otherwise you would fall into a trap, just thinking about the Soviet Union.

I will wind up with a couple of other comments. One that I was very impressed by their bravery in Belgrade, at having such a conference and panel discussion. Before I began my speaking engagements I asked the Canadian embassy official if there was any possible danger to me. He said, 'Well, of course not. It is however a very risky business for them.' The entire editorial staff of a major newspaper had just been fired because they were starting to discuss things which were considered too liberal. He said it would be interesting to watch the discussion after the film, to see what would happen. At the end of the discussion I was going to congratulate the panel on what I thought – that I was encouraged that they would raise such issues in their country, and that this boded well for the future. But I decided not to for the very obvious reason that it might only pour oil on the official fire. But it also reminded me of what Orwell had said – that the system was already creating some kind of self-censorship for me. I was already starting to think, perhaps I shouldn't say this; perhaps I shouldn't say that. I noticed that when any of my comments were translated the translator was very careful to preface the translation with, 'Professor Slater says this . . . . Professor Slater's view is so and so'. He was careful to put some distance between the translator and the commentator.

The last thing I want to comment on is the absence of popular critics in our time. While we have many academic critics because of the scholarly journals, I think there is a real lack of popular criticism, particularly in the North American media. Two of the reasons for this are economic and technological. Those of you who read Vancouver newspapers will know that it is much more economical to tear off reviews of books from the wire services from New York than it is to hire local reviewers. For a few cents a major newspaper chain can simply take reviews off the wire. A very few critics get a very large audience while many more potential critics are locked out. There are three publications in New York which can seal your fate as a novelist. One is *Publishers' Weekly*, the second is *John Barkham Reviews*, and the third is the *Virginia Kirkus Review Service*. They get advance copies of the book and if they give it good reviews, the book is away. Popular critical coverage is just icing on the cake. If they give it bad reviews, the result is catastrophic in the publishing house. The initial run is immediately cut to about a quarter – so there are not so many books out; there is little criticism and the whole thing is buried before it gets off the ground.

Peter Buitenhuis

I think the time has come to open the questions from the floor.

Questioner

Will the panel comment on the series of positions which Orwell marked out for himself throughout his career, since we tend to treat that career as a monolithic one.

Michael Ross

I can certainly see Orwell's novels as a kind of series that leads up to the best known of his novels, *Animal Farm* and *Nineteen Eighty-Four*. I would maintain that all his concerns are there in the earlier novels, at least in embryo and even more. For that reason I think those novels deserve more attention than they have received.

Bernard Crick

Can I just make a comment on that point. I don't see his novels as a series. I see him as thrashing around all over the place. It seems to me that it is even accidental that his first two novels got printed rather than the six or seven that got turned down and destroyed. *Burmese Days* is anti-imperialist, but it isn't necessarily socialist. *A Clergyman's Daughter* is about all kinds of things – really it is a hell of a muddle – but it's about the church, again not necessarily; it's secular. *Keep the Aspidistra Flying* is about the cult of failure. If you succeed, it is a sign that you are a right bastard or that you are selling out. Then comes Spain – crucial for his socialism and for his public commitments. *Coming Up For Air* is in a sense a socialist novel – it's a curious one – because the war is going to destroy everything, but from the ruins will come some sort of a future – a sort of Trotskyite pipe-dream. Tom Bowly is an engaging human figure, but he is rotten with nostalgia: Orwell makes him rotten. I think it is dangerous to look backwards on someone's life. We see series and sequences and we are picking out things that lead to *Nineteen Eighty-Four*, but I don't think that is the end of the sequence. It is a teleological fantasy. If you begin with *Nineteen Eighty-Four*, then you are assuming it is his last work, but of course it was because he died. He was already working on something else.

Ian Slater

I think that one common thread that you might find in Orwell before Spain – even though he might have been thrashing around – is his belief that the rich were always wrong and the poor were always right. That is an attitude he changed later on, after Spain. But I think in the three novels you mention that's a consistent notion.

Michael Ross

I just wanted to comment briefly on the question as to whether Orwell's earlier novels need to be reassessed. It seems to me that Orwell's criterion of survival might have some relevance here.

There is some good reason why *Nineteen Eighty-Four* and *Animal Farm*, in particular, are the novels that continue to be read. They are simply perceived to be more successful – more coherent and more relevant than the earlier ones. That is simply reaffirming the conventional wisdom, but I think there is something to be said for the view that those novels are more focused and more coherent and make their point much more effectively than the earlier ones did.

Ian Slater

I think there is truth in that, but it can go too far. I have the feeling that the early novels, *Keep the Aspidistra Flying, A Clergyman's Daughter*, and especially *Coming Up For Air*, will be much better known in the years to come. Just for editorial and financial reasons those books will be thrust forward much more than they ever have been before. Purely because of distribution they will become better known and valued. They are underrated novels and we will see them rise to some prominence.

Questioner

Would the panel explore the relation between literature and politics, which I believe has not been sufficiently explored at this conference, particularly in view of Orwell's idiosyncratic view of politics. Why does this intimate relationship between politics and literature seem to have diminished in our time as compared to the 1930s and 1940s?

Bernard Crick

Although it has a declining readership I think the novel is still the main carrier of political and moral ideas. We are perhaps too worried about this problem at the moment. Maybe the Marxist critics have really muddied the waters with the old belief that there should be, somehow, a socialist novel. The novel still pushes on about politics. Look at *The Lord of the Flies*, for example, or Doris Lessing's novels, and I don't mean her South African novels, but her Sci Fi ones, and *The Memoirs of a Survivor*.

There is a problem within literary criticism which the universities have created. As a political philosopher I find that everything that people have said about the internalisation of literary criticism completely parallels political philosophy. I mean we don't influence the man in the street. Very few of us review books in popular periodicals. We don't stand in public positions.

Ian Slater

I do want to respond to an earlier comment about *Nineteen Eighty-Four* being a state of mind. I think that is a very worthwhile observation – mainly because I made it in my book. But apart from that I think we are tempted to look too much at the mechanical structure of *Nineteen Eighty-Four* and forget what Orwell warned us – that that kind of madness doesn't belong either on the right or the left – that it can come from any direction, and that's what we have to guard against, in ourselves, not from anybody else.

Bernard Crick

It has suddenly struck me that there was an intellectual continuity between *Animal Farm* and *Nineteen Eighty-Four*. One is the story of the revolution betrayed and the other is the story of the ever afterwards. One could say that the pre-war novels are about the good old socialist novelist's projects about the rotten old order. *Coming Up For Air* is about the inevitability of its collapse. There is a kind of continuity there, I suppose.

Peter Buitenhuis

With that more or less ringing statement I will draw this panel session to a close. I wish to thank all the speakers in the conference, and the excellent and attentive audience. I'd like also to mention those people who put in so much work organising the conference, under the direction of Steve Duguid from Continuing Studies at Simon Fraser. All we have to do now is say farewell to 1984. Thank you.

Notes and References

Unless otherwise cited, the following texts by Orwell have been used:
The Collected Essays, Journalism and Letters of George Orwell, ed. Sonia Orwell
and Ian Angus, 4 vols (London: Secker and Warburg, 1968). Abbr. *CE*.
Nineteen Eighty-Four, ed. Bernard Crick (Oxford: Clarendon Press, 1984).

INTRODUCTION

ORWELL AND ENGLISH SOCIALISM

1. *Burmese Days*, p. 69. References to this text and to *The Road to Wigan Pier*, *Homage to Catalonia*, and *The Lion and the Unicorn* are taken from the Secker & Warburg Uniform Edition.
2. *The Road to Wigan Pier*, pp. 173–4 and 182.
3. Ibid., p. 214.
4. Bernard Crick, *Socialist Values and Time*, Fabian Tract 495 (London, 1984).
5. *The Road to Wigan Pier*, pp. 162–3.
6. *Homage to Catalonia*, pp. 26–7 and 69–70.
7. *The Lion and the Unicorn*, p. 67.
8. 'My Country Right or Left', in *CE*, I, 539–40. This essay was originally published in the Penguin *Folios of New Writing* (Autumn 1940), of which whole sections were re-used in *The Lion and the Unicorn*; see pp. 87–8 for example.
9. *The Lion and the Unicorn*, pp. 28–9.
10. Ibid., pp. 73–4.
11. Ibid., pp. 85–6. A fuller discussion of *The Lion and the Unicorn* can be found in this author's introduction to the Penguin edition of 1982.
12. As he did in addressing an American audience in 'Britain's Struggle for Survival', *Commentary* (New York, October 1948), then a left-wing journal. Orwell's own title was 'The Labour Government After Three Years'. This is another of those annoying omissions from the *Collected Essays* which create in the last volume the illusion that he 'went off' socialist writing while composing *Nineteen Eighty-Four*.
13. 'Toward European Unity', *CE*, IV, 370–5.
14. *CE*, III, 118–9.
15. *The Lion and the Unicorn*, p. 49. Elsewhere he speaks about the danger of 'oligarchical collectivism'.
16. 'Why I Write', *CE*, I, 6.
17. 'The Prevention of Literature', *CE*, IV, 60.
18. 'Writers and Leviathan', *CE*, IV, 412.
19. 'What Is Socialism?', *Manchester Evening News*, 31 January 1946; a particularly bad omission from the *CE*. For a discussion of this issue see this author's *George Orwell: A Life* (Harmondsworth: Penguin, 1982), p. 621.
20. *CE*, III, 64.

PART ONE: *NINETEEN-EIGHTY FOUR*

1. GEORGE ORWELL'S *NINETEEN EIGHTY-FOUR*:
THE FUTURE THAT BECOMES THE PAST

1. Compare, for example, the effect of the devil in 'The Devil in the Belfry', in Edgar Allan Poe, *The Complete Tales and Poems* (New York: Modern Library, 1938).
2. Samuel L. Macey, *Clocks and the Cosmos: Time in Western Life and Thought* (Hamden, Conn.: Archon Books, 1980), pp. 187–92.
3. Aldous Huxley, *Brave New World* (Harmondsworth: Penguin, 1955), pp. 177–80, *passim*; Yevgeny Zamyatin, *We*, trans. Mirra Ginsburg (New York: Viking Press, 1972), closing paragraphs and *passim*.
4. Samuel Taylor Coleridge, *Biographia Literaria*, ed. George Watson (London: Dent, 1965), pp. 91, 48, and Chapter VIII, 'On the Imagination, or Esemplastic Power'.
5. There are even more complex dreams. After telling us that 'The conspiracy that he had dreamed of did exist,' Winston is next involved in 'A vast luminous dream in which his whole life seemed to stretch out before him like a landscape on a summer evening . . . . It had all occurred inside the glass paperweight but the surface of the glass was the dome of the sky . . . . The dream had also been comprehended by – indeed, in some sense it had consisted in – a gesture of the arm made by his mother, and made again thirty years later by the Jewish woman . . . trying to shelter the boy from the bullets' (pp. 27, 130–1, 134). If Winston dreams of his whole life 'like a landscape on a summer evening', it may be worth noting that the only months mentioned in the year 1984 are April through August with the pointed exception of July. Julia – which means 'youthful one' – is the feminine form of Julius for whom July is named.
6. The title date of 1984 might well derive from a reversal of the last two digits of the date of writing in 1948. Since we learn on more than one occasion that the Party proposes to hold back the final version of Newspeak until 2050, it would seem that Orwell has presumed that the more normal period of a century must elapse until all human memory of what was occurring at the time of publication would be entirely eliminated by Ingsoc (pp. 44–6, 243, 251).

2. FROM HISTORY TO PSYCHOLOGICAL GROTESQUE:
THE POLITICS OF SADO-MASOCHISM IN *NINETEEN EIGHTY-
FOUR*

References to frequently cited texts, unless otherwise noted, are to the following editions:

The Collected Essays, Journalism and Letters of George Orwell, ed. Sonia Orwell and Ian Angus (Harmondsworth: Penguin, 1970), vols I–IV; abbreviated in notes as *CE*.

Nineteen Eighty-Four, ed. Bernard Crick (Oxford: Clarendon Press, 1984); cited as *Nineteen Eighty-Four*.

1. Isaac Deutscher, '"1984" – The Mysticism of Cruelty', *Russia in Transition* (New York: Coward McCann, 1957), pp. 230–45.
2. Paul Roazen argues convincingly that despite Orwell's reservations about psychoanalytic theory there is a surprising resemblance between some aspects of his thought and Freud's: 'Orwell, Freud, and *Nineteen Eighty-Four*', *Virginia Quarterly Review*, LIV (1978), 677–95. Other psychological critics tend to use the insights of depth psychology without distinguishing clearly between Orwell's intentions and the unconscious content of the novel. The most comprehensive interpretation of Orwell as novelist is Richard I. Smyer's *Primal Dream and Primal Crime* (Columbia and London: University of Missouri Press, 1979). Smyer establishes a broad affinity between *Nineteen Eighty-Four* and Freud's metapsychology, especially *Civilisation and Its Discontents*, but leaves open the question of how the novel's politics are related to its psychological content. Gorman Beauchamp provides a similar interpretation: 'Of Man's Last Disobedience: Zamyatin's *We* and Orwell's *Nineteen Eighty-Four*', *Comparative Literature Studies*, x (1973), 285–301. Gerald Fiderer sees all of Orwell's fiction as the projection of an unconscious sado-masochism; thus Winston's revolt is unconsciously hypocritical and doomed to ignoble failure: 'Masochism as Literary Strategy: Orwell's Psychological Novels', *Literature and Psychology*, xx (1970), 3–21. Marcus Smith attributes the positive force in the novel entirely to Winston's unconscious: 'The Wall of Blackness: A Psychological Approach to *Nineteen Eighty-Four*', *Modern Fiction Studies*, xiv (1968–9), 423–33. A recent feminist critique by Daphne Patai – 'Gamesmanship and Androcentrism in Orwell's *Nineteen Eighty-Four*', *PMLA*, xcvii (1982), 856–70 – uses games theory to analyse the interaction between Winston and O'Brien. Patai argues that Winston entirely shares O'Brien's values from the start, and that Orwell himself is compromised by them.
3. Further references to the essays will be given in brackets in the text.
4. James Connors finds some distortions in the direction of *Nineteen Eighty-Four* in Orwell's interpretation of *We*: 'Zamyatin's *We* and the Genesis of *Nineteen Eighty-Four*', *Modern Fiction Studies*, xxi (1975), 107–24. Connors argues in detail against the view that Orwell closely followed Zamyatin's novel.
5. Bernard Crick, *George Orwell: A Life* (Harmondsworth: Penguin, 1982), p. 403. Crick demonstrates that Orwell's political position remained substantially unchanged from *The Lion and the Unicorn* to the end of his life.
6. See especially *The Road to Wigan Pier* (Harmondsworth: Penguin, 1962), Chapter 12, p. 164 and pp. 185–8, and two essays concerning H. G. Wells: 'Prophecies of Fascism' (*CE*, II, 45–9) and 'Wells, Hitler and the World State' (*CE*, II, 166–72).
7. 'Never again will you be capable of ordinary human feeling . . . of

love, or friendship, or joy of living, or laughter . . . .' (*Nineteen Eighty-Four*, p. 380). Further references to the novel will be given in the text.

8. The parts of Erich Fromm's *Escape from Freedom* (New York: Avon, 1965) most relevant to O'Brien's lectures to Winston are the section on 'Authoritarianism' in 'Mechanisms of Escape' (Chapter 5, pp. 163–201) and 'Psychology of Nazism' (Chapter 6, pp. 231–64).

9. Orwell presented the proles as a satire on the British working class's passivity and lack of interest in politics, noted in *The Road to Wigan Pier*, but also as a repository of human values and source of potential revolt. I suggest that they fail in the latter respect because Orwell made them so masochistic in contrast to the aggression of the Party. The alternation between submission and domination is projected into the social structure of the future world.

10. The name 'Oceania' may contain a pun on Freud's diagnosis, at the beginning of *Civilisation and Its Discontents*, of the 'oceanic' sense of oneness with the world as a memory of the infant's assimilation of the outside world into the ego.

11. In the new final chapter added to his book on Orwell (*Orwell*, London: Fontana, 1984), Raymond Williams notes the anti-historical quality of Goldstein's book (pp. 111–14). Williams seems to feel that the perversities of 'the book' are related to confusions in Orwell's politics; I assume that Orwell was quite deliberately making 'the book' a part of the nightmare as well as a description of it.

12. This image links O'Brien to German fascism. In *The Lion and the Unicorn* Orwell comments on the 'vision' evoked by the goose-step: 'A military parade is really a kind of ritual dance . . . expressing a certain philosophy of life. The goose-step . . . is simply an affirmation of naked power; contained in it, quite consciously and intentionally, is the vision of a boot crashing down on a face' (*CE*, II, 81).

13. Sigmund Freud, *Civilisation and Its Discontents*, trans. Joan Riviere (Garden City: Doubleday, 1960), Chapter 7, p. 77 and p. 79.

14. Orwell described *Nineteen Eighty-Four* as 'a fantasy, but in the form of a naturalistic novel' (*CE*, IV, 378).

15. In a lecture delivered at the University of British Columbia, 24 November 1984, Bernard Crick pointed out the parodic quality of the novel's last paragraph.

16. William Empson argues that *Nineteen Eighty-Four* includes Christianity among its targets (*Milton's God*, London: Chatto and Windus, 1965, pp. 234–6).

17. James Connors (see note 4) contrasts the positive qualities of the world of *We* with the cynical cruelty of *Nineteen Eighty-Four*. I would point out that O'Brien does offer Winston the pleasure of mystical union, though of a far more perverse kind than the pleasure D–503 finds in the orderly world of *We*.

3. ROOM 101 REVISITED: THE RECONCILATION OF POLITICAL AND PSYCHOLOGICAL DIMENSIONS IN ORWELL'S *NINETEEN EIGHTY-FOUR*

1. Alex Zwerdling, *Orwell and the Left* (New Haven: Yale University Press, 1974), p. 206.
2. George Woodcock, *The Crystal Spirit: A Study of George Orwell* (New York: Funk & Wagnall, 1966), p. 221.
3. Ibid., p. 188.
4. Bernard Crick, *George Orwell: A Life* (Harmondsworth and New York: Penguin, 1980), p. 570.
5. John Wain, 'The Last of George Orwell', *20th Century*, CLV (January 1954) 71.
6. Murray Sperber, 'Gazing into the Glass Paperweight: the Structure and Philosophy of Orwell's *Nineteen Eighty-Four*', *Modern Fiction Studies*, XXVI (1980), 213–16.
7. T. R. Fyvel, 'A Writer's Life', *World Review* (June 1950) 7–20.
8. Czeslaw Milosz, the Polish poet who won the Nobel Prize in 1980, expressed his amazement 'that a writer who never lived in Russia should have such a keen perception into its life'. Cited by Edward M. Thomas, *Orwell*, Writers and Critics series (Edinburgh: Oliver & Boyd, 1965), p. 91.
9. *CE*, III, 222.
10. Ibid.
11. George Orwell [The 1943 outline of *Nineteen Eighty-Four*] in Crick, *Orwell: A Life*, pp. 582–5.
12. Orwell's personal letter to a Mr Moss of 16 December 1943, cited by Bernard Crick, *Orwell: A Life*, p. 468.
13. Edward M. Thomas discusses Orwell's comments on Koestler's Utopian tendencies. Thomas claims that in Winston's character Orwell did point out the flaws of Koestler's unrealistic, Utopian expectations – hence Winston's defeat (*Orwell*, p. 91).
14. Gerald Fiderer, 'Masochism as Literary Strategy: Orwell's Psychological Novels', *Literature and Psychology*, XX (1970), 3–21.
15. Paul Roazen, 'Orwell, Freud, and *Nineteen Eighty-Four*', *Virginia Quarterly Review*, LIV (1978), 690.
16. George Woodcock, *The Crystal Spirit*, p. 218.
17. Edward M. Thomas, *Orwell*, p. 94.
18. Murray Sperber, for example, focuses on Winston's paranoia ('Gazing into the Glass Paperweight', p. 22), while Gerald Fiderer concentrates on Winston's masochism and his 'homosexual resolution of the Oedipus triangle' ('Masochism as Literary Strategy', p. 20). Finally, Marcus Smith considers Winston's phobia of the rats the conclusion of a fixation on the mother. Since Winston also feels that he had offended against his mother, he seeks his punishment through the rats as a condition to be allowed to return to the womb ('The Wall of Blackness', *Modern Fiction Studies*, XIV 1968–9), 423–33.
19. Gerald Fiderer, 'Masochism as Literary Strategy', 20.

20. 'New Words', *CE*, II, 4.
21. Murray Sperber, 'Gazing into the Glass Paperweight', 222; Smith, 'The Wall of Blackness', 426.
22. Here I agree with Daphne Patai's 'Gamesmanship and Androcentrism in Orwell's *Nineteen Eighty-Four'*, (*PMLA*, xcvii, 1982, 856–70), where she discusses Orwell's tendency to use feminine stereotypes in the novel. Nevertheless, I believe that this tendency has little to do with 'sexism' or with the writer's overt or covert tendency for misogyny. Orwell's strategies in *Nineteen Eighty-Four* are directed to emphasise the difference between private and public personality, and he uses the family, with the woman in the centre, as a focus of private values. Also, the story deals with Winston's development – all the other characters are subordinated to his point of view.
23. Murray Sperber, 'Gazing into the Glass Paperweight', 226.

4. FALSE FREEDOM AND ORWELL'S FAUST-BOOK *NINETEEN EIGHTY-FOUR*

1. Bernard Shaw, *Back to Methuselah, A Metabiological Pentateuch* (London: Constable, 1931), Preface, pp. lxiii–lxix.
2. Gilbert Keith Chesterton, *The Everlasting Man* (New York: Image Books, 1955), pp. 202–66.
3. 'In our time the destiny of man presents its meaning in political terms – Thomas Mann'; epigraph to the poem 'Politics' by William Butler Yeats.
4. On the equivocal force of German tradition, see Glenway Wescott, *Images of Truth* (New York: Harper & Row, 1962), Chapter 7, 'Thomas Mann: Will Power and Fiction', esp. pp. 220–30.
5. Marc Angenot, 'Emergence du genre anti-utopique en France, Souvestre, Giraudeau, Robida *et al.*', paper presented to the Canadian Comparative Literature Association, June 1984.
6. David Garnett, (ed.), *Selected Letters of T. E. Lawrence* (London: Reprint Society, 1941), pp. 175–87.
7. James D. Wilkinson, *The Intellectual Resistance in Europe* (Cambridge, Mass.: Harvard University Press, 1981) p. 163.
8. Christian Bernadac, *Le Mystère Otto Rahn (Le Graal et Montsegur): Du Catharisme au Nazisme* (Paris: Editions France-Empire, 1978, esp. Annexe II 'Sources Secrètes de l'Hitlerisme'.
9. Wilkinson, *The Intellectual Resistance in Europe*, pp. 12–13 (without allusion to Orwell).
10. Bernard Crick, *George Orwell: A Life* (London: Secker & Warburg, 1980), p. 169.
11. Wescott, *Images of Truth*, Chapter 8, 'Talks With Thornton Wilder', pp. 280–3.
12. Wilkinson, *The Intellectual Resistance in Europe*, pp. 223–8.
13. Oswald Spengler, *The Decline of the West*, trans. C. F. Atkinson (New York: Knopf, 1926–8), vol. I, pp. 183–218 and vol. II, p. 294 ff.

14. Yevgeny Zamyatin, *We*, trans. G. Zilboorg (New York: Dutton, 1952).
15. *Burmese Days* (London: Victor Gollancz, 1935), Chapter 3. Cf. the syphilis of Mann's hero in *Doctor Faustus*, and of his original, Nietzsche.
16. See, for example, Arkady and Boris Strugatsky, *Definitely Maybe*, trans. A. W. Bouis (London and New York: Macmillan, 1978).
17. Evelyn Waugh, *Scoop* (London: Chapman & Hall, 1938), bk II.
18. See Arthur Koestler's summary of his 1932 report in *The Invisible Writing* (New York: Macmillan, 1954), pp. 52–8.
19. George Orwell, *CE* (London: Secker & Warburg, 1968), IV, 65.
20. Told to the writer by a correspondent, 1946.
21. Abbot Justin McCann (ed.), *The Cloud of Unknowing and Other Treatises* (London: Burns & Oates, 1952), pp. 90–3.
22. Hugh Kenner, *Paradox in Chesterton* (New York: Sheed & Ward, 1947), p. 26.
23. The 'Golden Bull' which promulgated the Constitution of Hungary in 1222 was influenced by the Magna Charta of England; both of them bound a king to justice and customary law.
24. John of Salisbury, *Policraticus*, trans. J. Dickinson (New York, 1927); in J. B. Ross and M. M. McLaughlin, *The Portable Medieval Reader* (New York: Viking Press, 1949), p. 256.
25. Ibid., p. 258.
26. The term 'proper analogy' used in this paper means a likeness existing between different actual things (e.g., tree and bush); the term 'metaphor' here means a likeness which does not so exist (e.g., Richard the Lion-heart).
27. Russell A. Peck, 'Number as Cosmic Language', in David L. Jeffrey (ed.), *By Things Seen: Reference and Recognition in Medieval Thought* (Ottawa: University of Ottawa Press, 1979), p. 50.
28. Pierre Daninos, *Major Thompson and I*, trans. W. M. Thompson (London: Jonathan Cape, 1957), p. 91.
29. René Descartes, *Meditations*, trans. John Veitch, in W. Kaufmann (ed.), *Philosophic Classics, Bacon to Kant* (Englewood Cliffs: Prentice-Hall, 1961), Meditation I, p. 36.
30. Feodor Dostoevsky, *The Brothers Karamazov*, trans. C. Garnett (London: J. M. Dent & Sons, 1927), vol. 2, bk XI, pp. 296–300.
31. Thomas Mann, *The Story of a Novel: The Genesis of Doctor Faustus*, trans. R. & C. Winston (New York: Alfred A. Knopf, 1961), pp. 11, 32, 96.
32. See note 9 above.
33. See, for example, Charles I. Glicksberg, *The Literature of Nihilism* (Lewisburg: Bucknell University Press, 1975).
34. Jean-Paul Sartre, *Existentialism and Humanism*, trans. Philip Mairet (London: Methuen, 1948), p. 34.
35. Shaw, *Back to Methuselah*, p. x.
36. 'I am certain of nothing but of the holiness of the Heart's affections' – John Keats' letter to Bailey, 22 November 1817; and in H. Bloom and L. Trilling (eds), *Romantic Poetry and Prose* (Oxford and New York: Oxford University Press, 1973), p. 765.
37. See notes 24, 25 and 27 above.

38. See, for example, I. V. Blauberg, V. N. Sadovsky, and E. G. Yudin, *Systems Theory: Philosophical and Methodological Problems* (Moscow: Progress Publishers, 1977).

PART TWO: LANGUAGE AND POLITICS

5. WORDS, DEEDS AND THINGS: ORWELL'S QUARREL WITH LANGUAGE

1. Cyril Conolly, *Enemies of Promise* (Harmondsworth: Penguin, 1961), p. 181.
2. Quoted in Erich Heller, *The Artist's Journey into the Interior* (New York: Random House, 1965), p. 218.
3. The classic rebuttal of this view is in the opening sections of Wittgenstein's *Philosophical Investigations*.
4. See H. L. A. Hart, 'The Ascription of Responsibility and Rights', in A. Flew (ed.), *Logic and Language* (Garden City, N.Y.: Doubleday, 1965).
5. *A Clergyman's Daughter* (Harmondsworth: Penguin, 1964), pp. 241–2.
6. Ibid., pp. 241–3.
7. Ibid., p. 245. Cf. Nietzsche on the case of George Eliot: 'They have got rid of the Christian God, and now feel obliged to cling all the more firmly to Christian morality: that is English consistency.' (*Twilight of the Idols*, Harmondsworth: Penguin, 1968, p. 69).
8. *The Road to Wigan Pier* (Harmondsworth: Penguin, 1962), pp. 159–60.
9. Nietzsche, *The Will To Power* (New York: Vintage, 1968), sec 513.

6. BENTHAM AND BASIC ENGLISH: THE 'PIOUS FOUNDERS' OF NEWSPEAK

1. George Orwell, 'INTERGLOSSA' – Make Do and Talk With 750 Words', *Manchester Evening News*, 23 December 1943, p. 2.
2. 'INTERGLOSSA', p. 2.
3. The memoranda are among the Ogden papers in the Bertrand Russell Archives, McMaster University, Hamilton, Ontario. I am deeply indebted to Mr Carl Spadoni, who kindly allowed me to examine the papers, and whose guidance through the archives was much appreciated.
4. John Atkins, *George Orwell: A Literary Study* (London: John Calder, 1954), pp. 313–14.
5. Richards' article 'Basic English and Its Applications', is included in

the anthology, *Basic English*, ed. Julia E. Johnsen (New York: H. W. Wilson, 1944), pp. 7–24.

6. C. K. Ogden and I. A. Richards, *The Meaning of Meaning: A Study of the Influence of Language upon Thought and of the Science of Symbolism* (London: Harcourt Brace Jovanovich, 1923), pp. 98–9.

7. Richards, 'Basic English and Its Applications', p. 9.

8. William Empson, 'Basic English and Wordsworth', *Kenyon Review*, II (1940), pp. 449–57.

9. L. H. Robbins, 'Eight Hundred and Fifty Words to Unite a World', *Basic English*, ed. Julia E. Johnsen, p. 103.

10. Richards, 'Basic English and Its Applications', p. 23.

11. C. K. Ogden, *Basic English: A General Introduction with Rules and Grammar*, 3rd edn (London: Kegan Paul, 1932), pp. 9–10.

12. Winston S. Churchill, 'Common Tongue a Basis for Common Citizenship', Address at Harvard University, 6 September 1943; rpt. in *Basic English*, ed. Julia E. Johnsen, p. 99.

13. Ogden, *Basic English: A General Introduction*. p. 43.

14. Quoted by C. K. Ogden, *Bentham's Theory of Fictions* (London: Kegan Paul, 1932), p. cvii.

15. Ibid., p. xxxvii.

16. Ibid., p. lii.

17. Ibid., p. lxiii.

18. Ibid., p. cxvi.

19. 'Panopticon; or the Inspection House', in *The Works of Jeremy Bentham*, ed. John Bowring (New York: Russell & Russell, 1962), IV, p. 44. Italics added.

20. Ibid., IV, p. 41.

21. Ibid., IV, p. 40.

22. Ibid., IV, p. 65.

23. Jonathan Swift, *Gulliver's Travels*, in *The Writings of Jonathan Swift*, ed. Robert A. Greenberg and William Bowman Piper (New York: Norton, 1973), Pt III, Chapter 5, p. 158.

24. Ibid.

25. Ibid., Pt III, Chapter 4, p. 149.

26. Ibid., Pt III, Chapter 5, p. 158.

27. Kenneth Burke, *The Philosophy of Literary Form: Studies in Symbolic Action*, 3rd edn (Baton Rouge: Louisiana State University Press, 1967), p. 164.

28. I. A. Richards, *Learning Basic English: A Practical Handbook for English-Speaking People* (New York: Norton, 1945), p. 44.

29. Ibid., p. 95.

7. ORWELL AND THE LANGUAGE: SPEAKING THE TRUTH IN *HOMAGE TO CATALONIA*

1. Q. D. Leavis, *Scrutiny* (September 1940) in *George Orwell: The Critical Heritage*, ed. Jeffrey Meyers (London: Routledge & Kegan Paul, 1975), pp. 187–90.
2. George Orwell, 'Literature and Totalitarianism' in *CE*, II, 134–6.
3. W. A. Hart, 'Speaking the Truth', *The Haltwhistle Quarterly*, vii (Spring 1979), 1–15.
4. Victor Gollancz quoted in Stephen Wadham's, *Remembering Orwell* (Markham, Ontario: Penguin, 1984), p. 102.
5. George Orwell, *Homage To Catalonia and Looking Back On the Spanish War* (London: Secker & Warburg, 1938; repr. Harmondsworth: Penguin, 1962), pp. 7–8. Page references are to the Penguin edition.
6. William Wordsworth, *The Prelude*, Book XIV, ii, pp. 446–50 in *Romantic Poetry and Prose*, ed. Harold Bloom and Lionel Trilling (Oxford and New York: Oxford University Press, 1973), p. 229.

8. ORWELL'S *NINETEEN EIGHTY-FOUR* AND MAO'S CULTURAL REVOLUTION

1. Simon Leys (Pierre Ryckmans) *Chinese Shadows* (Harmondsworth: Penguin, 1974), p. 52, note 8.
2. For example, see Roger Garside, *Coming Alive: China After Mao* (New York: McGraw-Hill, 1981). Also see Robert C. Tucker, 'Does Big Brother Really Exist?', *Psychoanalytic Inquiry*, ii, i (1982).
3. George Kateb, 'The Road to 1984', *Political Science Quarterly*, lxxxi (December 1966). Kateb refers especially to criticism by Anthony West and Isaac Deutscher.
4. Kateb, 'The Road to 1984', p. 85.
5. Liang Heng and Judith Shapiro, *Son of the Revolution* (New York: Knopf, 1983). According to Liang: 'One of my classmates rejected his old name, Wen Jian-ping ("Wen Establish Peace") in favour of Wen Zao-fan ("Wen Rebel"). My neighbor Li Lin ("Lin Forest") called herself Li Zi-hone ("Li Red from Birth") to advertise her good background. Zao Cai-fa ("Zao Make Money") became Zhao Wei-dong ("Zhao Protect the East"). Another friend got rid of the "Chiang" in his name because it was the same as Chiang Kai-sheck's' (p. 69).
6. Lian Hsiao was the group of writers in Beijing University and Qin Hua University. Phonetically it sounds the same as 'Two Schools'; thus the pseudonym. Ro Suding was the group in Shanghai. It sounds the same as 'screw'.
7. The attack on Imperial ministers was meant to be an attack on the state officials; while praising some cruel empresses was intended as a support for Jian Qing (Madam Mao).
8. Asian Research Centre, *The Great Cultural Revolution in China* (Hong Kong: Charles E. Tuttle, 1968), pp. 453–90.

9. First published in 1949. Between 1962 and 1966 its sales (15 million copies) far exceeded that of Mao's works (Garside, *Coming Alive*, p. 267, note).
10. For details of the plot to assassinate Chairman Mao see *A Great Trial in Chinese History* (Beijing: New World Press, 1981), pp. 184–90.
11. Liang and Shapiro, *Son of the Revolution*, Chapter 6.
12. Ibid., p. 45.
13. This was also related to the repression of the sex instinct, which went far beyond a normal concern for public decency. Not a single love lyric was sung or read in public; not even the most scientific mention of sex was permitted in print. See Garside, *Coming Alive*, p. 88.
14. Ibid., p. 103.
15. 'A common question abroad is – Why is Mao throwing it all away? After all, six years of careful rebuilding of the economy and the growing threat of the Vietnam war had given the Chinese government widespread support from its people within the country and from millions of Chinese abroad. Many Americans impressed by the Chinese Communists' extraordinarily powerful structure of organisation and their sophisticated methods of social control, wondered whether China was not committing political suicide for some obscure reason' wrote Franz Schumann in 1967. See 'The Attack of the Cultural Revolution on Ideology and Organisation', in Ping-ti Ho and Tang Tsou (eds), *China in Crisis* (University of Chicago Press, 1968), vol. 1, bk 2, pp. 526–7.
16. Samuel Hynes, *Twentieth Century Interpretations of* Nineteen Eighty-Four (Englewood Cliffs, N.J.: Prentice-Hall, 1971).
17. Liang and Shapiro, *Son of the Revolution*, p. 43.
18. D. W. Fokkema, *Report from Peking* (Montreal: McGill-Queens University Press, 1971), p. 163.
19. New China News Agency report, 3 November 1966, quoted in *The Great Cultural Revolution in China*, p. 385 (see note 8 above).
20. Quoted in Kateb, 'The Road to 1984'.
21. Fokkema, *Report from Peking*, p. 163.
22. This is binding a person's arms behind him over a piece of wood or pipe and then hoisting him up in the air letting him squirm in agony like a dragonfly with pinched wings. See Liang and Shapiro, *Son of The Revolution*, p. 79.
23. Garside, *Coming Alive*, p. 133.

PART THREE: LITERARY CRITICISM

9. ORWELL AND ELIOT: POLITICS, POETRY, PROSE

1. See Brian Matthews, ' "Fearful Despair" and a "Frigid, Snooty Muse": George Orwell's Involvement with T. S. Eliot, 1930–50', *Southern Review* (Adelaide) x, 3 (1977), 205–31. This is a good detailed account of the relationship, documenting Orwell's written comments on Eliot,

and discussing Eliot's influence on Orwell's poetry and novels of the 1930s. Matthews' theme is that Orwell saw Eliot's conversion as an alternative solution to the despair they both felt. In contrast, my focus is on their social thinking and creative work of the 1940s. See also Ralph Stewart, 'Orwell's Waste Land', *International Fiction Review*, VIII, 2 (1981), 150–2, for a thematic comparison of *Nineteen Eighty-Four* and *The Waste Land*; and Keith Alldritt, *The Making of George Orwell* (London: Edward Arnold, 1969), pp. 101–3, for a discussion of some parallels between *Four Quartets* and *Nineteen Eighty-Four*.

2. *Keep the Aspidistra Flying* (1939; repr. Harmondsworth: Penguin, 1973), p. 24.
3. Bernard Crick, *George Orwell: A Life* (London: Secker and Warburg, 1980), p. 133.
4. Ibid., p. 315.
5. The foregoing comments in this paragraph are based on unpublished correspondence between Orwell and Eliot held in the Orwell Archive, D. M. S. Watson Library, University College, London.
6. T. S. Eliot, *Notes Towards the Definition of Culture* (1948; repr. London: Faber & Faber, 1983), p. 84.
7. Unpublished letter from Orwell to Eliot, 5 September 1944, in Orwell Archive.
8. Unpublished letter from Eliot to Orwell, 15 September 1944, in Orwell Archive.
9. *Notes*, p. 9.
10. *Politics* (February 1944), p. 21.
11. *Notes*, p. 48.
12. *Notes*, p. 35.
13. *Notes*, p. 48.
14. Eliot, *Selected Essays* (1932; repr. London: Faber, 1972), p. 458.
15. *Selected Essays*, p. 458.
16. *The Road to Wigan Pier* (1937; repr. London: Penguin, 1974), p. 155.
17. *Notes*, p. 31.
18. *Selected Essays*, p. 288.
19. *Four Quartets* (1944; repr. London: Faber, 1970), p. 11.
20. Alan Sandison, *The Last Man in Europe: An Essay on George Orwell* (London: Macmillan, 1974), p. 10.
21. 'Little Gidding', lines 44–6.
22. 'The Dry Salvages', lines 199–200.
23. *Selected Essays*, p. 15.
24. 'Little Gidding', line 237.
25. 'Little Gidding', lines 162–5.
26. 'East Coker', line 1.

10. ORWELL AS LITERARY CRITIC: A REASSESSMENT

1. Keith Alldritt, *The Making of George Orwell* (London: Edward Arnold, 1969), p. 113.
2. Ibid., p. 115.

3. George Woodcock, *The Crystal Spirit*, rpt (New York: Shocken, 1984), pp. 312–13.

4. Bernard Crick, *George Orwell: A Life* (Harmondsworth: Penguin, 1982), p. 19.

5. John Wain, *Essays in Literature and Ideas* (London: Macmillan, 1963), p. 181.

6. Ibid., p. 191.

7. Woodcock, *The Crystal Spirit*, p. 303.

8. Ibid., p. 291.

9. Alldritt, *The Making of George Orwell*, p. 111.

10. Crick, *George Orwell: A Life*, p. 22, notes that Orwell 'was never insular. He was steeped in French and also in Russian literature through translation, though hardly at all in German'.

11. Wain, *Essays*, p. 190.

12. Alldritt, *The Making of George Orwell*, p. 114.

13. Woodcock, *The Crystal Spirit*, p. 301.

14. Orwell names 'Felix Randal' as the 'best short poem in English' in his review of W. H. Gardner's *Hopkins* in *The Observer*, 12 November 1944.

15. Woodcock, *The Crystal Spirit*, p. 297.

16. Woodcock, *The Crystal Spirit*, p. 298.

17. Graham Good, in a recent article, identifies the two dominant camps between which Orwell, in his role of critic, was caught as Marxism and 'Leavisism'. 'Although he could use the ideas of one to oppose the other he was essentially *against both* – Marxism as a political orthodoxy, Leavisism as an academic one' ('Ideology and Personality in Orwell's Criticism', in *College Literature*, xi (1984), p. 79). Crick comments concisely on the same dilemma in *George Orwell: A Life*, p. 362. I regret that I did not have the opportunity to read Good's stimulating essay until my work on the present paper was essentially completed.

18. Alldritt, *The Making of George Orwell*, pp. 112–13.

19. Ibid., pp. 131–2.

20. See Part III, chapter 3 of *Nineteen Eighty-Four*, where O'Brien elaborates on his thesis: 'Outside man there is nothing.'

21. *The Observer*, 6 February 1949.

22. The 'Quartet' omitted was 'Little Gidding'.

23. Alldritt, *The Making of George Orwell*, p. 113.

24. Ibid., p. 117.

25. *A Choice of Kipling's Verse Made by T. S. Eliot* (London: Faber, 1941), p. 6.

26. Good identifies this sort of progression as the 'basic strategy' in Orwell's critical essays: 'He tries to differentiate the author from his group, but only after working through the "group" features, the imprint of the writer's class, generation or political affiliation' (p. 83).

27. *A Choice of Kipling's Verse*, p. 10.

28. Alldritt, *The Making of George Orwell*, p. 112.

Index

GPSR Compliance

The European Union's (EU) General Product Safety Regulation (GPSR) is a set of rules that requires consumer products to be safe and our obligations to ensure this.

If you have any concerns about our products, you can contact us on ProductSafety@springernature.com

In case Publisher is established outside the EU, the EU authorized representative is:

Springer Nature Customer Service Center GmbH
Europaplatz 3
69115 Heidelberg, Germany

The manufacturer's authorised representative in the EU is Springer
Nature Customer Service Centre GmbH, Europaplatz 3, 69115 Heidelberg,
Germany. If you have any concerns regarding our products, please
contact ProductSafety@springernature.com

Printed and bound by CPI Group (UK) Ltd, Croydon, CR0 4YY

23/04/2026

02095595-0007